MINIMA MEMORIA

MINIMA MEMORIA

IN THE WAKE OF
JEAN-FRANÇOIS
LYOTARD

*Edited by Claire Nouvet,
Zrinka Stahuljak,
and Kent Still*

STANFORD UNIVERSITY PRESS
STANFORD, CALIFORNIA

Stanford University Press
Stanford, California

The following chapters were reprinted by kind permission:

Chapter 1, "Lyotard and *Us*" was originally published in Jacques Derrida, *The Work of Mourning*, ed. Pascale-Anne Brault and Michael Naas © 2001, University of Chicago Press.

Chapter 2, "Saving the Honor of Thinking: On Jean-François Lyotard" was originally published in *Parallax,* vol. 6, no. 4, © 2000, http://www.tandf.co.uk/journals.

Chapter 5, "The Writings of the Differend" was originally published in *Jean-François Lyotard: L'exercice du différend*, ed. Dolorès Lyotard, Jean-Claude Milner, Gérald Sfez © 2001, Presses Universitaires de France.

Chapter 6, "The Inarticulate Affect: Lyotard and Psychoanalytic Testimony" was originally published in *Discourse,* vol. 25, no. 1 & 2, © 2003, Wayne State University Press.

Chapter 7, "Jean-François's Infancy" was originally published in Yale French Studies 99, *Jean-François Lyotard: Time and Judgment*, ed. Harvey and Schehr, © 2001, Yale University Press.

Chapter 9, "Passages of the Maya" was originally published in *Jean-François Lyotard: L'exercice du différend*, ed. Dolorès Lyotard, Jean-Claude Milner, Gérald Sfez, © 2001, Presses Universitaires de France.

Printed in the United States of America on acid-free, archival-quality paper

Library of Congress Cataloging-in-Publication Data

Minima memoria : in the wake of Jean-François Lyotard / edited by Claire Nouvet, Zrinka Stahuljak, and Kent Still.
p. cm.
Includes bibliographical references and index.
ISBN-13: 978-0-8047-5111-7 (cloth : alk. paper)
ISBN-13: 978-0-8047-5112-4 (pbk. : alk. paper)
1. Lyotard, Jean François. I. Nouvet, Claire. II. Stahuljak, Zrinka. III. Still, Kent.
B2430.L964M56 2006 2007
194—dc22

2006017974

Typeset by Newgen in 11/13.5 Adobe Garamond

Contents

Abbreviations

CA	*The Confession of Augustine*, trans. Richard Beardsworth (Stanford, CA: Stanford University Press, 2000).
CdA	*La confession d'Augustin* (Paris: Galilée, 1998).
CS	*Chambre sourde: L'antiesthétique de Malraux* (Paris: Galilée, 1998).
CTGWB	"Can Thought Go On without a Body?" in *The Inhuman: Reflections on Time*, trans. Geoffrey Bennington and Rachel Bowlby (Stanford, CA: Stanford University Press, 1991).
D	*The Differend: Phrases in Dispute*, trans. Georges Van Den Abbeele (Minneapolis: University of Minnesota Press, 1988).
DF	*Discours, figure* (Paris: Klincksieck, 1971).
DP	*Des dispositifs pulsionnels* (Paris: Christian Bourgois, 1980).
DW	*Driftworks*, ed. Roger McKeon (New York: Semiotext(e), 1984).
E	"Emma: Between Philosophy and Psychoanalysis," trans. Michael Sanders et al., in *Lyotard: Philosophy, Politics and the Sublime*, ed. Hugh J. Silverman (New York: Routledge, 2002).
EL	*Économie libidinale* (Paris: Minuit, 1974).
ER	"L'extrême réel: Entretien avec Gérald Sfez," in *Rue Descartes*, special issue, "Passions et politique," ed. Gérald Sfez and Marcel Hénaff, 12–13 (May 1995): 200–204.
FD	*Flora Danica: La sécession du geste dans la peinture de Stig Brøgger* (Paris: Galilée, 1997).
H	*The Hyphen: Between Judaism and Christianity* (with Eberhard Gruber), trans. Pascale-Anne Brault and Michael Naas (Amherst, NY: Humanity Books, 1999).

HJ	*Heidegger and "the jews,"* trans. Andreas Michel and Mark Roberts (Minneapolis: University of Minnesota Press, 1990).
HLJ	*Heidegger et "les juifs"* (Paris: Galilée, 1988).
I	*The Inhuman: Reflections on Time*, trans. Geoffrey Bennington and Rachel Bowlby (Stanford, CA: Stanford University Press, 1991).
LD	*Le différend* (Paris: Minuit, 1983).
LdE	*Lectures d'enfance* (Paris: Galilée, 1991).
LE	*Libidinal Economy*, trans. Iain Hamilton Grant (Bloomington: Indiana University Press, 1993).
LI	*L'inhumain: Causeries sur le temps* (Paris: Galilée, 1988).
LL	"Levinas' Logic," trans. Ian McLeod, in *The Lyotard Reader*, ed. Andrew Benjamin (Oxford: Blackwell, 1989).
LR	*The Lyotard Reader*, ed. Andrew Benjamin (Cambridge: Blackwell, 1989).
MP	*Moralités postmodernes* (Paris: Galilée, 1993).
MPH	*Misère de la philosophie* (Paris: Galilée, 2000).
P	*Peregrinations: Law, Form, Event* (New York: Columbia University Press, 1988).
PC	*The Postmodern Condition: A Report on Knowledge*, trans. Geoff Bennington and Brian Massumi (Minneapolis: University of Minnesota Press, 1984).
PE	*The Postmodern Explained: Correspondence, 1982–1985*, translation ed. Julian Pefanis and Morgan Thomas (Minneapolis: University of Minnesota Press, 1992).
PF	*Postmodern Fables*, trans. Georges Van Den Abbeele (Minneapolis: University of Minnesota Press, 1997).
PLFE	*Pérégrinations: Loi, forme, énvénement* (Paris: Galilée, 1990).
PW	*Political Writings*, trans. Bill Readings with Kevin Paul Geiman (Minneapolis: University of Minnesota Press, 1993).
QP	*Que peindre? Adami, Arakawa, Buren* (Paris: Éditions de la différence, 1987).
RP	*Rudiments païens* (Paris: Union générale d'édition, 1977).
SH	"The Sign of History," trans. Geoffrey Bennington, in *Post-Structuralism and the Question of History*, ed. Derek Attridge, Geoffrey Bennington, and Robert Young (London: Cambridge University Press, 1987).

SM *Signed, Malraux*, trans. Robert Harvey (Minneapolis: University of Minnesota Press, 1999).

SMX *Signé, Malraux* (Paris: Grasset et Fasquelle, 1996).

SR *Soundproof Room*, trans. Robert Harvey (Stanford, CA: Stanford University Press, 2001).

TN "Translator's Notes," trans. Roland-François Lack, in *Pli: The Warwick Journal of Philosophy* 6 (Summer 1997): 51–57.

TP *Toward the Postmodern*, ed. Robert Harvey and Mark S. Roberts (Atlantic Highlands, NJ: Humanities Press, 1993).

TSWS "One of the Things at Stake in Women's Struggles," trans. Deborah Clarke, in *The Lyotard Reader*, ed. Andrew Benjamin (Oxford: Blackwell, 1989).

VT "Le visuel touché," *Rue Descartes*, special issue, "Passions et politique," ed. Gérald Sfez and Marcel Hénaff, 12–13 (May 1995): 219–35.

Introduction

MINIMA MEMORIA

Kent Still

The witness is a traitor.
—Jean-François Lyotard,
The Inhuman

The last words of Jean-François Lyotard's *The Inhuman*,[1] which serve as an epigraph to this introduction, are a rejection neither of any particular testimony, nor of testimony in general. They are an alert to the plurality of ways in which the singularity of an event may be eclipsed in the very testimony to it: the representation of an event can foreclose other ways of linking with it, attention paid to one event may cast a plurality of others into oblivion, and attentiveness to different events may obscure the singularity of each.

But attentiveness to such difficulties is not a pretext for not trying. Just because one is not—and cannot be—up to the task does not mean one is off the hook. Nor are the last words of *The Inhuman*—"The witness is a traitor"—the last words on the matter. In the words of "The Survivor," written shortly thereafter: "The witness is always a poor witness, a traitor. But he does, after all, still bear witness."[2] Indeed, Lyotard's writings are themselves testimonies, which is not to say that he lapses into a pious self-assurance, failing to heed his own warnings. For were one to take the last line of *The Inhuman* in its harshest sense—as a charge against a particular witness—the traitor in question would be none other than Lyotard himself. That line impugns the entire chain of phrases that lead up to it, acknowledging that they too are exposed to the difficulties to which they attest. The peculiar strength of his writings, however, resides precisely in this exposure.

Such exposure is not the end of testimony, but rather its infancy, the infancy of thought itself, of the multiple modes in which testimony is rendered:

> Differences between the fine arts proceed from differences between . . . the various ways, all contingent, the body has been threatened by nullity, of being anesthetized: deaf, color-blind, bedridden, etc. Aesthetics is phobic, it *arises* from anesthesia, belonging to it, recovering from it. You sing *for* not hearing, you paint *for* not seeing, you dance *for* being paralyzed. In each of these arts, the tiniest phrase is equivalent to a remission of pain.[3]

The event's resistance to memory motivates testimony in all its multiple forms. But, once attested, especially by works that take on the appearance of maturity and mastery, the event's resistance to determination risks being forgotten. The last line of *The Inhuman*, then, is both a reminder that mastery is imposture and a call for writings—in a maximally broad sense, including not only the phrases of articulated discourse, but also the gestures made in the media of the various arts—that attest to the event's resistance to determination, the "minimal, but intractable condition" of testimony.[4]

Let us call them *minima memoria*, these testimonies regarding the precariousness of testimony, these exposures of thought to what it cannot think. For they are *memoria*, reports, testimonies to events. They are, however, *minimal* ones. They do not present a grander, because more complete or adequate, representation of events. Nor do they claim to bring an end to the obligation to bear witness. Instead, they are all the more exposed: doubly so, attesting to their own shortcomings, and thereby the interminability of the obligation to bear witness. Yet, through their precariousness, they put forward, in their own representations, a stronger sense of what remains unpresentable.

Alerts to the event's resistance to determination may be heard in Lyotard's earliest writings, even those that are, perhaps, too early, such as his 1948 response to Karl Jaspers's *The Question of German Guilt*, written while still a student, which must be reevaluated in relation to the shifts in his thought that would come later.[5] While commending Jasper for responding to the questions raised by the events of World War II, questions that Lyotard himself will return to time and again over the next half century, perhaps most notably in *The Differend*'s discussion of "Auschwitz" (in quotation marks, so as to highlight the metonym of that proper name which has come to stand for the erasure of proper names),[6] Lyotard, even in that early essay, questions what he calls the "philosopher's confidence" in the ability to attain "salvation" through "self-awareness," challenging the effectiveness of "reflection upon the past as past" (*PW*, 131).

The problem with "reflection upon the past as past" is that it treats the past *as past*, treating the event in question as finished and already possessing a fully determinate (or, at least, fully determinable) meaning. Such a conception, of course, facilitates the attempt to break with that past and to inaugurate a new era, as well as the attempt "to tie the two together, to rely on the former to prepare for the latter" (*PW*, 133), which may amount to the same thing as breaking with the past, since it defines the epoch to come in terms of its determinate negation, or sublation, of the event that came before. In so doing, reflection upon the past *as past* forgets that the event retains a peculiar and insistent "presence" that was never fully present and determinate even when it was supposedly "the present." As Lyotard puts it in a later text, "what happens is always deferred and distanced right off the bat. . . . being forgotten is part of what it is" (*PF*, 168). Its meaning may be belatedly determined, by subsequent attempts to represent it. But, even then, what happened is, in a sense, still happening, still not yet determinate, awaiting and resisting further determination, due to an indeterminate "presence" that remains. Since this indeterminate "presence" was never inscribed in memory in the first place and hence cannot, strictly speaking, be forgotten, Lyotard calls it "unforgettable." This unforgettable "presence," however, is forgotten in a plurality of ways, reflection upon the past simply *as past* being one way of forgetting the unforgettable in the very act of remembering.

Such alerts resound throughout Lyotard's later writings, even those that are, perhaps, too late, like the posthumously published *The Confession of Augustine*.[7] Having long argued that Augustine's account of time—temporal order as determined from the fixed perspective of one's present consciousness—props up philosophy's confidence in reflection upon the past as past,[8] Lyotard nevertheless notes, in that posthumous work, that there are passages in the *Confessions* in which that confidence is stripped away and a different tone, vulnerable and exposed, can be heard. Of the visitation of God, Augustine writes: "where that light shineth into my soul there no space can receive, where that voice soundeth there no time is taken."[9] What, Lyotard asks, could be memorized of an event "that abolishes the natural conditions of perception and therefore cannot be perceived as an event?" (*CA*, 6). The upshot is that the event around which the narrative of the *Confessions* is supposed to be organized, then, cannot be situated in a determinate time-order—and hence cannot be situated in that narrative.

Such alerts can also be heard in Lyotard's most famous work, *The Postmodern Condition*,[10] although the polemics to which it gave rise threaten to deafen one to them. For citations of its Introduction's oft-quoted definition of postmodern as a state of "incredulity toward metanarratives" often omit Lyotard's important qualification of that definition, which, when quoted in full, reads: "Simplifying to the extreme, I define postmodern as incredulity toward metanarratives" (*PC*, xxiv). Lyotard, in short, acknowledges that such a definition remains too simple and must be complicated, lest it be taken for yet another attempt to inaugurate a new epoch that breaks from that past. Indeed, throughout that book and his later writings, Lyotard presents the postmodern not as a determinate temporal epoch, but as a mode of relating to—or recounting—events.

The postmodern, Lyotard contends, is already "undoubtedly part of the modern" (*PC*, 79). As he puts it, "the postmodern would be that which, in the modern, puts forward the unpresentable in presentation itself," that which "denies itself the solace of good forms . . . in order to impart a stronger sense of the unpresentable" (*PC*, 81). This attempt to throw out of sync the chronology—first modern, then postmodern—widely presumed to orient the distinction between the two is itself emblematic of a "postmodern" temporality: denying itself the solace of a neat chronological order, so as to impart a stronger sense of how the singularity of events are occluded when treated as if they neatly fit within the linear progression of a temporal process with a discrete beginning and end.

By contrast, the modern views events within all-encompassing frames. In his *Critique of Judgment*,[11] Kant claims that the "ultimate purpose" of nature is to produce a "culture" that allows humanity's rational capacity to develop, which in turn allows humanity to prescribe itself a "final purpose" (*C3*, 431), an end in itself, which, for Kant, consists in respect for the Moral Law. Kant's narrative, then, concludes when its addressee (humanity) enters that narrative as its hero, much as the Marxist metanarrative ends with its addressee (again, humanity, in the role of the proletariat) taking the stage.

Lyotard, however, calls attention to how even those narratives concede that the event around which they are organized (for the Enlightenment, the realization of humanity's moral reasoning, for Marxism, the realization of a classless society) is not presentable—not yet anyway. Both the modern and the postmodern, then, acknowledge that something exceeds representation. The modern, however, "allows the unpresentable to be put forward only as the missing contents" (*PC*, 81), posited at the end of the narrative, as the determinate goal to which recounted events are to lead. In such set-ups, it is a reassuring Idea that remains unpresentable. The postmodern, by contrast, attests to the extent to which the singular, contingent, and far from ideal events of history retain a remainder that cannot be appropriated into such edifying metanarratives.

Yet, further complicating any simple chronological ordering of the modern and the postmodern, Lyotard speaks of "rewriting modernity," citing passages in works such as Kant's *Critique of Judgment*, especially its Analytic of the Sublime, which acknowledge the resistance of events to determination. Considering objects so large that aesthetic comprehension in one intuition—i.e., in one representation—is impossible, Kant argues that, in such cases, it is not any one glance or representation of the object, nor even attempts at a progressive sequence of representations, that is sublime. Instead, what is sublime is the feeling that something exceeds representation. For Lyotard, this passage attests that events resist determination, even the seemingly minimal requirement of determination in time (what Kant calls "the form of inner sense"). In the First *Critique.* Kant argued that temporal ordering is performed by the transcendental "I"; the subject synthesizes, or links, one event with the following in a "progression," a synthesis which is said to be a condition of the possibility of any experience whatsoever. By contrast, in the Third *Critique*, Kant grants that the attempt to comprehend intuitively such large objects involves "a regression that in turns cancels the condition of time" (*C3*, 258–59), which he describes as a "violence to the inner sense" (*C3*, 259). But, in lieu of being inscribed within the progression of linked events constitutive of the form of inner sense, the feeling of the sublime cannot be said to be an "experience" and hence cannot be treated simply "as past," which is why Kant concludes that the sublime is capable only of a "negative presentation,"[12] signaled by the feeling that something exceeds representation.

Lyotard's emphasis on "rewriting modernity" demonstrates that his critique of the grand narratives of modernity and his call for "little narratives" (*petit récits*) is not an anti-modern throwback, a valorization of the stories that particular communities like to tell about themselves. Quite the contrary, in *The Postmodern Condition, petit récits* are defined as attesting to "singularities" and "'incommensurabilities'" (*PC*, 60), as establishing not communal consensus, but "dissension" (*PC*, 61). Such a definition is elaborated by the examples that Lyotard offers of such *petit récits*: unexpected scientific developments, which, while they may not seem to be narratives at all, nevertheless fulfill the function of such "little narratives" to the extent that they throw into question the assumptions of previous explanatory models (see *PC*, 53–67). From within the genre of scientific explanation, these *petit récits* would mark the extent to which events resist explanation by pre-existing explanatory schemas. Likewise, on such a definition, the Kantian sublime would itself be a *petit récit*. The relation of little narratives to the grand narratives, then, would be analogous to the way in which the postmodern may be read as already inscribed in the modern. Such little narratives would mark, from within, those moments when grand narratives implode, collapsing in on themselves.

In contrast, the stories communities tell about themselves—which establish communal identity by excluding others—threaten to further the forgetting of the singularity of events, constituting a danger that is at least as grave as the universal pretensions of the grand narratives.[13] Indeed, *The Postmodern Condition* argues that at stake in the narratives of particular communities is the formation (*Bildung*) of identity and the establishment of a "consensus" that "constitutes the culture of a people" (*PC*, 19). Neither *grand* nor *petit*, the term "normal" imposes itself here: for those narratives impose a set of norms by means of which identity and consensus are established, albeit without the universal pretensions of modernity. In the latter, the aimed-at consensus establishes the "emancipation" of "humanity as a collective (universal) subject" (*PC*, 66), whereas, in the former, it provides "customs" (a "know-how") making it possible "to distinguish one who knows from one who doesn't (the foreigner, the child)" (*PC*, 19). Because modernity's universal metanarratives and a particular community's normative stories both aim at consensus, both must be differentiated from *petit récits*, which aim at "'inventing' counter-examples" (*PC*, 54) that attest to the singularity of events.

The relation between *petit récits* with traditional narratives, however, is as complicated as that between the modern and the postmodern. Consider Lyotard's discussion, in *The Postmodern Condition*, of the child, who, not yet knowing the culture and its narratives, is said not to belong to that culture (at least, not yet). Narratives, however, will be addressed to the child, providing knowledge of the practices of that culture; they "recount what could be called positive or negative apprenticeships (*Bildungen*): in other words, the successes or failures greeting the hero's undertakings" (*PC*, 20). By identifying with the hero, the addressee (the child) enters the community and becomes an addressor, telling that narrative to others. Such narratives endeavor to fix a determinate meaning upon an event and to establish the identity of the community charged with saving the memory of the event. And, if education and remembrance are consequently tainted with the threat of ideology, attempts to resist ideology are, no doubt, similarly threatened, since a *petit récit* must be formulated in a particular language embedded with cultural meanings and presuppositions.

If Lyotard nevertheless calls for *petit récits*, it is not due to a confidence in the ability to break with the past, but to a childlike resiliency, proceeding *as if* it were still possible to attest to the forgetting perpetuated in such narrative set-ups. Indeed, this "as if" may be essential to narrative, which involves imagination, and which suggests that there might yet be resources for imaginative rewritings. For if *petit récits* are, in a manner analogous to the inscription of the postmodern within the modern, undoubtedly part of the culture formed by the narratives of particular communities; they must also involve a rewriting that attests, from within, to the indeterminacy of events in their singularity and other possible ways of linking with those singular events. Such rewriting, however, requires effort, obliging one to navigate the semantic field, attentive to the drives and tractions of sedimented meanings and presuppositions. It requires labor, nearly in the sense of obstetrics, as if attempting to give birth to an infant—in the etymological sense of *in-fans*, that which does not speak. In contrast to the notion of *Bildung*, which aims to produce a child with "know-how," confidently equipped with rules governing how to link one phrase to the next, the *petit récit* would transmit to its addressee an uncertainty regarding the linking of one phrase with the next, an uncertainty that conveys a stronger sense of the indeterminacy of the event to be narrated.

Lyotard's testimonies themselves take on narrative forms, as well as a multiplicity of other forms of representation: the argumentative discourse of philosophy, psychoanalytical writing, commentaries on literary and visual works of art, even the organization of museum exhibits, as in the case of *Les immatériaux*, the exhibition that he co-organized for the Centre Georges Pompidou. Through a rewriting of those forms of representation that strive to save memory by imposing a determinate meaning and identity upon what happens, Lyotard tries to inscribe the unforgettable "presence" of the event in precisely those forms of representation that prompt the forgetting of that "presence." The resistance to the forgetting induced by both the universal narratives of modernity and the particular narratives that communities tell themselves, then, can hardly presume to break with narrative, consigning such set-ups to the past as past. Instead, the task is one of rewriting them, working through them, in an interminable anamnesis that tries to put forward a stronger sense of the unpresentable:

> One must, certainly, inscribe in words, in images. One cannot escape the necessity of representing. It would be sin itself to believe oneself safe and sound. But it is one thing to do it in view of saving the memory, and quite another to try to preserve the remainder, the unforgettable forgotten, in writing.[14]

Petit récits, minima memoria—these do not involve a renouncement of representation in general or of narrative in particular (for it is not clear that such a renouncement would even be possible). But they do require the effort of experiments in representation, each time trying to inscribe the unforgettable forgotten within the forms that occlude it.

The contributors to this volume have taken up that challenge. Indeed, their essays are gathered together under the title of *minima memoria*, so as to highlight the ways in which each essay may be read as a response to Lyotard's call for *petit récits* and rewritings of modernity, attempts to preserve the remainder, the unforgettable forgotten, in writing.

Many of these essays were originally written for a colloquium held a little over a year after the death of Jean-François Lyotard. But I would urge readers not to assume that the volume's sub-title, with its invocation of a "wake," refers to a determinate period of time set aside for mourning. For the literary "wake" constitutes a distinct genre, one which attempts to establish a privileged viewpoint on an author's *corpus*, and to prescribe rules for future readings. It thereby facilitates a forgetting of the singularity of events, the forgetting of what—in a life, or, for that matter, a writing—keeps eluding such determinate representations. In short, it is the type of posthumous literary reception most ill suited to the philosopher of the postmodern, precisely the type of memorialistic forgetting that Lyotard—in life, and in writing—relentlessly resisted.

A passage from one of Lyotard's last works touches on such issues. It is important, at the outset, to note that the work in question, *Signed, Malraux*,[15] presents itself as nothing less than a biography of André Malraux, and, as such, is a model of the way Lyotard attempts to inscribe a testimony to the unforgettable forgotten in those genres that seem to most occlude the singularity of the event, its indeterminate "presence." And Lyotard's attempt to inscribe in the biographical genre a testimony to what escapes narration is only shortly underway when he launches into a discussion of the posthumous literary reception of Malraux's works, including, it should be understood, *Signed, Malraux* itself. The passage in question begins rather matter-of-factly with the reporting of a matter of fact, namely, that "*Man's Hope* was placed on the program for the *aggrégation* in literature four years after the author's death" (*SM*, 25). To which Lyotard adds: "But, with one final shove, that author had the time to parry the gesture that would embalm him" (*SM*, 25).

Why does Lyotard describe the inclusion of *Man's Fate* among the works upon which all French students seeking higher education would be tested as an "embalming"? In effect, it produces a market for interpretations that try to wrap up (*emballer*) an author's work for those seeking a reliable and definitive guide that provides rules for future readings—readings that would pass the test, as it were. Such attempts at authoritative interpretations attempt to fix the *corpus* in a static condition, a fixing assumed to be preservative, assuring the fabled literary immortality. Yet, by providing authoritative rules for reading, it assures instead that the work will not have been read—and not because such commentaries are often taken as alternatives to reading works on which one might be tested. More importantly, it is because reading involves questioning and judging how one phrase links with another. To read means returning to a state of *infancy*, like a child who does not yet know how to read, for whom the question of how to link phrases remains open. Predetermined rules for fixing links between phrases occlude that feeling of infancy: when approaching a work equipped with such rules, one need not read—that is, question and judge how one phrase links with another—because one is confident that one already knows what is at stake in the linking of phrases. In contrast,

Lyotard attempts to reopen the question of how to link phrases and, in so doing, to return readers to that unstable state and instant of infancy.

As for his "final shove," Lyotard finds it in a text Malraux wrote shortly before his death. In the epilogue to a volume where various contributors gave diverse assessments of his works, Malraux writes: "What should we call books like this one which we see more and more frequently these days? . . . Let us call them *colloquia*" (*SM*, 25). Here are Lyotard's remarks on Malraux's comments:

> Now, as "resolutely as Cubism broke with Leonardo's perspective," this genre breaks both with the erudite monograph and with the exhaustive biography. No representation. Assemblages, instead, of clippings taken either from an oeuvre or a life and mounted as a "picture" that imposes stylistic silence upon discourse. Malraux, after Braque, will repeat that "the most important thing in a picture is what cannot be said." Argued theses and "serious" biography aim to circumscribe their subject; the "colloquium's" Cubist ellipses will protect his breakaway. (*SM*, 25)

Perhaps, then, resources for opening up the question of reading instead of foreclosing it may be found in the more minimal requirements of the "colloquium" essay, requirements that, from the perspective of an attempt at a totalizing discourse, would be a liability, a vulnerability even. For the limited length of the "colloquium" essay forbids the pretense of saying it all, and imposes a more colloquial, even idiomatic, style of discourse. Instead of attempting to circumscribe the whole of an author's thought, contributors are constrained to cutting out bits and pieces, linking them up to present a striking picture, one published alongside other such collages. Incompossible perspectives of the same thing are thereby presented, as in Cubist pictures. It is, then, precisely the "colloquium's" constraints that make possible its "breakaways," its escape from the demand for a complete and authoritative representation, from the fantasy of a totalizing master discourse. In the tensions between its incompossible perspectives, the traces of these breakaways may be detected, like so many indexes, pointing to "what cannot be said."

Indeed, Lyotard, after Malraux, suggests that the most important thing in a "colloquium" is the way in which, like a picture, it may impose a "stylistic silence" on the attempt at a complete discourse, thereby attesting to "what cannot be said." "No representation," he said also. But the very fact that he *said* it betrays that it is through representation and discourse that this "stylistic silence" occurs. To stick with the analogy with

Cubism, it is precisely through representation—albeit a proliferation of incompossible representations of the same thing—that the Cubists' best-known break with the fixed and univocal view of "Leonardo's perspective" occurs. This proliferation of representations, however, does not constitute a more complete and coherent representation. Instead of becoming more fixed and determined, the picture begins to move, to break away. It is as if the opening of an "ellipsis," or a silence, were occurring in the heart of representation.

What Lyotard calls the "ellipsis" should not be confused with the absent object or missing content to which the picture would allude, according to a classic semiotic schema in which a present object refers to an absent one. The "ellipsis" does not occur as an absence, but as a "presence" that may be felt in the tension between the different perspectives that are represented. Neither absent from representation nor present in any determinate representation, it is an indeterminate "presence" that happens in the ebb and flow between determinate representations, in the drift or passage between them. In the trace of that passage, this indeterminate "presence" may be felt, provided that one is alert to the tensions between the determinate representations.

In defense of the "colloquium," Lyotard suggests that commentaries themselves may be like pictures: if, by presenting incompossible representations of the same thing, they impose a "stylistic silence" on the attempt at a complete discourse and, in so doing, provide the occasion for an affect that attests to this elliptical and indeterminate presence. Now, this volume tries to be just such a "colloquium," an ensemble of pictures, presenting multiple perspectives of the same "thing": the writings of Jean-François Lyotard. The ellipsis does not merely occur between the diverse pictures of Lyotard that the different contributors present but also, and more importantly, in each essay, insofar as each contributor brings out the different drives and tractions in Lyotard's work, goes to the sites of tension in Lyotard's work that the terms such as *differend, affect*, and *infancy* mark.

Thus, although Jacques Derrida, Rodolphe Gasché, Dorota Glowacka, Ewa Płonowska Ziarek, and Gérald Sfez all approach *The Differend* from different angles and thereby present multiple perspectives on that work, each of their essays brings out the incommensurable discourses operative in *The Differend* itself. And the account that Sfez renders of the works after *The Differend*, which he describes as "the second philosophy of the differend," differs from the approach taken by Claire Nouvet, who, for her part, accents the import that Lyotard's later supplements to *The Differend* have for psychoanalytical writing as a form of testimony. Each of them, however, traces the resistances that affect poses to articulation and writing. Analogously, what Lyotard calls infancy—in the sense of *in-fans*, which does not speak—would seem to resist articulation. Christopher Fynsk, Avital Ronell, and Geoffrey Bennington, each in his or her own singular way, attest to the inherent difficulties posed by a philosophical articulation of childhood and the rather unsettling effect that infancy will have on any attempt to do so. And, although Philippe Bonnefis, Michael Naas, and Bennington emphasize different aspects of Lyotard's late writings on Malraux, each confronts what is perhaps the central problem broached in those works: how can writing—by definition, reiterable—possibly offer resistance to what Lyotard calls *la redite*, translated as "the Redundant One," a term that conveys a sense of palpable uselessness of narrating singular events as finding their causes (be they psychological, cultural, etc.) in what had already come before, a set-up that often characterizes autobiography and other forms of commentary, such as the "wake."

Much as what Lyotard finds most important about Cubist pictures is the indeterminate "presence" to be felt in the ebb and flow between their multiple representations, what matters in the following discussions is precisely the tensions that they bring out between different discourses, or, for that matter, between discourse and that which does not let itself be articulated (affect, infancy), or between "the Redundant One" and the singular event. What emerges, then, is not a narrative of the life and work of Jean-François Lyotard but a stronger sense of the tensions, drifts, and displacements that traverse his work, its various currents and tractions. Consider, for example, Lyotard's description of his *Driftworks*, an English anthology of essays from the late 1960s and early 1970s: "Driftworks in the plural, for the question is not of leaving one shore, but several, simultaneously; what is at work is not one current, pushing and tugging but different drives and tractions."[16] Perhaps the best-known instance of such a figure is to be found in *The Differend*, in which Lyotard discusses Kant's division of the "field of philosophy" into distinct domains and territories, including his famous identification of the "immense gulf" that separates the domains of theoretical and practical philosophy. In place of Kant's "field," Lyotard proposes the figure of "a milieu—this would be the sea—the Archipelagos or primary sea as the Aegean was once called" (*D*, 131), a figure which opens Michael Naas's essay. The different genres of discourses—codifying rules for linking phrases, and, thereby, for representing events—would be islands that have emerged from the sea. The sea and its shifting currents does not only separate the various islands, it also allows one to peregrinate from one island to the other and, thereby, to map out their differences.[17] From which it follows that any maplike chart of differences between different discourses, which gives the sense of being above the fray, is only derived from that original drift. The "critical watchman," then, is immersed in the milieu, adrift, navigating different discourses, unable to pretend to judge from on high.

Perhaps the most important thing in the writings of Jean-François Lyotard, then, is not the multiple islands of discourses that he visits, but the passages he traces between them. The contributors to this volume have taken the risk of navigating the archipelago of Lyotard's work, each contributor, in his or her own singular way, taking the chance of retracing Lyotard's tracings and, in so doing, of charting new and unpredictable passages, breaking away to new vistas. They have indeed taken up the challenge of writing "in the wake of Jean-François Lyotard" in the English meaning of the expression "in the wake of," that is, in the trace of the passage of something through water.

In their own retracing of Lyotard's difficult tracings, they have lent an ear to the call for a critical "wakefulness" that resounds throughout his writings, a wakefulness that resists the forgetting induced by the more traditional genre of the literary or philosophical "wake." In *The Differend*, Lyotard notes Kant's contention that philosophy must be forever "alert" (Lyotard's term is *éveil*, Kant's *rege*), on guard against those who would attempt to bring philosophical debate to an end by lulling philosophers into a dogmatic slumber.[18] Indeed, Lyotard claims that justice requires such "wakefulness."[19] Whenever a phrase occurs, the question of how to link with it arises. And, given that there is no overarching and universal discourse, the critical watchman must be alert to the ways in which the hegemony of certain traditional ways of representing events occludes others. But justice also requires that one be alert enough not to lapse into a pious assurance in one's own discourse, critical enough not to let critique turn into doctrine, as if one were not also immersed in those difficult waters.

The essays in this volume immerse themselves in Lyotard's writings, alert to the plurality of different passages with their diverse pulls and tractions, alert to the trace of such passages, alert also to the critical "effort" that such tracing requires, an "effort" which, for Lyotard, may be the only "legacy," as can be heard in this remark on Adami's drawings, his drawing of rowers in particular: "Rowing is like drawing, one makes one's trace harshly in whatever waters; and the trace erases itself. Nothing will be disembarked on the shores of the next generation, but the effort of having traced."[20] Through these different and critical retracings of Lyotard's peregrinations, what is being transmitted, then, is not only a series of determinate pictures or memoirs of the works of Jean-François Lyotard but, more importantly, a feeling of the singular "effort," of the singular "gesture" that was made throughout this work in so many modes and voices, a gesture that necessarily retracts itself, in an insistent ellipsis, from the work to which it gives rise. Much as the trace of a passage through water is faced with oblivion, the gesture that his writings make against oblivion is itself precarious, passing. Yet, precisely in its fleeting fragility, it conveys a stronger sense of precariousness, serving as an all the more strident alert, calling out for further traces, more *minima memoria*. In the ebb and flow between the different representations of his writings, the indeterminate "presence" of the elliptical gesture that bore the name of "Jean-François Lyotard" may still, at least, be felt.

Lyotard and *Us*

Jacques Derrida

When, surviving, and so forevermore bereft of the possibility of speaking or addressing oneself *to* the friend, to the friend himself, one is condemned merely to speak *of* him, of what he was, thought, wrote, it is nonetheless still of *him* that one should speak.

It is of him we mean to speak, of him alone, of or on his side alone. But how can the survivor speak in friendship of the friend without a "we" indecently setting in, without an "us" incessantly slipping in? Without a "we" in fact demanding—and precisely in the name of friendship—to be heard? For to silence or forbid the "we" would be to enact another, no less serious, violence. The injustice would be at least as great as that of still saying "we."

For who could ever venture a "we" without trembling? Who could ever sign a "we," a "we" as subject in the nominative, or an "us" in the accusative or dative? In French, it is the same, the same *nous*, even when the second is reflected in the first: *nous nous*—yes, *oui, nous nous sommes rencontrés, nous nous sommes parlé, écrit, nous nous sommes entendus, nous nous sommes aimés, nous nous sommes accordés—ou non* [Yes, we met one another, we spoke with, wrote to, and understood one another, we loved and agreed with one another—or not]. To sign a "we," an "us," might thus already seem impossible, far too weighty or too light, always illegitimate amongst the living. And how much more so in the case of a survivor speaking of his friend? Unless a certain experience of "surviving" is able to give *us*, beyond life and death, what it alone can give, and give to the "we," yes [*oui*], its first vocation, its meaning or its origin. Perhaps its thought, *thinking* itself.

When, again at the last minute, I was asked about a title for this paper, I was roaming about the French and English words "we," *nous, oui, nous*, but someone inside me could not stop, and no doubt did not want to stop, this movement. It was impossible to endorse the strict authority exhibited by every title, even one made up of only two words, for example, *oui, nous*, "yes, we." I shall not propose any title here. I have none to propose. But you are well aware that the *nous*, the "we," was one of the most serious stakes of Jean-François Lyotard's thought, particularly in *The Differend*. Let us make as if, for us, the title had to be missing, even if "Lyotard and *us*," for instance, would have perhaps not been the most unjust phrase—a phrase to be risked, played out or played off.

"There shall be no mourning [*il n'y aura pas de deuil*]," Jean-François Lyotard once wrote.

This was about ten years ago.

I would never dare say, despite a couple of indications to be given in a moment, that he wrote this phrase for me. But it is certain that he addressed it to us.

That day, in the singular place where he published this phrase, he was pretending without pretending. The place was a philosophy journal. Perhaps he was then pretending to pretend. He was both pretending to address me and pretending to address some other, indeed any other. Perhaps you, perhaps us. Nobody will ever be able to ascertain this beyond a doubt. It was *as if*, in addressing me, he was addressing some other, or as if, in addressing no one in particular, he was also confiding to me: "there shall be no mourning."

He thus wrote what had to be written, and in the way it had to be written, for the identity of the destination to remain elusive, for the address to any particular addressee never to be, as we say, *proven*, not even by the one who signed it: neither publicly declared, nor obvious enough on its own, nor conclusively ascertained by means of a determining, theoretical judgment. In so doing, he asked publicly, in full light, and practically, but with reference to mourning, the question *of* the Enlightenment or the question *about* the Enlightenment, namely—in that Kantian space he tilled, furrowed, and sowed anew—the question of rational language and of its destination in the public space.

"There shall be no mourning" was thus like a drifting aphorism, a phrase given over, abandoned, exposed body and soul to absolute dispersion. If the tense of the verb in "there shall be no mourning" is clearly the future, nothing in what comes before or after the phrase allows one to decide whether the grammar of this future is that of a description or a prescription. Nothing allows one to decide between, on the one hand, the prediction: "it will be thus" (there will be no mourning, mourning will not take place, one will especially not plan for it, there will be no sign or work of mourning), and, on the other hand, the command or the prohibition of an implicit imperative, the prescription: "it must be thus," "there must be no mourning" (no sign or work of concerted mourning, of instituted commemoration), or even the normative wish: "it would be better if there were no mourning." For wouldn't the institution of mourning run the risk of securing the forgetting? Of protecting against memory instead of keeping it?

These hypotheses will remain forever open: is it a prediction or a prescription, an order, prohibition, or wish? What is more, all these "as if's" in these hypotheses come to be suspended through the detour of a negation. One must first pass through mourning, through the meaning of the word "mourning," enduring a mourning that befits its meaning, its essence, according to the very vision of what it will or must be, one must first cross this threshold and understand the meaning of what a mourning worthy of its name would or should be, in order to be able, afterward or thereupon, but in a second moment, to confer upon mourning or the meaning of mourning a negation, a "no" [*ne pas*]. As for mourning, there shall be none. There shall be *none of* it. And in the French syntax, "il *n'*y aura *pas de* deuil," the *de*, the partitive article, on the verge [*à l'article de*] of death and of mourning, is just as disturbing in the syntax of this extraordinary phrase: *of* mourning [*du deuil*], there shall be none, none of it, none at all, neither a lot nor a little, neither in whole nor in part—no matter how small the part; but also, *as for* mourning [*de deuil*], there shall be none, which means that mourning itself [*le* deuil] shall not be. No mourning, period.

But is there ever mourning itself, any mourning? Does such mourning exist? Is it ever present? Does it ever correspond to an *essence*? The very authority of the assertion "there shall be no mourning" can even, in its decontextualized isolation, lead one to think that Jean-François also meant to expose it to an analytical question. What is one saying in the end, what does one mean to say, when one asserts, in a suspended phrase, "There shall be no mourning"?

The impossibility of assigning any one single addressee to this phrase is at the same time the probably calculated impossibility of determining its context, including the meaning or the referent of the statement—which, in fact, *earlier* than a discourse, *before* being a statement, forms and leaves a trace. It is the impossibility of describing a context whose borders would be secure. No border is given, no shore [*rive*] at which to arrive or to allow this phrase to arrive. Later, I will explain what the apparent or manifest context was for this discreet [*pudique*] but public and published declaration. Yet, even as I give further surface information about the subject, the context will be far from saturated, far from saturable, secure on all its borders.

And so let us dream: "There shall be no mourning" could have been an apocalyptic repetition, the hidden or playful citation of John's Apocalypse; *ultra non erit . . . luctus, ouk estai eti . . . penthos*: "God shall wipe all tears from their eyes. Death shall be no more. Neither mourning, nor cries nor pain shall be, for the first universe (the first things of the world) has vanished [quia prima abierunt, oti ta prota apelthan]." This echo of the Apocalypse is infinitely far from exhausting Jean-François Lyotard's words, but it cannot but accompany, like a precursive double, like an elusive memory, at once clandestine and visionary, this "there shall be no mourning." It could be said that this spectral echo roams about like a thief of the Apocalypse; it conspires in the exhalation of this phrase, comes back to haunt our reading, respires or breathes in advance—like the aura of this "there shall be [*aura*] no mourning," which Jean-François will have [*aura*] nonetheless signed, he alone.

Earlier, I ventured the hypothesis, itself uncertain, that this "there shall be no mourning" may not be a constative but a normative or prescriptive phrase. Yet normative and prescriptive are not the same thing. *The Differend* offers us the means to distinguish them.[1] Speaking about the "We" after Auschwitz, Jean-François insists once more on the heterogeneity of phrases, and particularly on the subtle difference between a normative phrase and a prescriptive one. Whereas the normative phrase "resembles a performative" and in itself, by itself, in its immanence, "effectuates the legitimation of the obligation by formulating it," the prescriptive phrase requires another phrase, a further one. This further phrase is left to the addressee, the reader in this case; it is left to him or her, and thus to us here, to take it up or link on, even if it is, as is said elsewhere, with a "last phrase." Jean-François continues: "That is why it is customary to say that the obligation entails the freedom of the one who is obligated." And he adds—and I imagine him smiling mischievously as he wrote this remark about the freedom of the one obligated, playing with quotation marks—"This is a 'grammatical remark,' one that bears upon the mode of linking called forth by the ethical phrase." If the ethical phrase "there shall be no mourning" is taken as an obligation, it thus implies, in a quasi-grammatical way, that another phrase coming from an addressee responds to it. A phrase already called for in advance.

I would have followed this last recommendation, let myself be led by such an "obligation," had the phrase "there shall be no mourning" been determinable as a constative, normative, *or* prescriptive phrase, or if it had been possible, by either internal or external means, to identify its addressee. Yet not only is this not the case, but this phrase, unlike any other example of normative or prescriptive phrases given by Jean-François Lyotard, contains no personal pronoun. "There shall be no mourning" is an impersonal phrase, without an I or a you, whether singular or plural, without a we, he, she, or they. This grammar sets it apart from all the other examples given in *The Differend* in the course of the analysis just mentioned.

I thus did not know how to take this phrase, this phrase without a truly personal pronoun, when, about ten years ago, in an issue of *La revue philosophique*, Jean-François pretended to be addressing me by pretending not to address me—or anyone. As if there already had to be some mourning of the addressee of this phrase that says "there shall be no mourning." The reader must already go through mourning [*faire son deuil*] in his desire to know to whom this phrase is destined or addressed, and above all, with respect to the possibility of being, he or she or us, its addressee. Readability bears this mourning: a phrase can be readable, it must be able to become readable, up to a certain point, without the reader, he or she, or any other place of reading, occupying the ultimate position of addressee. This mourning provides the first chance and the terrible condition of all reading.

Today, I do not know any better, I still do not know, how to read this phrase, which I nevertheless cannot set aside. I cannot stop looking at it. It holds me. It will not let me go, even while it does not need me as addressee or inheritor, even while it is designed to pass right by me more quickly than it is to pass through me. I will thus turn round, turn back to these five words [seven in French] whose imbrication simply cannot be linked up, whose chain cannot be moored or fastened onto any constraining context, as if it risked—a risk calculated by Jean-François—being given over forever to dispersion, dissipation, or even to an undecidability such that the mourning it speaks of immediately turns back to the mute mumbling of those five [or seven] words. This phrase gets carried away all by itself. It holds itself back or withdraws; one can neither understand it nor be deaf to it, neither decipher it nor understand nothing of it, neither keep it nor lose it, neither in oneself nor outside oneself. It is this phrase itself, the phrasing of this unclassifiable phrase, drifting far from the categories analyzed even by its author, that one feels driven to get over mourning [*faire son deuil*], precisely at the point where this phrasing says to us: over me, there shall be no mourning. Over me, the phrase says, or at least the phrasing of the phrase says, you will not get over or even go into mourning. You will especially not organize mourning, and even less what is called the work of mourning. And of course the "no mourning," left to itself, can mean the perpetual impossibility of mourning, an inconsolability or irreparability that no work of mourning shall ever come to mend.

But the "no mourning" can also, by the same token, oppose testimony, attestation, protestation, or contestation to the very idea of a testament, to the hypothesis of a mourning that always has, unfortunately, as we know, a negative side, at once laborious, guilt-ridden and narcissistic, reactive and turned toward melancholy, if not envy. And when it borders on celebration, or *wake*, one risks the worst.

Despite all I have just said, and would wish to reaffirm, about the absence of a definite addressee for a phrase that was above all not addressed to me, in a context in which it may nevertheless have seemed to be, I could not completely avoid a temptation. The temptation to imagine Jean-François, one day in 1990, betting that the phrase "there shall be no mourning," which he wrote as he read it, and which I myself then read in a particular fashion in 1990, would one day, when the time came, be reread by one of the two of us (but which one?) both in the same way and differently, for oneself and in public. For this phrase was published. It remains public even if it is uncertain whether its public character exhausts it and whether there might not be a crypt forever buried and hidden within it. As if, published, it still remained absolutely secret, private, or clandestine—three values (secret, private, clandestine) that I would wish to distinguish carefully. I do not mean that this phrase is testamentary. I take all phrases to have a virtually testamentary character, but I would not rush to give this one, just because it says something about the death of the author, any specificity as a last will, as the instructions of a mortal being, even less of someone dying. Rather, it tells us something about the testamentary—perhaps that what the most faithful inheritance demands is the absence of any testament. In this respect, it says again or dictates another "there shall be no mourning." One would owe it to the loved one or the friend neither to be done mourning nor even to go into mourning for them.

I am going to put aside, though just for a time, this strange phrase. It will thus keep all of its reserve. I set it aside for a moment with the odd feeling that it will have been, one day, entrusted to me, intensely, directly, immediately addressed to me, while leaving me with no right over it, especially not that of the addressee. He who signed it is still looking at me with an attention at once watchful and distracted.

Reading Jean-François Lyotard, rereading him so intensely today, I think I can discern a question that would retain a strange, uncanny quality for him, a power that some might rush to call organizing, a force that I also believe to be radically disruptive. If I were to call it subversive, it would be not so as to take advantage of a facile word but so as to describe in its *tropic* literality (tropic, meaning turning, like the spiraling of a turn or a torment) and sketch out in its figural letter a movement that revolves, evolves, revolutionizes, overturns from the bottom up—as any subversion should. The effect of this question is not to radiate out infinitely from a center of thought, but would instead be, if one insists on keeping close to a center, like a whirlwind, like a chasm open as a silent eye, like a *mute* glance, as Jean-François liked to say about music, an eye of silence, even as it summons speech and commands so many words that crowd about the opening of the mouth. Like the eye of a hurricane.

This question of such vertiginous force, this thought like the "eye of a hurricane," would not be the question of evil, not even of radical evil. Worse, it would be the question of the worst. A question that some may deem not only apocalyptic but altogether infernal. And the eye of the hurricane, the hyperbole of the worst, is probably not foreign, in its excessive motion, in its blustery violence, to what sucks down from below, making it turn upon itself the phrase "there shall be no mourning." That there be no mourning—is that bad? Good? Better? Or is it even worse than mourning, like the mourning without mourning of mourning?

In at least two instances the thought of the worst is mentioned, both times quickly, in *The Differend*. First, through a quotation of Adorno: "In the camps death has a novel horror; since Auschwitz, fearing death means fearing something worse than death" (*D*, 88). I underline the word "worse," a comparative that can so easily turn into a hyperbolic superlative. There is worse than radical evil, but there is nothing worse than the worst. There would thus be something worse than death, or at least an experience that, in going further than death and doing more harm than it, would be disproportionate to what is too easily granted just after death, namely, mourning. A little further, the worse appears a second time, once again in relation to the survivors of Auschwitz, to the impossibility of bearing witness, of saying "we," of speaking in the "first person plural." Jean-François Lyotard wonders: "Would this be a case of a dispersion worse than the diaspora, the dispersion of phrases?" (*D*, 98). This would seem to imply that the dispersion of the diaspora is only half-bad; in fact, it is barely a dispersion—and dispersion in itself is not absolute evil. As soon as it receives a proper name, indeed a national name, this historical name, the *diaspora*, interrupts absolute dispersion. The Jews of the diaspora form, or at least think they form, a community of the diaspora; they are gathered together by this principle of dispersion, originary exile, the promise, the idea of a return, Jerusalem, if not Israel, and so on. The dispersion of phrases, however, would be an evil worse than evil since what these phrases forever lack—and this is the point of *The Differend*—is the very horizon of a consensual meaning, of a translatability, of a possible "to translate" (I use the infinitive form here for reasons that will become clear in a moment). What is lacking in this dispersion of phrases, in this evil worse than evil, is the horizon, or even the hope, of their very dispersion ever receiving a common meaning. What is inscribed in this worse, apparently, is the differend as everlasting difference between the wrong and the litigation, for example. But, as we will see, there may be something worse yet than this worse.

It is not certain that the "worse" is actually some thing, that it ever appears, is ever presently present, essentially, substantially, like something that "is." It is thus uncertain whether it can be approached by means of an ontological question. Nevertheless, I shall not refrain from asking, so as to pretend to begin: "What is the worse, the worst? Is there an essence of the worst? And does it mean anything else, and worse, than evil?"[2]

I would first like, for reasons I shall give later, to surround this old word *deuil*, "mourning," by a few phrases.

As if I were citing it—but I just cited it and I will cite it again.

There come moments when, as *mourning* demands [*deuil oblige*], one feels obligated to declare one's debts. We feel it our duty to duty to say what we owe to the friend. Yet being conscious of such a duty may seem unbearable and inadmissible. Unbearable for me, as I believe it would have also been for Jean-François Lyotard. Unbearable, no doubt, because unworthy of the very thing it means to give itself to unconditionally, the unconditional perhaps always having to endure the trial of death.[3] Inadmissible, not because one would have problems recognizing one's debts or one's duty as indebted, but simply because in declaring these debts in such a manner, particularly when time is limited, one might seem to be putting an end to them, calculating what they amount to, pretending then to be able to recount them, to measure and thus limit them, or more seriously still, to be able to settle them in the very act of exposing them. The mere recognition of a debt already tends toward its cancellation in a denial. The recognizing, grateful [*reconnaissante*] consciousness, all consciousness in fact, perhaps falls into such sacrificial denial: consciousness in general is perhaps the sacrificial and bereaved denial of the sacrifice it mourns. This may be why there must not be—why there shall be—no mourning.

I also wanted, for reasons that should become clear later, to surround the old word *garder*, "to keep," with a phrase.

As if I were citing it—and I will cite it.

For I know that the debt that binds me to Jean-François Lyotard is in some sense incalculable; I am conscious of this and want it thus. I reaffirm it unconditionally, all the while wondering in a sort of despair why an unconditional engagement binds only at death, or to death, to the one to whom death has come, as if the unconditional still depended on absolute death, if there is such a thing, death without mourning: another interpretation of "there shall be no mourning." I will thus not even begin to give an account of this debt, to give an accounting of it, whether with respect to friendship or to philosophy, or to that which, linking friendship to philosophy, will have *kept us* [*gardés*] together, Jean-François and me (kept us together without synchrony, symmetry, or reciprocity, according to a reaffirmed dispersion), in so many places and so many times that I cannot even begin to circumscribe them. I am not able here, relying on my own memory, to recall all the places, occasions, people, texts, thoughts, and words that, whether we recognized it or not, will have *kept* us together, to this day, together apart, together dispersed into the night, together invisible to one another, to the point that this being-together is no longer assured, even though we were sure of it, I am sure of it, *we* were together [*ensemble*]. We were sure of it, but sure with what was neither an assurance nor the surety of some certainty nor even a common accord [*ensemble*].

(One is never *ensemble*, never together, in an *ensemble*, in a group, gathering, whole, or set, for the *ensemble*, the whole, the totality that is named by this word constitutes the first destruction of what the adverb *ensemble* might mean: to be *ensemble*, it is absolutely necessary not to be gathered into any sort of *ensemble*.) But sure of being together outside any nameable *ensemble, we* were so, even before having decided upon it, and sure of it with a *faith* [*foi*], a sort of faith, over which we were perhaps together in accord, and in accordance with which we went well together. Yes, a faith, because Jean-François, like all those I like to call my best friends, also remains for me, in a certain way, forever unknown and infinitely secret.

For reasons that should become clear later, I have just surrounded the old word *foi*, "faith," with a few phrases.

As if I were citing it—and I will cite it.

In order to free myself, and you as well, from the narcissistic pathos that such a situation, the exhibition of such a "we," summons up, I was dreaming of being capable at last of another approach. I was dreaming of escaping genres in general, particularly two genres of discourse—and two unbearable, unbearably presumptuous ways of saying "we." First, I wanted to avoid the expected homage to Jean-François Lyotard's thought and oeuvre, an homage taking the form of a philosophical contribution fit for one of the numerous conferences in which *we* took part together, Jean-François and I, in so many places, cities, and countries (and right here, at the Collège International de Philosophie, a place that remains so dear to me for having been, since its origin, desired, inhabited, shared *with him*, as was also the case for other, more faraway places, for example, a particular house on the Pacific Wall). I really do not feel up today to such an homage in the form of a philosophical contribution, and Lyotard's oeuvre certainly does not need me for that. But I also wanted to stay away from an homage in the form of a personal testimony, which always tends toward reappropriation, and always risks giving in to an indecent way of saying "we," or worse, "me," when precisely my first wish is to let Jean-François speak, to read and cite him, him alone, standing back without, however, leaving him alone as he is left to speak, since this would amount to another way of abandoning him. A double injunction, then, contradictory and unforgiving. How to leave him alone without abandoning him? How, then, without further betrayal, to disavow the act of narcissistic remembrance, so full of memories to cry over [*pleurer*] or to make us cry [*faire pleurer*]?

I have just surrounded these words *pleurer* and *faire pleurer*, "to cry" and "to make cry," for reasons that will become clear later.

As if I were citing them—and I will cite them.

Set on giving in to neither of these two genres, neither of these two "we's," in a hurry to get away from them, knowing nevertheless that both will catch up with me at every instant, resigned to struggle with this fate, to fail before it, so as at least to understand it, if not think it, I had at first considered taking up again a conversation *with* Jean-François, addressing him as if he were here. For let me emphasize that it is *as if* he were here, in me, close to me, in his name, without fooling myself or anyone else in the least with this "as if," bearing in mind that he is not here and that, despite the different modalities, qualities, and necessities of these two incompatible but equally irrefutable propositions (he is here and he is not here, in his name and beyond his name), there is no possible transaction. And what I would have wished at once to discover and invent was the most just language, the most refined, beyond the concept, so as to do even more than describe or analyze without concession, so as to speak as concretely and tangibly as possible of the fact that Jean-François is here, that he speaks to us, sees us, hears us, answers us, and that we can know this, feel it, and say it without impugning any truth of what is called life, death, presence, or absence. And nothing attests to this better than the fact that I want to speak or address myself *to* him also, here, not knowing whether I should address him with the formal *vous*, as I always did, or with the informal *tu*—which will take me some time yet.

Later, perhaps.

This very time, this future, perhaps announces the attestation of which I am speaking. And the question I ask myself trembling, following him, concerns a certain right, always improbable, resistant to proof if not to faith—a certain right to say "we." As we will hear, Jean-François sketches a sort of answer to this question, but it is neither easy nor given in advance.

So, I had thought about taking up an interrupted conversation, the strangest of all. In fact all our conversations were odd and cut short, for all conversations are finite, nothing being less infinite than a conversation, and that is why one is never finished with the interruption of conversations, or, as he preferred to call them, "discussions." I had thus thought about pursuing, as if within myself but taking you as witnesses, a conversation that had ended not with Jean-François's death but well before, for reasons none other than those that knock the wind out of all finite speech. So I thought I could take up this thread again in order perhaps to declare, among so much else, a debt that nobody would have considered, not even Jean-François, not even myself, in truth, up until today. As for the many other debts that link us, you do not need me to declare them; they are readable in published texts.

I thus wanted to follow a thread of memory—and a particular recollection waiting for what could, one day to come, come to memory. What guided me, more or less obscurely, was an interweaving of motifs whose economy I came to see as necessary when most of the threads of the phrase "there shall be no mourning" appeared woven together silently within it. First, the thread of singularity, of the event and of the destination—of the "to whom it happens." Next, the thread of repetition, that is, of the intrinsic iterability of the phrase, which divides the destination, suspends it on the trace between presence and absence, beyond both, an iterability that, in dividing its destination, splits singularity: as soon as a phrase is iterable, and it is so right away, it can break loose from its context and lose the singularity of its destined addressee. A technical machinery comes in advance to strip it of the unicity of the occurrence and the destination. The tangled web of these threads (the machine, repetition, chance, and the loss of destinal singularity) is precisely what I would like to entrust to you along with this recollection. An easier choice, more cheerful, more modest, more in keeping with the adolescent modesty that always marked, and from both sides, our friendship. This modesty was characterized by a trait that was not in fact so assured, and left open its destinal singularity. I am speaking of the fact that, in a circle of old friends (in particular in the Collège International de Philosophie), where almost everyone addressed each other with the friendly or familiar *tu* form, we always refrained from this way of speaking by a sort of unspoken agreement. Whereas we both said *tu* to most of our common friends, who had been doing so among themselves, as well as with us, for a long time (such was the case, for example, with Philippe Lacoue-Labarthe and Jean-Luc Nancy, though there were many others), Jean-François and I, for decades, did not quite avoid but were careful *not to say* tu *to one another*. This could have suggested something more than the inherent difficulty I have using this form of address, much more so, to be sure, than Jean-François. It could have simply implied a polite distance, perhaps even a sort of neutralization of intimate singularity, of private intimacy, by means of the proper, plural quasi-generality of the formal *vous*. But this was not the case; if it somehow indicated a respect that also keeps a respectful distance, the exceptional character of this *vous* gave it a sort of transgressive value, like the use of a secret code reserved only for us. In fact one day, somebody in the Collège expressed their surprise about this in front of us ("How is it that after so many years you still say *vous* to one another, no one else here does that!"—or something to that effect). I can still hear Jean-François, who was the first to answer, demurring with that smile I would like to imitate and that you all know so well, speaking what I took right away to be a truth, grateful that he saw it so well and stated it so perfectly: "No," he said, "let us keep this; this *vous* belongs solely to us, it is our sign of recognition, our secret language." And I approved in silence. Henceforth, it was as if the *vous* between us had become an elective privilege: "we reserve ourselves the *vous*, that's what we do, we say *vous* to one another; it is our shared anachronism, our exception from time." From then on, this *vous* between us belonged to another language, as if it marked the passage, through a kind of grammatical contraband, in contravention of customary practices, to the idiomatic sign, the shibboleth of a hidden intimacy, one that would be clandestine, coded, held back, discreetly held in reserve, held in silence [*tue*].

Among so many other signs of this happy complicity, signs that spoke in silence like a series of winks, I would have liked to recall the moments when Jean-François made fun of me, feigning to take on and imitate the French-Algerian accent and gestures he pretended to recognize in me, precisely because, as you know, he too had his Algerian moment. And I learned rather late about the strange love he shared with me for someone whom I always tend to place back in his native Algeria: Saint Augustine. We were, in the time of these two memories, according to an anachronism of some fifteen centuries, Algerian compatriots of sorts by relation.

If I recall what was said and left unsaid, silenced [*tu*], in this unsaid *tu*, it is because the text from which I earlier drew the phrase "there shall be no mourning" puts center stage what had gone on behind the scenes between this *tu* and *vous*. The phrase appears in the section "Mourning" of a text entitled "Translator's Notes," in a special issue of a journal that was, as they say—dare I say it?—"devoted" to me.[4] In it, Jean-François plays at responding to texts that I had, upon his request, written in 1984 for the exhibition "Les immatériaux."

Instead of saying more about this, about, for instance, the calculated randomness of this exhibition and the chance Jean-François's invitation presented me, namely, the wonderful machinations that led me to learn to use, despite my previous reluctance, a word processor, which I have depended upon ever since. Instead of giving grand narratives about major debts, I prefer to speak of this apparently minor debt that Jean-François perhaps knew nothing about, just as I myself never knew whether he used a typewriter or a computer. This debt would appear to be merely technical or mechanical, but because of the techno-machinations effacement of singularity and, thus, of destinal unicity involved, its essential link will soon become clear with the phrase I had to begin with, the phrase that surrounded and besieged me in advance: "there shall be no mourning." I am thus returning to the important question of *tu*-saying. We never used, as I said, the *tu* form in speaking with one another, but in the serial text I had written for "Les immatériaux" (which consisted of defining and organizing in a computer network, through a more or less virtual discussion on early Olivetti computers among Jean-François's twenty-six guests, a series of words, motifs, concepts selected by Jean-François, the final result being the text later published under the title *Epreuves d'écriture*), I myself had played with a *tu* devoid of any assignable addressee, leaving the chance reader without the possibility of deciding whether the *tu* singularly addressed the receiving or reading position, that is, whoever, in the public space of publication, happened to read it, or, rather, and this is altogether different, altogether other, some particular private, if not cryptic, addressee. The point of all these both sophisticated and naive procedures was, among others, to make tremble, and sometimes, at the limit, tremble with fear, the limit itself, all borders, particularly those between private and public, singular and general or universal, the intimate or inner realm and the outside, and so on. In so doing, I pretended to challenge whomever was addressed by this *tu* to *translate* the idiomatic phrasing of many of my phrases, to translate it into another language (interlinguistic translation, in Jacobson's terms), or into the same language (intralinguistic translation), or even into another system of signs (music or painting, for instance, intersemiotic translation). Accordingly, after a phrase I considered untranslatable, I would regularly add the infinitive form of the ironic command or the imperative challenge: "to translate." Now, it is this challenge (*to translate*, which, if my memory is correct, was actually one of the words in the selected vocabulary) that Jean-François pretended to take up some five or six years later, in the text from which I took the "there shall be no mourning." The text in its entirety, many of you know it well, I am sure, is thus entitled "Translator's Notes." In it, Jean-François plays seriously not at translating but at imagining the notes of a virtual translator. He does so under four subheadings, which I will only mention, leaving you to read these eight pages worthy of centuries of Talmudic commentary. The four headings are: "Déjouer" [To frustrate, foil, outmaneuver, evade, play off], "Encore" [Again, more, yet, although, still], "Toi" [You], and "Deuil" [Mourning]. And right from the first phrase of the first heading, right from the *incipit*, Jean-François plays, plays off, replays the great scene of the *tu* and the *vous*, of the being-to-you [*à tu*] and the being-yours [*à toi*]. He addresses *me* as *vous*. I assume—no doubt rather imprudently, for the reasons I mentioned—that he is playing at answering me and is pretending to address himself to me, for such is the law of the genre and the contractual agreement of this text. Right from the first phrase, then, he addresses me as *vous*, leaving for the two final parts of the text entitled "Translator's Notes" the passage to the *tu*. Here are the first phrases:

> Your fear (you have left me the *vous*, for good measure, agreed) on the large and the small scale, of being made captive.

Before returning to the question of the worse, of the "worse than death," toward which all work of mourning tends (when the work of mourning seeks neither to save from death nor to deny it, but to save from a "worse than death"), I would like to follow in this eight-page text the trajectory leading from the first part, "Déjouer," to the fourth, "Deuil," through the second, "Encore," and third, "Toi." I will follow only its main outlines, for to do it justice would require an infinite analysis of the tight interplay of citations, quotation marks, responses, turns, and elliptical questions. Here, then, are but a few white pebbles to lead us from the scene of the *vous* and the *toi* to the scene of mourning, so that we might then come back to what *The Differend* will have already told us concerning a certain "we," one that is difficult to think, a certain "we" after Auschwitz, a "thinking we," a "we" that is neither the one related to what Lyotard calls "the beautiful death," nor the one that undergoes in Auschwitz what is, as he says, "worse than death." This "we," perhaps the last one, or the one before last, is neither that of the "beautiful death" nor worse than death, but—in a very particular sense of the word—a posthumous "we." In a passage I will read in a moment, Jean-François Lyotard says: "We only are 'we' posthumously."

My little white pebbles are only or mostly citations. I will cite Jean-François, and when he cites me in the citation as if playfully to add translation notes, I will make that little two-fingered gesture that mimics quotations marks. What comes between my little white pebbles (which you may think of as either those left by *le Petit Poucet* to mark his path,[5] or those left as tokens on graves by Central European Jews), I leave unspoken [*tu*]; that is, I leave it to you [*vous*] to read or reread on your own this extraordinary work of interwoven writing, this-more-than-sublime text.

Four times, then—according to the rhythm he chose to divide these "Translator's Notes."

1. *First time*, in "Déjouer," that of a *ductus*, one could say, or of *duction*. I select these lines, which already point, as it were—*between* the trans*duction* of translation [*traduction*] and se*duction*—to the passage from the *vous* to the *tu*, and, later, from a certain *tu* to a certain *nous*.

He writes:

> The untranslatable leaves something to "transduce," something still to be translated. "That we are expecting one thing or another, on arrival" is not "the essential thing," it is "that we are awaiting each other, you and I, on arrival." Not in the language of arrival, but in "the language of our country." (I defer this "you and I.") To await one another: reflexive, transitive? How to translate this out-maneuvering [*dé-jeu*]? In the language in which it is written. You resist capture thanks only to love of the language that captivates. Since language captures by means of its amphibologies, you mark them. In order to seduce language. (*TN*, 51)

2. The *second time* would be time proper, the time of time. Without waiting any longer for the passage to the singular and familiar, to the *toi*, this time announces it in what I would call a more "cutting" manner. I excerpt a few lines from "Encore," the title of this second time, by cutting even more brutally. By cutting, though, you are going to hear a certain "with you and me it's decisive, cutting" at the end. It decides resolutely with respect to a certain "we" or "us" produced by the mirror that Jean-François claims to hold up before "us":

> You give me your voice, your vote (*Voix*). But you have nothing to give. Except suspense. I try suspense. . . . You will smile. Yet another one who will have gotten it wrong. You watch me watching your gaze in the mirror I hold up before us (*Miroir*) . . . I run on time to Time to see if your desire to bend the matrix (to make it submit?) itself lacks time. . . . and yet you declare your "sentiment," your revolt or your ruse: there is simultaneity, beyond all temporal deferrals. There is some "full speed," some quasi-infinite speed, creating synchronies, political contemporaneities, for example, even "ignoble" ones, but above all there is the

reprieved, absolute "at the same time" of a being-together outside the network, as "dyad," which eludes any third party (*Miroir*). That is *toi* [you]; I'll come back to this.

The importance of the telephone for this speed. . . . loving caress, diligent too. I wonder whether full speed, your "hollow certainty" (*Simultanéité*) of possible simultaneity, so to speak delivered from *différance*, spirited away from every *de*-term, is to be taken as a free-ness or frankness, a freedom at least expected by the captive of delays and postponements, or else to be taken as a forcing of desire by desire itself, the effacing of its *encore*, a ruse of patience simulating absolute impatience. Resolution. It would decide, cut. With you and me, it's decisive, cutting. (*TN*, 53)

3. Entitled "Toi" [You], the *third time* thus cuts; and if its title is, directly, if I may say so, *toi*, it does all it can to avoid, as you will hear, a "thesis on the *toi*." In a few lines that I should not have the right to isolate in this way, I wish to underscore the theme of simulation and simulacra, the question of right ("the right to address one another as *toi*"), and above all the appearance of a "we" as "posthumous we," a phrase that should, I believe, not only make us hear the testamentary postmortem but inhale [*humer*] in advance the humus, the soil, the earth, the humid earth, humility, the human and the inhuman, the inhumed, which will resonate at the end of the text, in what will be the fourth time and last act. Jean-François writes:

Frankness or simulation: the opposition must be played off [*déjouer*] against itself. If we simulate suffering it is because we suffer from the infinite possibility of simulation (*Simulation*). . . . I mean: none of these partners could be you [*toi*]. "Do we have the right to address one another as *toi*? (*Droit*). . . . You are the one who signs, only you. "These words that I address only to you but that you sign, of which you are the addressee, the address-she, or as he would say: the mother" (*Sens*). . . . . With you, "I want to take my time, all my time" (*Vitesse*), you [*toi*] who "[give] me my time and [tell] me what it's like out at the time [*le temps qu'il fait*], *if you see what I mean* [in English in original]" (*Temps*).

There is immortality between you and me, whom we shall see die (*Immortalité*). To translate. But you were translating yourself (?) "The essential thing [is] that we expect, you and I, the arrival, that we await one another, you and I, upon arrival, in the language of our country" (*Traduire*). To translate, again. I am trying. But I'm afraid of forcing, of forcing you and forcing me into a thesis of and on the *toi*. . . . "We shall see us die." You will see me and I will see you die. Or, dying will come [*arrivera*] to the two of us together, and we will know it together. Coming ashore [*La rive*] . . . (*TN*, 53–54)

And later (but I suffer so much at not being able, for lack of time, to read everything, rushing as I must toward a certain posthumous "we"):

I pause at this *toi et moi*, "you and me," which you dissect . . . since the body that's yours and the body that's mine, at which neither you nor I can arrive, we will not get there, we will arrive at the other body. It would be another country. Sunk in darkness? To translate. Where we won't see each other, or ourselves, or the two of us together. Where we will only see each other, or ourselves, sinking, being blinded, un-writing, delivered up to translators and those who guide across borders. We are "ourselves," or "we," only posthumously. You and I await it, or ourselves, there. Not that language will ever sink or go under. It is on the boat of every transit. But it is its image in me. . . . You sign this desire, with my signature? (*TN*, 55)

4. It is in the last breath of this text, in the *fourth time*, entitled "Mourning," that one can find at once the words I said I wanted to cite—"mourning," "keep," "cry," "faith"—and the phrase that is now slightly more, but still not totally, re-contextualizable, "there shall be no mourning," which keeps silent [*se tait*], mute, and keeps it down [*se terre*] between humus, inhuman and inhumed. I tear a few more strains from this mourning lament. Jean-François writes:

"A sign from you, my everyday tongue. What I cry for. To translate" (*Signe*). Already translated: you make me cry, I cry after you, I shall always cry, right up to the arrival. There shall be no mourning. Memory will be preserved. "My luck: that the only form of unhappiness would be to lose, not to preserve, memory." . . . It is not for this supposed loss that I cry, but for and after your presence, language, never deserted. Which will always have happened as long as I will have written, out of place. This gap gives space and time for tears. . . . You are asked: "We shall efface the harm." The harm done by writing. But damages call only for litigation and a decision, not forgiveness, which escapes rules and settlements. Forgiveness would forgive only the wrong. But it is not a gesture and makes no gestures. Forgiveness "has already let it [the wrong] *of itself* efface itself: what I call writing." This is why there is no proof of it. As I write, you do me wrong and I forgive you, but it will never be proven, not even by my tears. As you haunt my writing, without holiness asking anything, I do you wrong. Do you forgive me? Who will prove it? Mute. . . . That is why there is this gap, "melancholy," a wrong exceeding declared forgiveness, consuming and consummating itself in writing. Of which you have no need. That is why mourning is never lifted, the fire never put out. It is vain to count on acquitting yourself of your unseizability through incineration . . . through the consumption of writing in an immediate fire and by a signature in cinders. To satirize, to singe this signarizing [*singerie de cette signerie*]. Cinders are still matter. I sign in humus. Of the inhuman, I bear witness inhumed. False witnesses. "I love only faith, or rather, in faith, its irreligious trial." (*TN*, 55–56)

I still do not know how to interpret these words. I do not know how to identify them through, in, and despite the dispersion of phrases that he claims to be worse than a diaspora. My fragmentary citations will have only made things worse. I do not know how to interpret "there shall be no mourning," followed at a distance by the phrase "that is why mourning is never lifted, the fire never put out." The impossibility of interpreting, of deciding about or disposing of these phrases no doubt comes from their radical, irreversible dispersion, as well as from their forever undetermined addressee, whether public or not.

These "Translator's Notes" have the remarkable status of a *response.* They wish to breathe or exude the "yes" [*oui*] of a response that appeals to a certain "we" [*nous*], a response with, however, no assignable or demonstrable addressee. And yet I do not consider this impossibility of interpreting, which is not a hermeneutical impotence, to be an evil. It is the very chance of reading. Beyond all destination, it bespeaks the very destiny or fate of mourning. It offers this destiny over to *thinking*, specifically to thinking, if that is possible, better than an interpretative decision or an assignable destination could have.

For if, to reassure myself in this deciphering, I were to seek some help from *The Differend*, written a decade before these "Translator's Notes," which are themselves about a decade old, I would be able to find there all the necessary premises for a thinking of this destiny without destination. And particularly when it is a question of us, of you and me. *The Differend* already put to work the very language of these "Translator's Notes," thus confirming yet again that these *Notes*, and their "there shall be no mourning," cannot be confined to their context or apparent destination.

Hence, in closing, let me come back to the three occurrences of the "worse" I mentioned earlier:

1. Adorno's phrase: "since Auschwitz, fearing death means fearing something worse than death" (*D*, 88).
2. Lyotard's phrase some thirteen pages later, which, commenting upon Adorno's phrase, says of the death sentence at Auschwitz: "This death must therefore be killed, and that is what is worse than death. For, if death can be exterminated, it is because there is nothing to kill. Not even the name Jew" (*D*, 101).
3. And between these two occurrences, this third one: "Would this be a case of a dispersion worse than the diaspora, the dispersion of phrases?" (*D*, 98). There is indeed another name for the worse,

> for the "worse than death." And when, while preparing for this gathering, I read the title chosen by Jean-Luc Nancy, "From One End to the Infinite" [*D'une fin à l'infini*], I assumed that he would cite the following phrase, which I simply recall here without comment: "What makes death not yet the worst is its being not *the* end but only the end of the finite and the revelation of the infinite. Worse than this magical death would be a death without reversal, an end which is simply the end, including the end of the infinite" (*D*, 89).

In all these pages, which are also powerful readings of Hegel and Adorno, but above all, meditations on Auschwitz, on the impossible possibility of bearing witness, on survival and the "we," a "we" that may go beyond, as Lyotard says so well, what he calls a "transcendental illusion" for which the "we" would be a "vehicle" (*D*, 99), the law of the magical death, that is, the "beautiful death," is opposed to the *exception* of Auschwitz.

In both cases, I will venture to say, there is no—there shall be no—mourning. But for diametrically opposed reasons. What Lyotard calls the "beautiful death" or the "magical death" is the one that gets meaning, and gets it as an order given to an addressee. It is a beautiful death because the order thus given to a dying or mortal addressee, the verdict addressed to him, signifies to him that this death has meaning because it is *preferable*; and since it is preferable, it is, in sum, as if it did not take place and thus can do without mourning. This is the case, Lyotard says, when the private authority of the family, the political authority of the state or the party, the authority of religion, gives its members, that is, its identifiable addressees, the order to die the preferable death, the order to prefer death: "Die rather than escape" (Socrates in prison) (in the background are the analyses of the *Apology* and the *Menexenus* in the "Plato Notice," often with reference to Nicole Loraux's work); "Die rather than be enslaved" (the Paris Commune); "Die rather than be defeated" (Thermopylae, Stalingrad).

This beautiful death does not, in the end, I would say, take place, insofar as it claims to make sense, to remain meaningful, oriented by an end that goes beyond it, and thus by an economy, even if it is an economy of sacrifice: "Die with a view to . . . ," and you shall not die. And Lyotard concludes: "Such is the Athenian 'beautiful death,' the exchange of the finite for the infinite, of the *eschaton* for the *telos*: the *Die in order not to die*" (*D*, 100).

But "this is not the case for 'Auschwitz'" (*D*, 100), Lyotard notes, taking pains—and with very good reason—to put quotation marks around this name that also names the "extinction of that name" (*D*, 101), but which of course—and this is an enormous problem that I must leave open here—can only play its role of absolute exception if it loses the quotation marks that make it a metonymical or exemplary name, and as such not exceptional, able to stand in for other possible "Auschwitzes." At any rate, "Auschwitz" would be the exception to the law of the "beautiful death." This is indicated in section 157, whose title is in fact "Exception," and which begins: "'Auschwitz' is the forbiddance of the beautiful death" (*D*, 100). It is an exception first of all because the victim is not the addressee of the order—and let me note in passing that all the deaths in question here are deaths following an order, "Die," which means that these deaths (whether beautiful or not) are never, as one says of illnesses, natural—supposing that an illness is ever natural. The choice here, if I may use this word precisely where there is no longer a choice, is between "Die, I decree it" and "That s/he die, I decree it" or "That I die, s/he decrees it" (*D*, 100). Both of these deaths, which are no more natural than any other, are also forms of putting to death, ordered deaths, whether we are talking about Socrates, Athenian soldiers, World War II, or Auschwitz. But between these two deaths, these two "Die's," the heterogeneity is absolute, so that "Auschwitz" cannot, except through an abuse of rhetoric, be turned into a "beautiful death," or a sacrificial holocaust in which the Jewish people come to replace Isaac on Mount Moriah. "Rhetoric" is the word Lyotard uses in his analysis of these terrifying hypotheses in the paragraphs about Abraham (161, 170), which I wish I could have meditated upon at greater length.

In all these pages on the *Result*, on the "after Auschwitz," on the witness, the third party, the survivor, on the enormous question of the "we," on the two "Die's," the two orders of dying and the two orders that say "Die," that of the beautiful death and that of "Auschwitz," mourning never comes up. "Mourning" never appears, and the word "mourning" has no grounds for appearing. As if the phrase "there shall be no mourning" had already been heard, and taken into account, in its most extreme consequences. I wouldn't swear that the word "mourning" never appears in the whole book, but if it does, it is not in the passages dealing with death, the beautiful death, or the death that is worse than death. The word and concept "death" appear twice in the index ("death," "beautiful death"), but "mourning" does not appear at all. If there are no grounds for mourning, if there are no grounds for having to get over mourning these two ordered deaths, it is for diametrically opposed reasons. In the "beautiful death," it is because death has meaning: it brings to fulfillment a life full of meaning; this death gets over itself, overtakes or sublates itself, in this meaning. In the case of "Auschwitz," on the contrary, "worse than death," it is the extinction of the very name that forbids mourning, given that this murder of the name constitutes the very meaning of the order "die," or "that he die," or even "that I die." In both of these orders, the "there shall be no mourning" is implicitly so radical that the word "mourning" does not even need to be uttered. Which would seem to suggest that whenever the word is uttered we are perhaps—we are no doubt—dealing with another case, where mourning is at least possible enough to be averted by the "there shall be no mourning."

I would like to inscribe here, as a programmatic indication of a reflection to come, a reference to two of Jean-François Lyotard's remarks, apparently quite distant from one another (*D*, 106, 56), which, without referring to mourning, give us a great deal to think about the empty place left to mourning in *The Differend* and about what is worse than death. It is as if—or at least this will be the hypothesis of my reading—mourning implied either a litigation concerning damages, or else some kind of wrong, that is, some differend. Without litigation or differend, there can be no mourning. In a way, then, what is worse than death, as well as non-mourning, is that there *not even be a differend*. As if what is "worse than death" were what comes, if not to erase, at least to marginalize or subordinate the nevertheless unerasable limit between a wrong and damages, differend and litigation: an alternative or alternation that, as you know, marks the rhythm, pulse, and heartbeat of this great book, *The Differend*.

I take the risk of sketching this hypothesis about mourning based on what Lyotard himself says, without mentioning mourning, about a certain duel, or even divorce, between "Auschwitz" and "Israel." In establishing damages that can be repaired, in thinking that it can translate the wrong into damages and the differend into a litigation, which is and remains impossible, it is as if Israel had meant to complete its mourning. In so doing, the state of Israel would have sought to signify the mourning of Auschwitz, precisely there where mourning has no meaning. All I can do here is juxtapose these two series of statements from *The Differend*:

1. First, "Auschwitz":

Between the SS and the Jew there is *not even* a differend, because there is not even a common idiom (that of a tribunal) in which damages could at least be formulated, be they in place of a wrong. Thus there is no need of a trial, not even a parodic one. (This is not the case with the communists.) The Jewish phrase has not taken place. (*D*, 106; I emphasize "not even")

2. Now Israel, the state that bears or takes this name, signifying something like the mournful misunderstanding of this truth, namely, the absence of a common idiom and the impossibility of translating a wrong into damages. Some fifty pages earlier, we read:

By forming the State of Israel, the survivors transformed the wrong into damages and the differend into a litigation. By beginning to speak in the common idiom of public international law and of authorized politics, they put an end to the silence to which they had been condemned. But the reality of the wrong suffered at Auschwitz [no quotation marks here] before the foundation of this state remained and remains to be established, and it cannot be established because it is in the nature of a wrong not to be established by consensus. (*D*, 56)

I now want to recall something obvious throughout: the absence of the word "mourning," the alternative between the "beautiful death" and the exception of the "worse than death" are related to an institution of *ordered* death, to some imperious verdict: "die," "that he die," or "that I die." Should we deduce from this that mourning, the experience of mourning or simply the hypothesis and the naming of mourning—even if it is only to say "there shall be no mourning"—are reserved for the endurance of a death that, while never natural, would nevertheless not be murder, not the terrifying result of some order to die, whether given to oneself or the other? Yes, of course, and this is precisely what we are discussing tonight. Whether we accept it or not, whether we endure it or not, whether we name it or not, mourning here does not follow an order to die. If mourning does still follow, hypothetically, some order, wish, prayer, request, or desire, it would instead be, still tonight, a "do not die" or a "that he not die." And the "there shall be no mourning" could thus be heard as a response to, or echo of, some "do not die," "that he not die." To go into mourning, on the contrary, and even more so, to organize mourning, would always run the risk of confirming the order or the wish ("die," "be dead," "stay dead," "that you die, that you be or remain in death"). (We should never forget, however, that what *happens* to us, what comes to *affect* us, at the death of the friend, goes beyond the order, the wish, even the promise, beyond any performative project. As does any event worthy of this name.)

But we know that this "do not die," which nothing will silence, even when it would not be heard, even when it would forgo mourning, is *threatened* on all sides: threatened by the "beautiful death" itself, with its consoling image, like the figure of a life that was indeed fulfilled, successful, so full of accomplishments and reminders left for future generations, so abundant in meaning and work in the service of thinking, of loved ones, of humanity, etc.; but threatened too by the always open risk of a "worse than death," the disguised extinction of the name always lying in wait. For there are a thousand different ways, as we know, for a name to vanish; it can lose itself at the point where there would no longer even be a differend, as in the "not even a differend" I just recalled. But the name can also be effaced, in another perversion of the worse, precisely insofar as it is kept or keeps itself back, *through* what it keeps for itself or through the one who keeps it, or insofar, as we read in *Signed, Malraux*, in the last chapter entitled "Witness," as "the names remain," or what remains is the "Signature from beyond the tomb. As always. The only one."[6] Names keep, watch over, but these spectral sentinels remain always as threatened as they are threatening; "In and around names, vengeance is on the prowl" (*D*, 56), says *The Differend* on the same page as the passage about Israel I cited a moment ago. Consequently, would this threat be "worse than death"? Would the "worse than death" be this, and worse than the worst? Would what is worse than the worst be this threat of the *contamination* of all these deaths, and all the forms that might be taken on—and yet also denied—by this mourning of mourning?

This is why, in his "Translator's Notes," Jean-François linked with so much insight his reflection on mourning to the question of wrong and forgiveness. Faced with the threat of equivocation, forever pressing and necessary, between all these orders of death, we are all, we, Jean-François's friends, in the impossible—some may even say unforgivable—situation of those third parties or surviving "we's" who must survive not only death but the disappearance or disqualification of the "witness," of a certain "we" and a certain "third."

In guise of a conclusion, I would like to read an extraordinary passage, the passage to hyperbole in *The Differend*, in the apparently furtive moment in which, so to speak, Jean-François Lyotard signs his book by giving us to think what is perhaps here thought, the very thinking of thought. It is also precisely the moment of the leap toward a thinking "we" that signs, seals, leaves its seal and its legacy, goes on to survive or lives on beyond all the "we's" that it demystifies. This "we" will have been, in the end, the only one to have inspired me tonight, to have whispered to me everything I say and address to Jean-François, to those who love him and those whom he loves. The fact that Lyotard almost always (though there are exceptions) puts this "we" into quotation marks does not mean that he is neutralizing it. It is simply being torn out of an all-too-easy understanding of so many other "we's" and given over to a type of thinking that should be called reflection, the reflexive thinking of an impossibility. What happens when one thinks and reflects an impossibility? Is this possible? For instance, so close to the experience of the worse, whenever it becomes nearly impossible to distinguish between a wrong and damages, between a differend and a litigation? Does this experience of the impossible become possible? What possibility is there for another *we* announcing itself to us through the impossibility of the *we*? And even through the "affirmation of nothingness"?

Here is the passage to the hyperbole of the "we." It comes at the end of section 158, entitled "Third Party?," in the course of a powerful reflection on the coexistence of two secrets and on the troubling equivalence between the third and fourth party. These pages deserve a much closer analysis than I can provide here. As you will hear, this thinking *we* is *presupposed* by the critique, by the overcoming or sublating [*relevante*] disappearance of all the other *we*'s. Rhetoric here develops an "objection" attributed to the "speculative." But it is unclear whether the speculative gains or loses itself here, whether it wins or loses its mind. This thinking *we* survives all the *we*'s it thinks. It thus indeed resembles a Hegelian presupposition (*Voraussetzung*), a speculative *we*. But does it not also survive this survival? Does it not survive as survival itself, through a subtle and infinitesimal excess of thinking? Does it not rather think the speculative, even before thinking in a speculative mode? A beautiful risk to run, once again, at the instant of death. With or "without a result" ("Without a Result" is the title of the following section, which I would have wanted to follow step by step). Let us listen:

> But the third is there, objects speculation. The dispersion without witnesses that "we" have characterized as the extinction of the third needed to be expressed by a third. That *we* [in italics, while most of the other "we's" are within quotation

marks] has vanished at Auschwitz, "we," at least, have said it. There is no passage from the deportee's phrase universe to the SS's phrase universe. In order to affirm this, however, we needed to affirm one universe and then the other as if "we" were first the SS and then the deportee. In doing this, "we" effected what "we" were looking for, a we [this time, neither italics nor quotation marks]. In looking for it, this we was looking for itself. It is expressed then at the end of the movement as it had effected itself since the beginning. For, without the presupposition of this permanence of a thinking "we," there would have been no movement in search of a whole. This we is certainly not the totalization of the I's, the you's, and the s/he's in play under the name of "Auschwitz," for it is true that this name designates the impossibility of such a totalization. Instead, it is the reflective movement of this impossibility, that is, the dispersion that comes to self-consciousness and is sublated out of the annihilation and into the affirmation of nothingness. The we composed at least of *I* who write and *you* who read. (*D*, 102–3)

There it is. Running the risk of what *The Differend* elsewhere calls the "last phrase" (*D*, 11), that is what I would have wanted to say. Perhaps I was still speculating.

And yet would I have stopped addressing myself to you?

To "us"?

Would I be abusing fiction or desire if I were to say to Jean-François, here and now, as if for the first time in my life, still not daring to address him as *tu*, still keeping to the *vous*, keeping it, keeping him faithfully alive in our *vous*, there it is, Jean-François, this is what, I tell myself, I today would have wanted to try to tell you.

Translated by Boris Belay
Translation edited by Pascale-Anne Brault and Michael Naas

Saving the Honor of Thinking

ON JEAN-FRANÇOIS LYOTARD

Rodolphe Gasché

Through all the distinct displacements undergone by Jean-François Lyotard's thought—from the philosophy of desire in *Discours, figure* and *Libidinal Economy*, to the pragmatic turn culminating in *The Differend*, and, finally, to the further inflexion of his thought on the differend in *The Inhuman* and his sudden interest in writing—one concern in particular not only has remained unchanged, but has progressively gained in importance, and has with increasing urgency taken front stage.[1] This one concern is the concern of philosophy with thinking itself. The question regarding the nature of thinking, and especially philosophy's responsibility for thinking, is one of the central issues—or indeed, I would hold, *the* central issue—that Lyotard has relentlessly pursued in his later work. By way of evidence, I will limit myself to referring to *The Inhuman*, where Lyotard says quite unambiguously that "the philosopher asks only: 'What is thinking?'"[2] It is precisely this preoccupation with thinking that also leads him, in the preface to *The Differend*, entitled "Preface: Reading Dossier," to formulate the problem arising from the grounding assumption in his pragmatic approach to language that he has made his own in this work, namely, that "there is no language 'in general'."[3] The sole object of Lyotardian pragmatics is what he calls the "phrase."[4] This notion is much broader than the linguistic act of speech; even though Lyotard's analysis of this notion in *The Differend* centers largely on articulated phrases, the notion of the "phrase" itself places the accent on the occurrence of an event in the kind of utterances under investigation.[5] Whether linguistic or not, phrases happen, and they "do" something. Their doing is a function of the instances that together constitute phrase universes—referent, sense, addressor, and addressee—instances that are "the pragmatic posts" of a phrase, and are somewhat akin to categories or genera that form nothing less than the event.[6] The same principle is valid for the rules of the phrase regimens, as well as for those of discourses. In all cases, these are pragmatic rules that constitute phrases as cognitive, descriptive, prescriptive, narrative, deictic, and so forth, or that derive from what a specific discourse seeks to accomplish. Understood as events, phrases "do" things. They have actual effects as well as side effects, and inadvertent effects, and therefore trigger other responses, other events that may clash with the initial phrase event. But there is a particular consequence of the fact that phrases come about according to heterogeneous rules (the rules of phrase regimens, and genres of discourse) for which, in the absence of "a language 'in general,'" there can be no universal unifying rule. While Lyotard holds that linking onto a phrase that has happened is necessary, the follow-up to a phrase inevitably brings with it the risk of wronging the phrase event—the singular phrase—that has occurred, thus causing a differend. In a section entitled "Problem," Lyotard therefore asks:

> Given 1) the impossibility of avoiding conflicts (the impossibility of indifference) and 2) the absence of a universal genre of discourse to regulate them (or, if you prefer, the inevitable partiality of the judge): to find, if not what can legitimate judgment (the "good" linkage), then at least how to save the honor of thinking. (*D*, xii)

As one can gather from the 1980 essay "Discussions, or Phrasing 'After Auschwitz,'" Lyotard's turn to pragmatic linguistics sought first and foremost to secure a possibility for thought in the face of "the impossibility to think Auschwitz,"[7] that is, in face of speculative thought's failure, including through negative dialectics, to continue to link onto this event. *The Differend*, published three years later, includes a modified version of this essay in the chapter "Result," a chapter on Hegelian dialectic. But within the context of the book, the attempt to secure a possibility for philosophical thinking has become aggravated by the fact that the very presuppositions of pragmatics tie phrasing up with an inevitable risk of wronging the event onto which it links. Hence the concern with saving thinking and, more precisely, its honor.

As a maxim, however, the expression "to save the honor of thinking" may come across as oddly antiquated. In referring to the norm of honor,

Lyotard seems to evoke a rather ambiguous ideal which lies at the heart of traditional social relations—based on a familial model in the Mediterranean countries, or on social order and privilege in North and Middle Europe. Considering that honor has diminished its central normative role in egalitarian and democratic societies, the expression seems bound to provoke some irritation. We may ask whether Lyotard's evocation of honor is not involved in a dubious revalorization, if not even rearchaicization, of this outworn norm; a gesture that is all the more disquieting as the theme of honor is making a regressive comeback today, in the form of a mythicized national honor in eastern and southeastern European countries, as well as in the form of a resurgence of family and gender honor in Islamic fundamentalism.[8] From antiquity onwards, the concept of honor has been primarily a social and cultural regulator, setting rules for the behavior of individuals, groups, or nations. Such behavior can also include the activity of thinking; Jean-Jacques Rousseau provides an example of this when he writes in *Emile*: "I am not simply a sensitive and passive being but an active and intelligent being; and whatever philosophy may say about it, I shall dare pretend to the honor of thinking [*l'honneur de penser*]."[9] Lyotard's gesture of linking honor and thinking is thus not without precedent. However, Lyotard no longer shares Rousseau's self-assurance; rather, for him the problem has become one of *saving*, and reclaiming, the honor of thinking—especially of thinking philosophically. Nevertheless, the call for saving philosophical thinking in the name of a value as atavistic as the exalted and ceremonial "honor" makes one wonder all the more why Lyotard would have resorted to this notion.

In an essay from 1982, "Answering the Question: What Is Postmodernism?" Lyotard speaks of the need "to save the honor [not of naming, but] of the name" (*PC*, 82). However, on the occasion of his "Postscript to Terror and the Sublime" (1985), published in *The Postmodern Explained: Correspondence, 1982–1985*, he refers explicitly to the requisite of saving the honor of thinking as such. He writes: "The avant-gardes' unremitting work of anamnesis has, for a hundred years, saved the honor of thought, if not of humanity, without compromise and everywhere."[10] One can thus assume that what is at stake in the call to save the honor of thinking is not so much the honor of the thinker, but that of philosophical thought itself. But does not such talk not amount to an intimation of anthropomorphism, and ironically in a work that systematically takes great pains to avoid humanizing language and thinking? Lyotard is fully aware of the threat in question. Given that phrases are heterogeneous, and that there is no universally valid rule for linking onto them, any and all such linking can inevitably wrong a phrase. Indeed, Lyotard voices the following question in *The Differend*: "How can a phrase offend a phrase, or do it wrong? Do phrases have honor, or pride? An anthropomorphism; now, it's your turn [*anthropomorphisme; à votre tour*]?" He then goes on to respond: "In simple terms, you never know *what* the *Ereignis* is. A phrase, in which idiom? In which regimen? The wrong is still in anticipating it, that is, in prohibiting it" (*D*, 85). As Lyotard contends, it is necessary to link onto a phrase that has happened; but that phrase is a singular event in a singular idiom, and with its own regimen. Linking onto it implies anticipating the *what* of something which, *qua* singular event, defies cognitive appropriation. To prejudge *what* the phrase presents—without which another phrase is not possible—causes any linking phrase to deprive the prior phrase of its singularity as an event. The phrase in response to which another phrase arrives is missed or wronged necessarily, because of the very nature of its event quality. But not only does a responding phrase wrong the phrase onto which it links, it also wrongs all other phrases that could have arrived in its place. Lyotard asks: "In the absence of a phrase regimen or of a genre of discourse that enjoys a universal authority to decide, does not the linkage (whichever one it is) necessarily wrong the regimens or genres whose possible phrases remain unactualized?" (*D*, xii). Injustice (*adikia*), according to Anaximander, has come about by the very fact that existing things have come into existence in lieu of others, thus preventing those others from manifesting themselves; the result of this injustice is that things need "to give justice and make reparation to one another for their injustice, according to the arrangement of Time."[11] But just as this injustice is not to be understood in a moral sense, so the wrong that the arriving phrase causes to the phrase onto which it links, and to the phrases it ousts or represses, is a sort of "objective"—or, more precisely, ontological—wrong. Although it is still far from clear why the injustice in question damages an honor that is specific to phrases, such honor cannot be understood as an anthropomorphism, but must, of necessity, be just as "objective" or ontological as the wrong it suffers. Since one wrongs a phrase, necessarily and for ontological reasons, by linking onto it, a phrase event must have, by extension, something of the order of an honor that calls to be saved. This much should already be obvious at this point: that similarly to the wrong that is done to a phrase, the honor of a phrase must be retraced to the phrase's character as an event.

If the traditional role of philosophical thought has always been one of establishing a universal genre capable of settling all disputes, the problematic broached by *The Differend*—precisely the kind of conflict for which no universal mediating genre exists—would seem to entail the outright abdication of philosophical thinking. The question with which *The Differend* is concerned is whether, given the impossibility of ever providing universal rules for "good" linkage, philosophical thought can still have a role to play. After the prevailing philosophical kind of thinking has proven its shortcomings, is there another task of thinking that only philosophical phrasing can fulfill? Even though no role will ever match philosophy's initial privilege, is there not still a way for philosophy to claim a task which is still honorable; in other words, a task that compares favorably to philosophy's previous employment? And is this indeed the sense in which we have to understand the talk concerning the honor of thinking? Here too honor would refer to the integrity of thinking itself, and would thus characterize the state of thinking. At this point, it may be appropriate to remark that if all linking onto a phrase inevitably wrongs that phrase, then philosophical thinking must uphold its honor in testifying to the differends that arise from this situation. But it is also obvious right from the outset of *The Differend* that there are ways of linking onto phrases, and hence there are differends, that are brought about by precisely thinking. The chapter entitled "The Differend" opens with examples of situations in which thinking itself serves to cause and perpetuate injustice: historical revisionism, editorial rationality, and communist rhetoric. By providing the logically impeccable argumentational schemes that serve to wrong parties and plaintiffs, this employment of thinking actually disgraces thinking; but it also induces the call to save the honor of thinking and demands that thinking testify to those differends for which thinking itself is responsible.

Before further elaborating on this response to thinking's self-disgrace, let me return again to the notion of honor that is linked, for Lyotard, to the very fate of philosophical thinking. In light of the archaic connotations of this term, and also of the marginalization of the notion of honor in modern society, one might have had reason to expect that Lyotard would speak of the dignity of thinking rather than of its honor. Indeed, whereas honor concerns identity in relation to institutionalized social roles and socially imposed norms, dignity refers to the intrinsic values that pertain to the self or individual as such, independent of any institutional context.[12] However, if honor, rather than dignity, is emphasized here, one can safely assume that this is not by accident. Could it perhaps be that in calling on the notion of honor, Lyotard is not gesturing at all toward the institutional codex of traditional societies which serves to secure identity by way of social roles? What if he were not invoking honor in the sense of its Latin derivations, namely as implying an official recognition by a public institution, but were instead suggesting that honor in "the honor of thinking" would first have to be retraced to the Greek *time*? Unlike the Latin *honor, time* signifies simply the recognition and respect shown, through words and deeds of fellow citizens, to someone who merits such esteem because of his excellence (*arete*). In distinction from *eudozia*, which refers to the fame or good reputation enjoyed by an outstanding person, *time* is the respect shown to someone whose reputation derives from outstanding services he has rendered for the well-being of the community. In the *Rhetoric*, Aristotle explains that "fame (*eudozia*) means being respected by everybody, or having some quality that is desired by all men, or by most, or by the good, or by the wise. Honour (*time*) is the token of a man's being famous for doing good."[13] Because *time* is "the end of political life," Aristotle labels it, in *Nichomachean Ethics*, "the greatest of external goods."[14] The public life of the *polis*, the life in common, provides the horizon within which the Greek conception of honor is properly situated. Understood in this sense, honor is the ultimate end and highest good for a life devoted to the state and the well-being of its citizens. In other words, honor is of the order of the *bios politikos* and is, so to speak, a concept of practical reason.[15] By speaking of the honor of thinking, Lyotard therefore situates thinking immediately on the level of the practical, and more precisely of the "political." If, according to Lyotard, the honor of thinking is at stake, it is because the involvement in public and political life not only of the thinker, but especially of thinking itself, is in jeopardy. When it is no longer evident that thinking intends what is just and good with respect to the life in common, then nothing less than the honor of thinking needs to be saved. Throughout *The Differend*, this task—which is the task par excellence of thinking—is understood as a political task. Nevertheless, as Lyotard remarks in *Just Gaming*, the "political" is something that needs to be redefined and completely overhauled in light of the point of departure of the pragmatic approach to language, according to which "all discourses [are to be conceived] as moves [*coups*] in language games."[16] As we know, *The Differend* inquires into the inevitable conflict that derives from the fact that, *qua* events, phrases are incommensurable, and that all universal rule for regulating this conflict is lacking. Lyotard defines the "Stakes" set by this inquiry thusly: "By showing that the linking of one phrase onto another is problematic and that this problem is the problem of politics, to set up a philosophical politics apart from the politics of 'intellectuals' and of politicians" (*D*, xiii). What such a philosophical politics consists in—a politics intrinsically called upon by the pragmatic approach to "language" at work in *The Differend*—will become somewhat clearer hereafter.

This is an appropriate point at which to return to the question left in abeyance: the question concerning the need to save the honor of thinking from the disgraceful and dishonoring forms to which thinking lends itself. First, however, a brief detour is warranted through the last section of Adorno's *Negative Dialectics*, entitled "Meditations on Metaphysics," and his lectures from the summer of 1965 when he was completing this last section. These lectures have been published under the title *Metaphysik. Begriff und Probleme.* The reason for this detour is that not only are the "Meditations" a constant reference point throughout Lyotard's pragmatic turn, but even the maxim "to save the honor of thinking" may refer back to Adorno. In *Negative Dialectics*, Adorno concludes a discussion of nihilism by remarking that "thought honors itself by defending what is damned as nihilism."[17] "Honor" is invoked at one point in *Metaphysik. Begriff und Probleme* as well, when Adorno calls for saving the honor of the history of philosophy.[18] But most important, in connection with Lyotard, is the fact that "saving" (*retten, Rettung*) is a leading concept in Adorno's work. The "idea of rescue" in *Negative Dialectics* is linked to the conception that metaphysical thought "conserves," in transformed fashion, what it criticizes and is intrinsically bound up in the question of whether metaphysics is still a viable possibility.[19] In the face of the atrocities of Auschwitz, that have irreparably damaged traditional metaphysical thought, Adorno's overall concern in *Negative Dialectics*—and furthermore in *Metaphysik*, where he unfolds the concept of saving in greater detail—is the attempt to foster "a respect for the possibility of the spirit for its ability to raise itself, in spite of everything, and be it just slightly [*um ein Geringes*], above what is."[20] For Adorno, not only is thinking's ability to transcend the given the sole thing that merits respect; this ability is what secures the possibility of a new metaphysical experience, in spite of the irremediable ruin of traditional metaphysical thought.

"Saving," for Adorno, represents a constitutive moment of this ruined traditional metaphysical thought. As we shall see in a moment, despite the collapse of such thinking in consequence of Auschwitz, the effort to elicit a new metaphysical experience and a new kind of philosophical thought can also only be achieved by way of a "saving." First, however, we need to understand how traditional metaphysical thought and the "idea of saving" are intertwined. The first part of the lectures of the summer 1965 is devoted to Aristotle's *Metaphysics*, and Adorno holds here "that the essence of metaphysics is made up by the double intention of critique and saving."[21] Metaphysics has "the double character of the critical, or, as one also likes to say, the destructive, and, of the apologetic and the salvaging,"[22] or conservation.[23] Adorno assumes that the concepts of metaphysics, that is, concepts in general, are secularized phenomena, or abstractions of empirical intraworldly givens, but that these concepts are to have a pertinent relation to the empirical. Given this assumption, the inevitable rupture with the empirical, which is implicit in conceptual secularization and abstraction, needs constant mending. This takes place in the attempt to save the phenomena that have been critically overcome or destroyed by being transformed into concepts. Consequently, metaphysics is double:

> On one side, metaphysics . . . is always rationalistic insofar as it is a *critique* of a view about what-is-in-itself, true, and essential which, however, has not been justified before reason. But it is, on the other side, also and always an attempt to *save* that which the genius of the philosopher feels to be fading and disappearing. In fact there is no metaphysics, or only very little metaphysics, that would not be the attempt to save, by way of the very means of the concept, that which for its part appears to be threatened by the means of the concept, or that runs the danger of decomposing at the hands of the concept, or that faces the danger of being corrupted, as it has been called in an age-old antisophist impulse.

Adorno thus concludes that "metaphysics would have to be defined as the effort of thinking to rescue what, at the same time, it dissolves."[24] Metaphysics, he continues, "is always present where on the one hand enlightenment criticizes some handed-down representations and, above all, some ideas, some being-in-itself, for being mythological, while, at the same time, it seeks to save somehow, restore, or even newly produce from itself, or *through* reason, the concepts destroyed *by* reason, and this not only because of a desire to apologize, but as well from the interest taken in truth."[25] Saving is intimately linked to critique—the gesture by which thinking raises itself to the level of the concept—and is thus the conceptual answer to what metaphysical thought, as conceptual thought, must put into question, jeopardize, or squarely demolish in order to become conceptual. Although this concept of saving is an intrinsic feature of the traditional metaphysics that has become obsolete with Auschwitz, the different kind of metaphysical experience, and a new mode of philosophizing that is to replace traditional metaphysical thought, also form a mode of thinking that saves. Furthermore, this different mode of thinking saves precisely that remnant of metaphysics which has "passed through the portal of its death"; and this includes its ways of saving.[26] Against the backdrop of this Adornian notion, Lyotard's talk of "saving the honor of thinking" will reveal a further aspect, in addition to those which we have already teased out.

We have begun to see how, by taking the phrase in a pragmatic sense as its starting point, *The Differend* is led to recognize an inevitable conflict between phrases, a conflict that admits of no arbitration. Because phrases arrive, and it is necessary to link onto them by way of another phrase event, a wrong occurs with respect to the "first" phrase, and all the phrases in lieu of which the "second" phrase comes into being. Given the absence of a universal genre of discourse to regulate the conflicts in question, the problem formulated in the "Preface: Reading Dossier" is "to find, if not what can legitimate judgment (the 'good' linkage), then at least how to save the honor of thinking" (*D*, xii). Two tasks, therefore, need to be distinguished: two tasks that "bear witness to the differend" (*D*, xiii). The first task is to seek a "good" linkage, and this would consist in finding ways to address or voice the wrong that a phrase or party has incurred. The second task would seem to be much more modest, but at the same time it is an almost desperate one. It seeks to accomplish the minimal goal of saving the honor of thinking, but in the face of a wrong so radical that the task of bearing witness to it by providing a "good" linkage is at the limit of what is possible for thinking.[27] The two tasks are clearly distinct from one another. Notably, the second task, intent on saving the honor of thinking, is not to be explained primarily, or exclusively, on the basis of the ontological differend caused by phrasing as such.

In an essay entitled "Lyotard: Differend, Presence," Jacob Rogozinski has distinguished "two figures of the wrong, two versions of silence, two modes of necessity" in *The Differend*.[28] This distinction is between a restricted wrong, and the "radical wrong designated by the name of Auschwitz"; in other words, between a wrong that, in principle, can be repaired by other phrases, and one in which the possibility of phrasing is threatened or even destroyed. Rogozinski remarks:

> One [regimen of the wrong] concerns only the choice of possible phrases, and another which strikes a blow at the *power to phrase*, at the "capacity to speak or to be silent." The first case would be ontological. It designates the inevitable discarding of the possible for the real, the impossibility of "saying everything," the *impossibility of possibilities*, their exhaustion. It is the pathos of finiteness. This case pleads in the name of the multiple, of the profusion of possibilities sacrificed each instant by an actualization of one of them. The second case would be an ethical wrong. It would plead in the name of uniqueness, of a *power to phrase* each time unique and threatened with interruption. It signifies the *possibility of the impossible*, that which cannot happen, in any case, and which happens nevertheless. While the ontological wrong can be repaired, and can cease to be a wrong, the ethical wrong would be radical, that is to say, beyond repair. It would not arise from *every* sequence, but only when the very possibility of a linkage is menaced.[29]

This suggestive distinction seems, at first glance, to correspond to the two tasks of thinking that Lyotard has distinguished; however, Geoffrey Bennington has criticized it, arguing that even a restricted wrong cannot be repaired, because no later phrase can ever come close to being the very phrase that was sacrificed for the benefit of the actualized phrase. I would also add that it cannot be repaired because any phrase that links onto another one anticipates the *what* of the initial phrase, and thus inescapably wrongs it. Lyotard himself, significantly enough, also wonders whether "the threat with interruption [Rogozinski referred to] could at all be thought under the title of a wrong."[30] What is at stake in this question is the status of Auschwitz in *The Differend*. Even though "Auschwitz appears in every chapter of the book" as the "principal example," and even though it may form its very starting point, "Auschwitz seems to be a problem," Bennington remarks in *Lyotard: Writing the Event*. Indeed, he points out, "the *différend* cannot describe Auschwitz," since as even Lyotard acknowledges in the work in question: "Between the SS and the jew there is not even a differend, because there is not even a common idiom (that of a tribunal) in which even damages could be formulated, be they in the place of a wrong."[31] Auschwitz "itself," if one can put it this way, does not yield to the key concepts of "wrong" and "differend." In *The Differend*, Auschwitz is the name, par excellence, for the event; in other words, it names that which requires phrasing, and in the process of which radical wrongs occur—wrongs such as those that the revisionists inflict on the Holocaust survivors when they put into question *that* it happened. As Lyotard remarks in an interview with Elizabeth Weber, entitled "Devant la loi, après la loi": "Auschwitz appartient éminement à l'ordre de l'événement. Il *est* la question: *Arrive-t-il?* Premièrement; on n'en finit pas d'établir que c'est arrivé. . . . Mais surtout, deuxièmement, Auschwitz est l'événement parce qu'on n'arrive pas à établir son *sens*."[32] Still, Rogozinki's distinction points to a real problem in *The Differend*, namely the absence of any systematic differentiation between types of differends. Such differentiation is a task that the pragmatic origin of the differend and the action it requires compel one to perform. Undoubtedly, there is the general ontological differend that is inherent to the very event character of all phrases. But if the name "Auschwitz" designates a wrong, it is not an irreparable wrong that would contrast the ontological differend—for the ontological differend cannot be repaired either—but a wrong, and not just any wrong, that has occurred for reasons other than ontological reasons. Indeed, in addition to the ontological differend, or against the backdrop of what explains it, there are a host of other kinds of differends; they derive from the specific rules for linking two phrases with heterogeneous regimens, a process by which the various genres of discourse submit phrases to a single finality. These genre-based rules alone are the reasons that cause "Auschwitz" to name an irreparable wrong and to be a paradigm of the differend.

There are many differends that derive from the "shift [of] the differend from the level of regimens to that of [the] ends" pursued by the genres of discourse (*D*, 29). But among the various types of genre-based differends, Lyotard lingers in effect almost exclusively on the differend brought about by the cognitive discourse.[33] This is, as we will see, particularly palpable in the opening chapter of *The Differend*, the chapter entitled "The Differend"; but it is also evident in the subsequent chapters, which explore one after another the four instances that constitute phrases—the referent ("The Referent, The Name," and "Presentation"), meaning ("Result"), addressor, and addressee ("Obligation")—before taking on the issue of the genres themselves. As Alain Badiou has noted in his review of Lyotard's book, "tout se joue pour lui dans la question du référent."[34] In what follows I will not take issue with this prioritization of the differend that arises from the cognitive genre or question the degree to which it may affect the theory of the differend itself. I will only be interested in figuring out why the differend caused by the cognitive discourse presents such a challenge to thinking that it puts the honor of thinking itself into question. To put it differently, what will occupy me are the reasons why it is precisely the cognitive differend that causes Lyotard to invoke an honor of thinking and to call for its salvation.

The first chapter of *The Differend* opens with three examples of differends: the testimony of the Holocaust survivor faced with the revisionist historian Faurisson's demand for proofs; the assertion that major works of art have remained unpublished and the press editor's demand to name one such work; and the Ibanskian witness and the Communist authorities. In each case, the differend is shown to be owed to the impossibility faced by the plaintiff of demonstrating the existence of what is in question. The kind of demands for verification that are made of him stifle the plaintiff's ability to furnish proof. To all appearances, these demands come with phrases that belong to the genre of discourse whose aim is cognition. However, let me state right away that it is entirely possible in all three examples that some other goal is at stake—that, as the text suggests, Faurisson "is 'playing' another genre of discourse, one in which conviction, or, the obtainment of a consensus over a defined reality is not at stake" (*D*, 19); that the play of the editor is primarily one of "defending his or her profession" (*D*, 4); and finally, that for the Communist authorities the real issue is the maintenance of their monopoly over what is or is not to be accredited as real. But the differend that results from the possible manipulation or monopolization of the cognitive discourse by the revisionist historian, the professional editor, and the Communist authorities is of another kind than the one demanded by the discursive genre of cognition itself; this forms already a third kind of difference, wrong, and silence. If the victim of the Holocaust is further victimized by Faurisson, it is not primarily because the latter may be playing another game but is a consequence of the preliminary discursive demands of cognition. Now the reason why the Holocaust survivor cannot furnish proof for the existence of what he or she reports is not the same as the reason why the Ibanskian witness cannot hope to sustain his testimony. In the latter case, the differend arises from reasons other than those that pertain to the case of the Holocaust victims, who would have to be dead in order to render their testimony credible. It is thus necessary to distinguish still further kinds of differends. In the case of the Ibanskian witness, the supplementary differend results from the demand for proof of the existence of what, by definition, is a nonobservable entity: the "idea of historical-political reason" called Communist society. Lyotard writes:

> As a general rule, an object which is thought under the category of the whole (or of the absolute) is not an object of cognition (whose reality could be subjected to a protocol, etc.). The principle affirming the contrary could be called totalitarianism. If the requirement of establishing the reality of a phrase's referent according to the protocol of cognition is extended to any given phrase, especially to those phrases that refer to the whole, then this requirement is totalitarian in its principle. (*D*, 5)

The differend here arises from the illicit application of one genre of discourse to a phrase whose regimen excludes cognitive verification. It is a differend that comes from a disregard for, or blindness to, the differences that distinguish phrase regimens, and from the illegitimate extension of the expectations and competences of one genre of discourse to heterogeneous phrase regimens. But this differend due to an illicit extension of the scope of scientific cognitives has to be kept separate from the differend that arises as the result of legitimate applications of cognitive discursivity. Both, however, derive from the rules of cognitive rationality and have their origin in established discursive procedures. Similarly to the ontological differend inherent in the event character of phrases, these differends are "objective." They are rooted in the intrinsically heterogeneous nature of phrase regimens and of genres of discourse, and come with the rules that constitute such genres of discourses.

If the plaintiffs in the three examples are wronged for reasons which, when they are owing an investigator's or judge's oblique intentions, could certainly have been avoided,[35] it is precisely because their testimony is met by the demand to furnish evidence for what they assert—the existence of the gas chambers, unpublished major works of art, the existence or nonexistence of a communist society. As should already be evident by now, this demand is the distinctive trait of cognitive discourse. Indeed, as Lyotard recalls, this discourse also obeys the rule that "reality is not what is 'given' to this or that 'subject,' it is the state of the referent (that about which one speaks) which results from the effectuation of establishment procedures defined by a unanimously agreed upon protocol, and from the possibility offered to anyone to recommence this effectuation as often as he or she wants" (*D*, 4). It is thus not possible to contend that something exists because one has seen or experienced it, unless that contention is backed up by well-formed phrases whose operators have been clearly distinguished and rendered completely explicit, and consists of unanimously agreed-upon "effectible procedures whose reiterable effectuation authorizes the consensus between addressor and addressee" (*D*, 17). Others must be able to verify or falsify the contention made, at a different time and a different space. Without following these established procedures, no cognitive claim can be made and upheld. If one ignores these rules, there is, as Lyotard remarks in the context of the Ibanskian witness, "no more credit to be accorded to [someone's] testimony than that of a human being who says he has communicated with Martians" (*D*, 4). Now let us remind ourselves that this constitutive demand of the cognitive discourse—the demand to prove the existence or reality of the claim one makes according to established rules, so that they can be verified by others—is a very reasonable demand. Indeed, it is reason itself. Furthermore, as the Gorgias and Plato Notices will argue, it is the kind of thinking that came into being in early Greece, and whose rules as a whole have changed little over time.[36] As Lyotard will say, this is "our way of thinking," the way *we* think since philosophy's inception in Greece (*D*, 9). The expectations and rules of this thinking are manifest in paradigmatic fashion in the genre of the cognitive discourse; it requires, first and foremost, that any statement one makes (regarding, especially, the existence of something) be accounted for according to universally agreed-upon procedures—which means, in essence, publicly, in the open, for all to be able to agree or disagree about. This request for clarity, transparency, and public openness is at the heart of Western thinking. The Greeks called this demand to make oneself intelligible *logon didonai*. It is a request to which it is difficult to object.

From this characterization of "our way of thinking that reality is not a given, but an occasion to require that establishment procedures be effectuated in regard to it," (*D*, 9) several things follow that need to be underlined. If reality is not to be thought of as a given, that is to say, as something that shows itself immediately to a subject without the latter's contribution, and which, consequently, could serve, as such, as the unquestioned foundation and reference point from which inferences and judgments are made; if, on the contrary, reality is discursive and rests on rational demonstration, then its assertion always puts the subject in the position of a plaintiff before a public court, of sorts. Lyotard writes that "reality is always the plaintiff's responsibility." "The one who says there is something is the plaintiff, it is up to him or her to bring forth a demonstration, by means of well-formed phrases and of procedures for establishing the existence of their referent" (*D*, 8). If reality is discursive, then there can be no exception to this rule: "That is why it is [even] up to the victims of extermination camps to prove that extermination" (*D*, 9); and furthermore, "the proof for the reality of gas chambers cannot be adduced if the rules adducing the proof are not respected" (*D*, 16). Lyotard contrasts this in noting that, "for the defense, it is sufficient to refute the argumentation and to impugn the proof by a counter-example" (*D*, 8–9). In our thinking, therefore, the discursive status of reality brings with it the further implication that even a successful plea for the reality of a referent can always only be temporary. It means merely that "until further notice it has not been falsified" (*D*, 10). Reality is always potentially in suspense, or in dispute. Since it has not yet been refuted, it has always only been given credence until further provision is made.

The Notice on Gorgias follows Lyotard's analysis of the conditions under which a victim's silence—for example, before Faurisson's demand to give evidence about the existence of gas chambers—could be lifted. The Notice brings out additional presuppositions that underlie "our way of thinking." The text states that "the silence of the survivors does not necessarily testify in favor of the non-existence of gas chambers, as Faurisson believes or pretends to believe," and then argues that in order to prove the existence of the gas chambers, the plaintiff's silent denials of the four instances that make up a phrase (referent, sense, addressor, and addressee) would have to be withdrawn (*D*, 14). Having just called for new idioms to do justice to a victim's silence, this suggestion that to prove the existence of the gas chambers, it is necessary to lift the silence concerning the four instances in question, Lyotard seems to intimate that even the assessment of reality in the cognitive mode of thinking is a kind of phrasing that occurs only after a silence. The Notice on the sophist serves to sustain this point. Lyotard writes that "in its form, the argumentation establishing reality follows the nihilist reasoning of Gorgias in *On Not-Being*: 'Nothing is; and even if it is, it is unknowable; and even if it is knowable, it cannot be revealed to others' " (*D*, 14). Analyzing Gorgias's "simultaneously nihilistic and logological standpoint" (*D*, 16) regarding Being (that nothing happens), Lyotard points out that this argumentation rests on the concession granted to the opponent, in what he calls a "logical retreat," and in the process of which the four instances of a phrase universe are successively negated. Lyotard notes that "the logical retreat, absurd when it is isolated from the course of the prosecution's argumentation, unveils the rules for the family of cognitive phrases: determination of the referent . . . , attribution of a predicate to the subject of the utterance . . . , display of a case which proves conclusively" (*D*, 15). The matrix of the establishment procedures that philosophical thinking adopts in arguing for reality correspond to the four steps that serve Gorgias's refutation of Being; the only difference is that in the cognitive discourse, the four silences induced by the sophist are to be withdrawn "in reverse order." If the reality of a referent is to be discursively established, it must be argumentatively ascertained that "there is someone to signify the referent and someone to understand the phrase that signifies it; the referent can be signified; it exists" (*D*, 16). But what also becomes clear in the process is that although this procedure is not nihilistic, as in the case of Gorgias' refutation, it shares the sophist's denial of Being, in that it entails a fundamental doubt concerning existence. This doubt is the prime reason why, in Western thinking, anything which can be shown to exist can only hold on to that claim as long as it has not been invalidated by some counter proof. As a result, our way of thinking, the way that requires a discursive establishment of reality—and a way that is not easily to be surrendered—pays a price. It is fundamentally suspicious of the event. The discursive genre of cognition, which is largely responsible for shaping philosophical thought, is intrinsically skeptical of the "Does it happen?"—the "Arrive-t-il?"—and thus is bound to produce differends.[37]

But what about the third Notice in the chapter "The Differend"? The context in which this Notice on Plato is inserted concerns the suspicion that bad faith and prejudgment of the plaintiff may hamper any consensus over a defined reality. Given that rules of scientific cognitives are intended precisely to prevent prejudgment, the question that arises is whether those who establish these rules are not "prejudging their competence to establish them" in the first place (*D*, 19). Lyotard recalls here that the proper rules "to allow a consensus between partners concerning a phrase that identifies its referent as it should" become instituted by Plato in response to "the loss or decline of the referent's reality" (*D*, 22). This decline occurs by dint of the paralogical operations employed by those who seek to make weak arguments win over the stronger ones, as well as through mimetic poetics, all of which engage in operations that manipulate the instances in phrase universes. The Plato Notice inquires into the kind of discourse, within the dialectical genre, in which the rules of consensus become established. Since the quest for consensus is not the aim of eristics or of sophistics, nor even of peirastics or the dialectic of experimentation, consequently "the rules for forming and linking phrases and the adducing of proofs are far from established and far from being the object of a consensus even for those who seek the true through discussion" (*D*, 23). As Lyotard shows, the Platonic solution to finding a consensus about the adducing of proofs concerning a referent is the living, and (in principle) infinite, dialogue between two, the *dialegesthai*. This Platonic solution to the problem is to "separate the *mathematikoi* from the *politikoi*" (*PE*, 107); and this means that the consensus about the rules for public discussion is sought out of sight of the public sphere. But instituting the rules in question within living dialogue is not only a matter of eliminating the third party—both the witness and the judge—at a remove from public places (*D*, 23). This living dialogue is also selective (i.e., undemocratic) in that it admits as partners only those who agree to seek agreement, and excludes idiots, infirm brutes, and any one who is in bad faith. Ultimately, the living dialogue intent on producing the rules that are to govern phrases and their linkage takes place only among friends; and, to be entirely specific, between simulated interlocutors who, through simulation, have been made more civilized (as Plato says with respect to the materialists with whom he pretends to dialogue in the *Sophist*). In the Plato Notice, this narrative procedure of Plato's dialogues is thematized in terms of metalepsis. This is also the device by which we readers are kept at a distance from the truth-seeking living dialogue, especially if, as Lyotard remarks,

> we are incapable of coming to an agreement concerning the rules of the dialogue, whose principal rule is that the agreement concerning the referent ought to be obtained for ourselves by ourselves. We believe in the decision of the third party in matters of reality. We think that success in the eyes of the third party is the sign of the true. We believe in agonistics. We allow the lesser argument to prevail, under the right conditions. (*D*, 25–26)

What follows from this is that the genre of discourse that "seeks to institute the rules for what we call scientific discourse" (*D*, 26)—that is, the rules for our prevailing mode of thinking in the West, whose values of clarity and public openness are not negotiable—is instituted at a remove from the public sphere, and by exclusion of the third. Therefore, it is bound to produce still further inevitable wrongs. This attempt to establish the rules for cognitive phrases brings about the differend between, on the one hand, those who share the values of cognitive thinking and wish to arrive at a consensus about its rules by way of public discussion and via third parties, and, on the other hand, the partisans of the living dialogue. This differend "between the partisans of agonistics and the partisans of dialogue" irreducibly inhabits the institution of the dialogue in which the rules in question are set forth. Lyotard concludes that none of Plato's attempts to defuse the threat of agonistics, and hence to reduce the differend caused by the dialogic approach to the rules, has been successful.[38]

So much for the necessary evils that beset from within the principal mode of "our" thinking. As we have seen, the demand to establish the reality of a phrase's referent according to unanimously agreed-upon procedures—a demand which in itself is rational, and without which thinking (in its cognitive mode, at least) is not possible—can thus wrong a witness or plaintiff; in situations such as those that *The Differend* evokes, this demand can produce unsolvable conflicts, or radical differends. A wrong, according to Lyotard, is "a damage accompanied by the loss of the means to prove the damage" (*D*, 5). It is thus a privation to which "there is added the impossibility to bring it to the knowledge of others, and in particular to the knowledge of a tribunal" (*D*, 5). To make matters worse, and in addition to all the differends it causes, philosophical thought has supplied a mode of argumentation that manipulates the rules for the cognitive discourse, and shuts up any victim of a differend that derives from the rules of cognitive phrases, and who yet dares speak up.

> Should the victim bypass this impossibility [of bringing the wrong it has incurred to the knowledge of a third party] and testify anyway to the wrong done to him or her, he or she comes up against the following argumentation: either the damages you complain about never took place, and your testimony is false; or else they took place, and since you are able to testify to them, it is not a wrong that has been done to you, but merely a damage, and your testimony is still false. (*D*, 5)

Lyotard formalizes this argument, and then traces it back, in the Protagoras Notice, to this most important sophist, the friend of Pericles and Euripides, who was held in respect by Socrates and Plato. What is the role of this first Notice on Protagoras in the context of the chapter on "The Differend"? It is to argue that the sophist's argument is also the philosopher's response to the differends that philosophy cannot fail to produce. Protagoras is both a sophist and a philosopher, but the mechanism of the *double bind* contained in the argument is also, as Lyotard argues, "a linchpin of Hegelian dialectical logic" (*D*, 6), that is, of speculative thought (speculative dialectics). But this kind of response is not worthy of philosophical thinking. It is a mode of coping with thinking's inevitable shortfalls that, in seeking to attain legitimate goals, in fact disgraces thought. The demand to account in verifiable ways for the claims to reality cannot but produce inescapable wrongs, and philosophy's disgraceful response to these inevitable wrongs adds, as it were, insult to injury. In light of this situation, Lyotard's prime concern in *The Differend* becomes visible. Given that the established procedures for proving reality cannot be relinquished without condoning the worst, and given furthermore that an inevitable evil arises from the demands of rational thinking, and finally, given that speculative thought, for instance, covers up disgracefully the wrongs caused by thinking, the problem, as defined in "Preface: Reading Dossier," becomes indeed one of how "at least . . . to save the honor of thinking." The nature of the differends in question means precisely that the very honor of thinking itself is at stake. If thinking disgraces thinking, the good standing of thinking is in question. It is in a differend with itself, and though no solution offers itself, yet it must respond to this differend if it is not to lose face.

At this point, where the true stakes of the question of the honor of thinking come into view, let me briefly circle back to Adorno. For Adorno, all major concepts of metaphysical thinking have become obsolete in the aftermath of the genocide of the Jews, and therefore the question concerning the possibility of metaphysical experience—that is, a transcendence of what he calls in *Negative Dialectics* "the closed system of immanence"—is a question of saving thinking from stupidity and the triumph of realized unreason.[39] Metaphysics, according to him, is characterized from its inception in Greece by a double movement: the movements of conceptual destruction, and conceptual saving of what has thus been destroyed. To save the possibility of a metaphysical experience in the aftermath of Auschwitz, the traditional form of metaphysics must be surrendered unreservedly and in its entirety. A new metaphysical experience can be won only by metaphysics, and on condition that metaphysics throw itself away (*Metaphysik möchte gewinnen allein, wenn sie sich wegwirft*).[40] "If rescue is the inmost impulse of any spirit," Adorno writes, "there is no hope but that of unreserved surrender: of that which is to be rescued as well as of the hopeful spirit."[41] In light of what happened in the extermination camps, it has become plain that within all venerable metaphysical concepts and values "the destruction of nonidentity is teleologically lurking."[42] According to Adorno, "thinking must measure itself at what is the most extreme, at what is absolutely unthinkable, in order to have thinking as a right to begin with." It achieves this task by bringing to light the destructive potential inherent in all prior and current metaphysical conceptions. The form of thinking that survives the Holocaust is a thinking of uncompromising resistance to any affirmation, and "that drives the process of demythologization or of the enlightenment to the extreme"—indeed, to the point where thinking turns to "thinking against itself."[43] The *Negative Dialectics* insists that thinking must become "a thinking against itself."[44] Lyotard shares with Adorno the insight into the price attached to concept formation. Yet the two also differ, in that for Adorno the concept inevitably does injustice to what it conceptualizes, with the effect that thinking acquires the additional task of saving what has been condemned (or as he puts it in *Negative Dialectics*, what has "passed the portal of its death"),[45] including metaphysics as a whole, in the aftermath of Auschwitz when all metaphysical concepts have become exposed. However, Lyotard's pragmatic analysis of philosophical thinking displaces the question of saving onto an entirely different level.[46] For Adorno, the question is one of saving the possibility of metaphysical thinking by thinking against it; and although Lyotard agrees that concept formation comes with a high price, according to him the rules that govern it are rules that cannot be rescinded for fear of the worst. For Lyotard, the task is not to save thinking by thinking toward a new metaphysical experience, but rather to thinkingly address the evils of thinking, while allowing that no enlightening critique can ever hope to completely free thinking of its potential for the worst. The extreme against which thinking is staked, according to Lyotard, is the fact of the inevitable wrongs to which thinking itself subjects witnesses and plaintiffs—those who make existence claims that, according to the rules of the cognitive discourse, cannot be validated, or who phrase according to the rules of other genres of discourse than the cognitive discourse, and who are further victimized by the speculative thinking that robs them of the very power to speak. For Adorno, saving a minimal metaphysical experience for thinking is aimed at preventing the total closure of the system of immanence; for Lyotard, the question is one of responding, by thinking, to the worst in which thinking inevitably gets caught up when it seeks to avoid the worst, and thus it is a question that concerns the honor of thinking.[47]

In order to address this question, Lyotard must reconceive and reformulate the task of thinking. In *The Differend*, he asks: "What if the stakes of thought (?) concerned differend rather than consensus?" (*D*, 60). This task is distinct from what thinking has hitherto considered to be its role, and may thus also imply that with this new task, thinking is no longer thinking. Implicitly, Lyotard is asking here whether philosophical thought is intrinsically, or in truth, about consensus; about establishing universal rules to solve (dialogically, as Gadamer and Habermas would have it, falling into line with Plato) conflicts that are of the order of litigations between damaged and damaging parties. What if philosophical thought would not be true to its essence if it understood conflicts solely in terms of litigations, nor be faithful to its own task if it engaged in finding rules for solving them? Against the philosophers who understand philosophy "as the pursuit of conciliation or as obedience to its principle," Lyotard "pleads inconsistency [with respect to such a principle] which is not only the risk that thinking and writing runs, but the honor (honesty and probity) of thinking and writing."[48] As the analysis of the differend has shown, "at the far end of univocality, something announces itself (through feeling) which that 'unique voice' cannot phrase" (*D*, 86). This feeling, according to Lyotard, is a sign signaling that a differend must be put into phrases, though it cannot yet be done (*D*, 13); and philosophical thought must link onto this feeling if the honor of thinking is to be saved.

> To give the differend its due is to institute new addresses, new addressors, new significations, and new referents in order for the wrong to find an expression and for the plaintiff to cease being a victim. This requires new rules for the formation and linking of phrases. . . . Every wrong ought to be able to be put into phrases. A new competence (or 'prudence') must be found. (*D*, 13)

To give the differend its due requires finding ways of phrasing the wrong that a victim has incurred, and that inhibits the victim's overall power of doing things with words. Given that there are no universal rules for linking onto the silence to which the victim has been condemned, the competence Lyotard calls for can only be the practical wisdom of *phronesis*, which in Latin is called *prudentia*. What is required of any thinking that tries to save the honor of thinking by seeking to give the differend its due is not the theoretical elaboration of rules (not a *bios theoretikos*), for no differend is reducible to litigation, but a praxis, a *bios politikos*, on the level of linguistic pragmatics. Lyotard writes:

> A lot of searching must be done to find new rules for forming and linking phrases that are able to express the differend disclosed by the feeling, unless one wants this differend to be smothered right away in a litigation and for the alarm sounded by the feeling to have been useless. What is at stake in a literature, in a philosophy, in a politics perhaps, is to bear witness to differends by finding idioms for them. (*D*, 13)

I would like to recall here Lyotard's definition of philosophy: the philosophical discourse, he says, "has as its rule to discover its rule: its *a priori* is what it has at stake. It is a matter of formulating this rule, which can only be done at the end, if there is an end" (*D*, 60). If in philosophical thought "the links from phrase to phrase are not ruled by a rule but by the quest for a rule" (*D*, 97), then the search for new rules—rules for forming the phrases that may link onto the silence caused in differends—is philosophy's task par excellence. Rather than proceeding according to established rules, thinking is properly thinking only in the absence of preestablished rules. Its fate, therefore, is necessarily linked to the differend—that is, to the task of phrasing what cannot be said.

Lending an Ear to the Silence Phrase

LYOTARD'S AESTHETICS OF HOLOCAUST MEMORY

Dorota Glowacka

> You who aren't afraid of me
> Because I am little and I'm not even there
> Do not deny that I was
> Give me back the memory of me
> These post-Jewish words
> These post human words.
> —Jerzy Ficowski, "Seven Words"

> It takes a poet to describe it, I don't have the words.
> —Aba Beer, Holocaust survivor

In his lecture "Discussions, or Phrasing after Auschwitz," delivered in August 1980 at Cerisy-la-Salle, Lyotard announced that a new task for philosophy in the post-Holocaust era would be to link onto the name "Auschwitz," yet without obtaining a speculative result.[1] Auschwitz is a proper name that cannot be subsumed by *Aufhebung* because it is a nonnegatable negative (*un négatif non niable*) that can yield no meaning. When speculative dialectics can derive no profit, "were it a minimal one of the beautiful soul" (*LR*, 364), it grinds to a halt, its theoretical operators in disarray. In that case, what does it mean to speak about "Auschwitz"? How to present a phrase that connects to that name "otherwise"? In this essay, I will engage in "phrasing after Auschwitz," guided by Lyotard's precept.

In my work in the area of Holocaust literature and art, I have been aided by Lyotard's own responses to the Shoah in at least two ways. My first debt to him is intertwined with a personal narrative. Since I see myself as straddling two cultures, North American and Eastern European (Polish, to be exact), I have searched for ways to construct "passages" (*Übergänge*), to draw on Lyotard's use of Kant's vocabulary, over the abyss that seems to separate North American and Polish accounts of the annihilation of Jews in World War II. Lyotard stipulates, in *The Differend*, that two national narratives belong to the same genre of discourse, and therefore between them there is a litigation and not a differend. Because, for Lyotard, litigation implies an imminent resolution of the conflict, the application of this model to diverse instances of Holocaust testimony offers hope that the survivor's tale can be shared—indeed, translated and retranslated into a collective idiom that carries the message of "Never again!" Yet, the disputes over the different ways of memorializing the Shoah have been acrimonious, and one has a feeling that the conflict has eluded adjudication in the common language of the ethical imperative to remember. Lyotard bids us to heed such inexpressible feelings, since they often signal that something cannot be phrased in the language present at hand: a remainder, an intractable untranslatable that resists all efforts to share the Holocaust story.

Secondly, this personal experience of incommensurability between different ways of narrativizing the Holocaust has attuned me to a multitude of "differends" that often become suppressed within what I would like to call the Holocaust genre of discourse. The stakes of this genre are to remember the atrocities of the Shoah for the sake of the future, as expressed in the imperative "Remember!" In order to legitimate this wager and constitute itself as a genre of discourse, the Holocaust genre of discourse must continue to seal the gaps opened up by unresolvable conflicts.

The last decade has witnessed an exponential growth in the number of Holocaust productions, many of which have been deemed controversial for lack of a better term to designate the liquefaction of boundaries between creditable responses to the Shoah and "mere" aesthetic production. Some examples of contentious representations of the Holocaust include Art Spiegelman's graphic novel on the Holocaust, *Maus*; Binjamin Wilkomirski's (alias Bruno Doesseker's) *Fragments: Memories of a Wartime Childhood*;[2] Norman Finkelstein's polemical study, *The Holocaust Industry*;[3] Roberto Benigni's Oscar-winning film *Life Is Beautiful*; the Memorial to the Murdered Jews of Europe in Berlin; and the exhibition *Mirroring Evil: Nazi Imagery/Recent Art* at the Jewish Museum in New York, among others. The controversies surrounding all of them have spawned lengthy academic debates and leaked into popular media, signaling a crisis in the realm of Holocaust memory and Holocaust memorialization. Holocaust literature and art, as well as the debates surrounding these works, have become the site where the relationships between ethics and aesthetics enter a hiatus. I propose to call this radical discrepancy between the piety of memory and the iconoclastic impetus of art called upon to convey that memory the differend between the ethical and the aesthetic phrase. I will insist that a Holocaust scholar today, as well as anyone wishing to remember the Holocaust for the sake of the future, is confronted with the task of bearing witness to that differend.

Lyotard's critics often find him guilty of collapsing the realms of ethics and aesthetics, of politics and art, into a panaestheticism of the sublime, under the aegis of the avant-garde artist. This often translates into the critic's frustration with the logic (or paralogic) of Lyotard's arguments; Allen Dunn, for instance, objects to the irremediable contradiction inherent in Lyotard's articulation of the differend: it stands for both an ethical call for justice and the aesthetic celebration of incommensurability.[4] Such criticism, however, seems possible only within the purview of the game, whose stakes are to maintain traditional boundaries between ethics and aesthetics. It necessarily skirts, for example, Levinasian inflections of Lyotard's take on ethics, that is, Lyotard's own efforts to articulate heterogeneity "otherwise," and the fact that he is writing both within and against the contexts of post-Heideggerian critiques of mimesis (most notably by Jacques Derrida and Philippe Lacoue-Labarthe).

Lyotard's "pagan" forays into philosophy involve continuous negotiations in the border zone between ethics and aesthetics, where he continuously redraws their respective territories.[5] In the context of renewed debates about the limits of representation and the politics of Holocaust memory, Lyotard's most notable contributions to the idea of postmodernity, that is, his resuscitation (via Longinus and Burke) of the Kantian sublime—a term after all from the provenance of traditional aesthetics—and his formulation of the notion of the differend, arguably an ethical concept, are gaining new currency.

In order to situate Lyotard between ethics and aesthetics, I will retrace the slippage between three terms in Lyotard's oeuvre: the sublime, the differend, and "the jew." The thought of the sublime, the category that already in Kant stretches between aesthetics and ethics, informs many of Lyotard's texts, culminating in an extensive exposition of Kant's *Critique of Judgment* in *Lessons on the Analytic of the Sublime.*[6] Engaging in a multiple exegesis of the Kantian text, Lyotard reads the sublime over and against Kant as the moment that upsets the architectonics of the faculties and fractures the unity of the transcendental subject instead of grounding it. According to Kant, the sublime results from the imagination's failure to provide a representation corresponding to the idea; taut at its very limits, imagination plunges into the abyss, and it can do no more than signal the frustration of its incommensurability with what exceeds it as the faculty of presentation. This signal comes as a shock, "the feeling of a momentary checking of vital powers,"[7] and erupts in the sensation of simultaneous pleasure and pain—the distress of imagination's sacrifice and the satisfaction of having gestured, even if only in a negative fashion, toward the suprasensible. This sensation of imagination striking against its limit never becomes present to the perceiving mind, which means that the sublime affect cannot be experienced as a moment in the temporal continuum, to be retained in memory or prehended in anticipation of a concrete shape. Irrecoverable in representation, the sublime "cracks open . . . a framework placed over the manifold," eluding schematism.[8] The sublime is then the experience of bearing witness to the intensity of feeling when the event of presentation, of mind putting into shape, is happening. Abandoning the fixity of the beautiful form, the *Formlösigkeit* of the sublime is the aesthetics of movement, of an endless play of the figure's absence. Yet, always awaiting the future of possible presentation, it signals the infinite possibility of figuring.

Lyotard revisits Kantian aesthetics in order to articulate the postmodern: if Kant's evocation of the sublime as the presentation of the unpresentable betrays nostalgia for the ineffable presence (and, as Lyotard says in "Answering the Question: What Is Postmodernism?," the yearning for the solace of good form), the postmodern sublime is the presentation that the unpresentable *is*, and as such, it signals, through an indeterminate feeling, the minimal occurrence of the question "Is it happening?" *(Arrive-t-il?)*. The sublime is therefore an affective testimony to "Is it happening?" that averts the terror of ultimate privation, that is, of nothing further happening. That it happens, says Lyotard, precedes the cognitive question pertaining to what happens: "Or rather, the question precedes itself. . . . The event happens as a question mark 'before' the happening as a question" (*LR*, 197). The occurrence is infinitely simple, and it can only be approached in a state of privation—an inner ascesis or sacrifice (Kant's *Be-*

raubung [spoliation]) of pathological interest. It does not mark a transcendent moment of an unattainable elsewhere but the here-and-now of the occurrence, the intensity of feeling. In a later text, entitled "L'inarticulé ou le différend même," Lyotard has referred to the singular sensation of the sublime as an "affect phrase"; the affect phrase is inarticulate because it does not present a phrase universe and its time is always the time of the "now"—"a feeling appears and disappears entirely at every instant . . . it is completely new each time."[9]

That is why this feeling, which Barnett Newman once called "a sensation of time," poses a conundrum for memory: how will the mind remember it? Lyotard writes, in *Heidegger and "the jews"*: "When the sublime is 'there' (where?), the mind is not there. As long as the mind is, there is no sublime. This is a feeling that is incompatible with time, as is 'death'" (*HJ*, 32). Yet, it signals that something in excess of consciousness has touched the mind.

In *The Differend*, Lyotard deploys the idiom of the sublime, the sensation that marks the discord between the faculties, to communicate the sense of the differend's resistance to representation. The first "Kant Notice" identifies the primal conflict inherent in every act of representation: there is a disparity between "nature," which is the first addressor, and the perceiving "subject," the addressee affected by sensations. The subject "knows," or rather intuits, that something seeks to phrase itself, but it fails to do so in the idiom of space-time categories. The indeterminate affect of the sublime then signals, without occluding it, the differend between the faculty of understanding and the otherness of nature, which appears to the subject as a multitude of sensations. It is a feeling that "there is a first phrase, and it does not come from the subject" (*D*, 63).

In the "Preface: Reading Dossier" to *The Differend*, Lyotard defines the differend as "the unstable state and instant of language wherein something which must be able to be put into phrases cannot yet be" (*D*, 13). Bearing witness to the differend entails the necessity of respecting the experience of heterogeneity between phrases. Between instances within each phrase, and between genres of discourse. Since phrases can only arrive one at a time, that is, the possibility of all the other phrases is foreclosed with the arrival of the current one, the relation of the current phrase to the phrases from different phrase regimens is agonistic. Further, the phrase universe of each phrase is marked by the disunity between the addressor and the addressee. As it comes along, a phrase enters into a conflict between different genres of discourse, and when the stakes of one genre of discourse prevail, the others are obliterated or repressed, as is the differend between them. The very fact that the phrase is taking place, the event of its current arrival into speech, is occluded. Genres of discourse are modes of forgetting the very fact that "it" happens as a phrase here and now, in the singularity and simplicity of its occurrence. The differend remains nevertheless, demanding that it be articulated. The only potential linkage or passage between the various incommensurables is an indeterminate affect, "the silent feeling that signals that the differend remains to be listened to" (*D*, 141). The proleptic "yet to be phrased" of the differend, currently signaled by silence, is what calls upon possible future phrases.

In *The Differend*, Lyotard pays special attention to obligation, the phrase that places emphasis on the addressee while leaving empty the pole of the addressor. In the phrase of obligation, the "I" instance of the transcendental subject, the one who both prescribes the ethical norm and responds to the "you ought to" of the categorical imperative, is displaced from its privileged site as the addressor of the prescriptive and situated in the position of a hostage to the voice that commands. Obligation, according to Lyotard, is therefore a preeminently Jewish phrase, as witnessed in the injunction "Listen, Israel!" The Jews, as Lyotard explains in *Heidegger and the "jews,"* are the community bound by the "law of listening, which cannot spare it the despair of never hearing what the voice says" (*HJ*, 22). They are the people who bear witness to the occurrence of the command as the voice that commands. To convey the sense of the absolute nature of this obligation, Lyotard quotes Levinas, from *Quatre lectures talmudiques*: "They act before they harken!" (*D*, 111). The imperative "Listen, Israel!" is empty of content, yet the necessity of responding or a demand for further phrasing is always already inscribed in it. Obligation is at the farthest remove from the Aryan narrative. Unlike the phrase of the Jewish law, in which the instances of the addressor of the command and its addressee are radically separated, in the Aryan narrative all the instances in the phrase universe are conflated in the single name "Aryan." The Aryan myth is formulated as a self-referential prescriptive, tightly closed upon itself: "If you are Aryan, tell, hear and carry out the Aryan 'beautiful death.' . . . If you hear, tell or do. If you tell, hear or do. If you do, tell or hear. The implications are reciprocal" (*D*, 105). The time of the transmission is already folded into the mythical past of the events it is conveying. The stakes of the Aryan narrative are thus waged upon the foreclosure of the very event of phrasing.

It is no coincidence, therefore, that the post-Holocaust attempts to phrase the inexpressible wrong perpetrated on the Jews and to restore to the victims their extinguished phrase have surfaced as another phrase of obligation: "Remember!" (*Zakhor!*). Within the horizon of Lyotard's phrastics, however, there arises a question: what happens to the phrase "Remember!" when it comes along? Further, does the command "Remember!" make sense, is it "a meaningful phrase?" (*D*, 17). In the Holocaust genre of discourse, the differends proliferate on the edges of this memory phrase, where we cannot yet know what it is that we must remember or how we are to remember "it." Unlike in the phrase "Listen, Israel!", which prohibits the name of the addressor while the addressee is clearly designated ("chosen"), the addressee instance of the imperative "Remember!" is also left unmarked. Who is its addressee? Is the addressee singular or plural? Although phrasing is necessary and the next phrase is immediately presupposed, it is contingent on how the addressee chooses to link onto the command. By analogy with Lyotard's example in which the officer shouts "Avanti!" and jumps out of the trench, to which the soldiers reply "Bravo!" and do not move, the addressee of "Remember!" can respond with an approving "Well said!" or with a dismissive "Why should I care?" Both of these utterances signal that the addressor of these rejoinders withdraws himself or herself from the addressee instance of what was to be a phrase of obligation; the addressee has not listened, although he or she may have heard. A phrase is obligatory, Lyotard explains, only "if the addressee feels obligated" (*D*, 108).

Secondly, if the addressor instance of the obligation is empty, unknown, where is the phrase "Remember!" arriving from? Who bids me to never forget? One can imagine it as a voice from the gas chamber of Bergen-Belsen, as in the poem quoted in the epigraph, or from a bunker in the Warsaw ghetto in the last days of the uprising, that is, from the place of death. In the memory phrase "Remember!" the addressor has withdrawn, commanding the addressee absolutely by this absence. "Remember!" then signals absolute transcendence of the voice that demands remembrance, and the abyss between the sender of the prescriptive and the receiver of the command is unbridgeable. The phrase "Remember!" is marked by indeterminacy, bidding "us" to engage in memory events without the criteria that would determine who is a competent rememberer, adequate to the task of witnessing. Bearing witness to the indeterminacy of "Remember!" requires respect for the alterity of the non-place from which the command arrives and acceptance of its inconvertibility into known categories. If this is the case, no one, not even a survivor, is vested with the absolute authority to prescribe it or, as has been evident in the debates about Wilkomirski's fictional memoir, to judge the substance of someone else's memory. Yet, many of us, especially those who teach in the area of Holocaust studies and often consider ourselves to be the appointed guardians of Holocaust memory, do so. Yet, as David Carroll explains in his introduction to *Heidegger and "the jews,"* Lyotard's work cautions against succumbing to piety that elevates the Shoah to a moral absolute; such a sacrosanct stance prohibits discussion and is no longer remembrance but "a way of granting oneself the authority to speak . . . a means of silencing those who are claimed not to have the authority to speak about it."[10]

What is the referent of "Remember!"? The reality this phrase designates is not signified in the phrase, but this radical obliteration of the referent demands that the command be followed by descriptives, by infinitely possible recitations of "I will never forget" this or that, as in Elie Wiesel's famous passage from *Night*:

> Never shall I forget that night, the first night in camp, which has turned my life into one long night, seven times cursed and seven times sealed. Never shall I forget that smoke. Never shall I forget the little faces of the children, whose bodies I saw turned into wreaths of smoke beneath a silent blue sky.
>
> Never shall I forget those flames which consumed my faith forever.
>
> Never shall I forget that nocturnal silence which deprived me, for all eternity, of the desire to live. Never shall I forget those moments that murdered my God and my soul and turned my dreams to dust. Never shall I forget these things, even if I am condemned to live as God Himself. Never.[11]

Lyotard says, "Impertinence is to link onto the command by a commentary on a command, and not by its execution" (*D*, 85). But we do engage in commentaries, and in that sense, Wiesel himself is impertinent, albeit his "betrayal" is a necessary one, for "one must, in any case, speak (*dire*)" (*LR*, 364). The incommensurability between "Remember!" and knowledge phrases about the Holocaust is inevitable; yet, the possibilities of linking onto "Remember!" are infinite. They can be such as to uphold the hegemony of cognitives, to perpetrate the erasure of the differend and suppress the very occurrence of the memory phrase—or they can bear witness to indeterminacy and foreground the conflict. Lyotard writes that "the presentation entailed by a phrase-case is not presented in the universe that this phrase presents. . . . But another phrase-case can present it in another universe and thereby situate it" (*D*, 71); it is possible, therefore, to create, in the utterance that ensues, the conditions for phrases from heterogeneous families to meet.[12] I would argue that, alongside a great number of texts whose authenticity has been nevertheless deemed impeccable, Binjamin Wilkomirski's "testimony," its dubious status as a memoir notwithstanding, was a case of such presentation, although it must be rejected under the cognitive regimen. Since it is this regimen, grounded in knowledge claims, that most often adjudicates what constitutes acceptable Holocaust testimony, the debates about Holocaust literature often turn into attempts to legitimate the phrase "Remember!" whereby it vanishes as the phrase of obligation. History, the genre of cognitives, the depository of things remembered, forgets the event; it is necessary that it forget so that it can continue narrating. But, says Lyotard, "the silence imposed on knowledge does not impose the silence of forgetting, it imposes a feeling" (*D*, 58), a sign that something is happening, but it cannot be articulated with a historian's "game." In order for a historian to become attentive to the silence coming from the phrases in abeyance, whose possibility of arriving has been eclipsed, he or she must "break with the monopoly over history granted to the cognitive regimen of phrases, and he or she must venture forth by lending his or her ear to what is not presentable under the rules of knowledge" (*D*, 57).[13]

Holocaust literature frequently illustrates the preponderant silence imposed upon the survivor's phrase. For example, in a dramatic piece titled "The Table," by Ida Fink, a Holocaust survivor now living in Israel, a prosecutor is trying to establish the truth about an *Aktion* in a small-town ghetto, during which twelve hundred Jews were murdered. He solicits corroborative evidence, required in order to bring the murderers to justice before the law. The eyewitnesses' accounts during the interrogation, however, are inconsistent, even contradictory, and it becomes frustratingly obvious that no positive proof of the crime will ever be established. Instead of proof, the witnesses offer descriptive judgments:

> WITNESS: "The square was black with people."
> PROSECUTOR: "'The square was black with people' is not completely accurate."

> WITNESS: "It was a sunny, cold day. There was snow in the streets. The snow was red."
>
> ANOTHER WITNESS: "Oh, you want proof, don't you? The snow on the town's streets was red. Red! Does that satisfy you?"
>
> PROSECUTOR: "Unfortunately, Mr. Zachwacki, snow does not constitute proof for judges, especially snow that melted twenty-five years ago."[14]

What really matters—the nightmare of the selection process and the enormity of the crimes—cannot be ascertained. It is signaled, however, outside all the evidence that the witnesses can provide, in the silences that cloak the prosecutor's frustration and the witnesses' anguish as they desire to procure such "proof." It is the affect phrase, inadmissible under the rules that constitute the genre of history, that resists the hegemony of knowledge phrases.

My second question to Lyotard is about the name "Auschwitz," a proper name that has become an overarching symbol for the atrocities of the Holocaust. In the universe of phrases, says Lyotard, the proper name occupies a unique position: "A single proper name, whether singular or collective, designates an entity astride two heterogeneous situations" (*D*, 99). The differend flourishes around names, although they themselves remain fixed throughout the sequences of phrases. Lyotard notes that names, unlike common nouns, are untranslatable, but they have the property of attracting to themselves phrases belonging to different regimens and to heterogeneous genres of discourse. The name cannot be ultimately validated: its reality cannot be established because in order to do so subsequent phrases must signify it, name it, and show it. Because the name is "an empty and constant designator" (*D*, 44), the number of possible phrases that can attach themselves to a single name is infinite, even if such inflation of possible senses around a name can be halted by history phrases (cognitives).

In the chapter "The Referent, the Name," Lyotard provides an example (and the philosopher is not unaware of the politics of examples in his book) of a descriptive phrase that attaches itself to the name Auschwitz: "Auschwitz is a city in southern Poland in the vicinity of which the Nazi administration installed an extermination camp in 1940" (*D*, 44). For those who band around the collective name "Polish people," this example is disquieting. Lyotard would find himself in litigation with Polish historians over the criteria for establishing the reality of the referent for this well-formed expression. According to Polish sources, "Auschwitz" is not a name of the town in Poland, and it is debatable whether it has ever been. Since the first settlements there in the twelfth century, the name of the town has been Oświęcim, although it was called Auschwitz by German settlers and merchants who were passing through the town on the way to Kraków. According to Polish sources, one can hear the transformation of Oświęcim—the root of the name is ostensibly Slavic—into Germanic "Auschwitz" through the permutations of the name in the fourteenth century: Auswintzen, Auswieczin, Awswiczin. The town was referred to as Auschwitz in legal documents after the first partition of Poland at the end of the eighteenth century, when Oświęcim became part of the Austro-Hungarian Empire. In October 1939 the Germans changed the name of Oświęcim to Auschwitz, and when the town and the concentration camp were liberated on January 27, 1945, the Polish name was returned. The battle for the name of the town has been central to the Polish nationalist narrative and the country's struggle for political independence. In today's Poland, it is known that Auschwitz was the name of the death camp, Kontzentrazionlager Auschwitz, yet the place is remembered as Oświęcim. Polish narratives of camp survival are titled, for instance, *Przeżyłam Oświęcim* (a memoir by Krystyna Żywulska).[15]

Polish historians, who have written extensively on the historic town of Oświęcim, have been irked by the obliteration of the Polish name. The elision of the name Oświęcim, around which Polish memory of the Shoah has congealed, from the Holocaust genre of discourse has virtually excluded Polish historians, philosophers, and writers from participating in the dialogue on the subject of post-Auschwitz thought, post-Auschwitz philosophy, post-Auschwitz theology, and post-Auschwitz poetry writing. Is this feud over the name a sign of a certain "geophilosophy," the kind that Lyotard attributes to Heidegger, opposing it to "'the jew's' hatred of geophilosophy" (*HJ*, 93)? To what extent does it signal a "translation differend" between the languages in which the Holocaust genre of discourse is formulated and in which its narratives are embedded? It should also be noted that the stakes involved in the politics of the name Auschwitz do not admit a certain Jewish phrase. The Holocaust survivor Moshe Weiss, a former Jewish inhabitant of the town of Oświęcim, reminds us, in a memoir entitled *From Oświęcim to Auschwitz*, that "Auschwitz, a name that has seared itself on the collective memory of humanity as the place of ultimate horror, is called by the Poles Oświęcim, but we Jews, who in those days constituted two-thirds of its population of 12,000, called it

Oshpitzin, a word that means guests."[16] In the post-Shoah battle for the name, the Jewish name has been forgotten, buried under the Polish name Oświęcim and the German name Auschwitz. The stakes placed in a name are not necessarily cognitive; they can be aesthetic, ethical, political, or other, and the same goes for the stakes of the genre of history in which the etymology of the name Oświęcim is being established.

Lyotard diagnoses, as did others before him, the impossibility of "after-Auschwitz" aesthetics; yet, it is important, even if perhaps somewhat naive, to share Lyotard's "faith" that art persists nevertheless—dead as a beautiful form and devoted only to delivering the "nothing" of the event. The task of the artist is to perpetuate art through bearing witness to the gesture of art, to the event that signals its own unpresentability. Because, for the last several decades, the events of the Shoah have been often evoked as the ultimate unpresentable, it is obvious how their representations would yield themselves to an analysis in terms of the sublime, defined by Kant as negative presentation. I have avoided this route of negative theology for fear that the post-Auschwitz call to "present the unpresentable" has become so much of a cliché in Holocaust studies that perhaps it does not move us anymore. And, as Lyotard reminds us, it is important to pay attention to feelings, a host of sublime feelings that compel us to search for idioms to express them. Sorrow (*der Kummer*), says Kant in *The Critique of Judgment* (quoted in *D*, 179), is one of those vigorous emotions that move the mind.

I would argue simply that it is imperative for Holocaust art and literature, as well as for the debates that surround them, to acknowledge and pursue both "the pain of silence and the pleasure of invention," the affective paradox of the sublime. It is this sensation that announces the advent of "Is it happening?" which, in bearing witness to the differends surrounding the memory phrase "Remember!," ungrounds both ethics and aesthetics. Elie Wiesel's litany of horror moves us not only as a graphic description of little children being murdered but also as an event, an incantation, a dirge whose rhythm, complemented by the rhythm of my reading, probes the immeasurable depths of grief. Although Wilkomirski's *Fragments* must be carefully contextualized and exposed as fictitious, it has proved its extraordinary capacity for moving us. For many readers, the exposure to "the facts" of the Wilkomirski affair does not deaden the emotional impact of this vicarious testimony to human pain, engulfed by silence. Let us return to this silence.[17]

The silence that occasioned the phrasing of Lyotard's own book was the silence of Holocaust survivors and their inability to prove the wrong they had suffered vis-à-vis the Holocaust denier Robert Fourisson and his cohort. The differend is surrounded by silence; yet, Lyotard insists, silence is also a phrase in which one or more instances have been muted. Silence in place of an utterance can signal the addressor's inability to speak because of constraint or the lack of authority to do so, or the language's failure to communicate the meaning of the event. It can also indicate the nonexistence of the referent, and this is how a Holocaust denier chooses to interpret a survivor's silence. Finally, as Lyotard remarks in *Heidegger and "the jews,"* it may suggest the addressee's lack of authority or even his or her incapacity to listen, as in the case of Heidegger's silence, "mute, leaden silence that lets nothing be heard" and that stifles the imperative to do justice. In each case, however, silence is not a cessation of speech but a relation of speech, a sign that further phrasing is necessary.

The motifs of stunned silence in the wake of the Shoah, the strife between speech and silence in testimonies, and the challenge of rendering the disastrous in language have been central to debates about representing the Holocaust. In order to find an idiom to express the wrong suffered by the Jewish victims, the injustice that has deprived the survivors even of the ability to express their grievance, the negations bearing upon their stunted phrases have to be withdrawn—in the phrases issuing from "us." Speech arrives from the abyss of silence, from the threat of the absolute cessation of speech; these silences come to us who speak them. Yet, if the questions of moral responsibility that infuse the discussions about representing the Shoah hinge upon the question of silence, it must not be overlooked that in Holocaust literature and art, including memoirs and diaries, silence is the most powerful rhetorical figure, the figure of the sublime, as Longinus already knew when he was writing *Peri Hupsos*. The example many will recall is the barbershop episode during Abraham Bomba's testimony in Lanzmann's *Shoah*; a lesser-known example from the history of Holocaust cinema is a moment in Andrzej Wajda's *Korczak*, a film about the Jewish doctor and director of the orphanage in the Warsaw ghetto, who fought for the survival of his wards until the very end and followed them to the gas chambers of Treblinka. Following the sequence when the children from the Warsaw ghetto orphanage board the cattle train, there are several empty frames—the cinematic equivalent of the silence phrase that summons "Remember!"

In print, such silences are usually marked with ellipses, and some Holocaust memoirs (for instance, Isabella Leitner's *Fragments of Isabella*) are punctuated by more ellipses than "regular" full stops.[18] In the published transcripts of diaries written in the midst of horror, whose authors often perished without a trace, the ellipses indicate the missing pages or the sentences broken off in the middle (and many Holocaust diaries end haltingly that way). Similarly, the style of much Holocaust literature is marked by a strong tendency toward parataxis, as if all the modes of linking that indicate logical causality had failed. As Lyotard remarks, referring to Auerbach's famous comparison between the Greek and the Hebrew styles of writing (in *Mimesis: The Representation of Reality in Western Literature*), parataxis connotes the abyss of Not-being that opens between phrases. In the context of Holocaust literature, it is especially poignant that the writing style should bring us to the brink of that abyss, where we are shocked and surprised that *it* is being said, even if instead of an "and" there should be nothing. Parataxis is "the conjunction that most allows the constitutive discontinuity (or oblivion)" (*D*, 67).

Yet the considerations that fall under the domain of rhetoric and aesthetics are often excluded from the debates on the memory after the Shoah, echoing Emmanuel Levinas's pronouncements that aesthetics, "the games of art," are injurious to ethics. The suppression of the aesthetic phrase in commentaries on Holocaust literature and art, of the judgment of taste of the beautiful and the sublime, allows for the hegemony of the ethical phrase. Subsuming the memory phrase "Remember!" under the ethical phrase occludes, therefore, the differend inherent in the analogy between the sacrifice of human life and the sacrifice of imagination striving to present the unpresentable, although it is this differend that makes further phrasing necessary. As Lyotard reminds us in his critical reading of Kant, the bridging every analogy performs, its "as if" (*als ob*), maintains the separation in the very act of attempting to span it. I would argue that bearing witness to the incommensurability between the ethical and the aesthetic phrase allows us to discuss, teach, read, and experience Holocaust literature and art as memory events rather than as "mere" substantiations of the paradox of negative presentation. Lyotard's "anaesthetics"—his negotiations between ethics and aesthetics—bid us to acknowledge the sensation of "Is it happening?" as both an ethical expression of injustice and an aesthetic gesture of what he calls "avant-gardes," a gesture of free imagination, presenting nothing. The law of "Is it happening?" does not rely on any set of criteria or prescriptives because it is indeterminate and new each time. The constitutive power that takes up that law and strives to "present" it Lyotard calls, after Kant, imagination: "Imagination is not only the power to judge; it is a power to invent criteria."[19] Imagination is that which searches without a rule, which reaches for an untried possibility, for the next possible phrase. Its task is not, as Kant may have desired, to wrestle the unity of the subject out of the heterogeneous, but to bring the faculties into movement, into agitation which "presents" that there is indeterminacy. This is the law that "Remember!" is calling forth. The occurrence of "Is it happening?" is, for the memory phrase, a glimpse of its own persistence and the affirmation of its own ability to continue. This does not mean that we are awaiting a Gertrude Stein of Holocaust literature or a Marcel Duchamp of Holocaust art for this to happen; it has happened already, in many of the works I am familiar with—although in each instance of remembering we have to allow it to happen again.

Holocaust memory today is seized with the terror of its own imminent disappearance, of its not happening anymore, and it hastens to absorb that terror into all-too-familiar representations and mantras of "so it never happens again." Lyotard reflects, "One will say, It was a great massacre, how horrible! . . . one cries out 'never again' and that's it! It is taken care of" (*HJ*, 26). On the other hand, by the very event of its being written, Holocaust literature "as if" says "Remember!" in an instance of the here-and-now of the memory phrase, keeping it alive. It is this recalcitrance of the memory phrase with respect to any one genre of discourse, also reflected in its resistance to literary classifications into genres such as fiction and nonfiction, that defies the impersonality and anonymity of Holocaust memory, the features that allow its referent to sink into oblivion. The hysteria around Wilkomirski's fictional memoir was a symptom of that absolute terror of the vanishing of memory, its dispersal in representation with the death of the last witness. We despair of our inability to remember truly if we can no longer distinguish between the authentic voice of a legitimate victim and the chaff of constructed memory.

For those who care, it is terrifying that no phrase might attach itself to "Remember!," to the posthumous phrase issuing from the dead, who insist on becoming phrased. The shock, the sublime "intensity producing ontological dislocation" (*LR*, 206) that some, but certainly not all, of Holocaust literature is capable of producing, is an index of this anxiety. Yet, at the same time, it gives the pleasure of warding off that fear, in the here-and-now of the memory event, signaling the interval in which bearing witness occurs. It offers the assurance that not only is linking necessary but also, as Edmund Burke already knew, "it is in our power to effect with words combinations that would be impossible by any other means" (*LR*, 205).

Heidegger and "the jews" is largely Lyotard's own effort to phrase on the edges of "Remember!". He knows that forgetting is not a failure of what was first constituted as memory but that it precedes memory itself as a starting point that has erased the very possibility of memory. That is why he would probably concur that the memory phrase is marked by indeterminacy: the only thing remembered is that something has disappeared into oblivion. In *Heidegger and "the jews,"* Lyotard spells "jews" in lowercase, in distinction from "the real Jews," who paid the real price for the Nazi attempt to eliminate the occurrence. "The jews," for Lyotard, represent the unpresentable, that which is constitutively always already forgotten in Europe's memory yet which resists the foundational thinking of the Occident. "The jews" are the people who guard the memory of what cannot be represented, witnesses to the non-place from which thinking proceeds. Analogously, in the essay "The Survivor," Lyotard argues that the survivor is an inscription of the occurrence of "Is it happening?," a witness that "something indeterminate still happens, when in fact it should be no longer, not be capable, not be able to stand it any longer."[20] The survivor, therefore, is in a paradoxical position in relation to speech, since by continuing to be, he or she bears witness to the elimination of the possibility that he or she was supposed to have stopped speaking, the possibility decreed by the Nazi prescriptive that he or she die!

Lyotard writes that "philosophy as architecture is ruined, but a writing of the ruins, micrologies, graffiti can still be done" (*HJ*, 43). For Lyotard, philosophy is a genre of discourse whose stakes are in a rule that remains to be sought, and the indeterminacy of the sublime is, in a sense, the critical essence of philosophy.[21] Yet, should we not think about the Holocaust genre of discourse as also such writing of the ruins whose task, like that of the philosophical genre, is to proceed without a rule? Lyotard asks, "But what if the stakes of thought concerned differend rather than consensus?" (*D*, 84). I would argue that the same question pertains to Holocaust literature and art, summoned into existence "after-Auschwitz" by the memory phrase "Remember!" whereby the links from phrase to phrase are determined not by the rules of how to remember the victims of the

Holocaust but by "a quest for a rule" (*D*, 97). The art of memory, marked by the *Formlösigkeit* of the sublime, is seized and dispossessed by the urgency of the indeterminate it is trying to capture. Holocaust literature is not only about knowing, but also about feeling, always posing anew the challenge of how we can share an affect that is unexchangeable. This literature breaches speculative logic because, as David Carroll has written, it is "indebted to the memory of fundamental non-memory and . . . obliged to recognize this debt."[22] To Allen Dunn's warning that "it is dangerous to conflate the artist's need for discontinuous originality with a death camp victim's plea for justice,"[23] one should answer, "Yes, I am running that risk each time I link onto 'Remember!'; nevertheless, I ought to."

Lyotard himself proposes that the unforgotten, which endures in the forgetting of where the voice is coming from, cannot be represented without being missed, being forgotten again:

> Whenever one represents, one inscribes in memory, and this might seem a good defence against forgetting. It is, I believe, just the opposite. Only that which has been inscribed, can in the current sense of the term, be forgotten because it could be effaced. . . . One must, certainly, inscribe in words, in images. One cannot escape the necessity of representing. But it is one thing to do it in view of saving the memory, and quite another to try to preserve the remainder, the unforgettable forgotten, in writing. (*HJ*, 26)[24]

The withdrawn referent of "Remember!," like "the jew," cannot be remembered for what it was, but must be remembered as something that never ceases to be forgotten, anamnesis and amnesia at the same time. The occurrence of the memory phrase is withdrawn from representation, "but this concealment lets something else show, this contradictory feeling of a 'presence' that is certainly not present, but which precisely needs to be forgotten to be represented; this is the theme of not only avant-gardes but also 'the jews'" (*HJ*, 4). While ordinary memory merely accomplishes forgetting, as has been the case with the forgotten Jewish names in Poland, Lyotard, as if taking his cue from Elie Wiesel's Hasidic tale, admonishes that "it must even be sufficient that one remembers that one must remember, that one should" (*HJ*, 38).[25]

Holocaust literature—the art of the excess of memory and the ruin of memory—becomes the writing of the differend. It searches for the ways to express the impossibility of either remembering or forgetting what cannot be remembered, although, yes, we know now, and we fear, that it can be forgotten. I see the task of Holocaust literature, art, and criticism today as bearing witness to the "Is it happening?" of the memory phrase "Remember!" so that the question mark is not snuffed out. The artist, critic, or teacher is a guardian of memory, whose duty is to listen to the rumblings of the differend, allowing herself or himself to feel the tremors along the fault lines of memory, even if all the instruments for the measurement of their impact have been destroyed, to evoke Lyotard's famous seismic metaphor.[26] What remains when the apparatuses of knowledge malfunction and words turn up fallow, is "the interstice, without extension, which is the instant of judgement, reading, learning, and writing, of growing up undisturbed, for the child."[27] Lyotard writes that it is not by chance that Wiesel's witness in *Night* is a child, but the same goes for many other prime examples of Holocaust literature and art, from Anne Frank's *Diary of a Young Girl*, Henryk Grynberg's *The Jewish War*, and Imre Kertész's *Fateless* to Wilkomirski's book, all of which try to capture the moment of childish wonder, the innocence of the mind, and thus release the unremembered of memory, not yet buried by the piety that seeks to annex the memory phrase "Remember!"

The above reflections are intended to convey my belief in the importance of lending an ear to "Remember!" today. Let me end with a quote, which could serve as a gloss on Lyotard's differend in the realm of popular Holocaust art, from Art Spiegelman's *Maus*. In his graphic novel Spiegelman, an adult child of a Holocaust survivor, uses comic-strip drawings, in which Jews are mice and Germans are cats, to work through his father's recollections of his ordeal in the ghettos of German-occupied Poland and then in Auschwitz. In one of the panels in the second volume we see the cartoonist, drawn as a diminutive child mouse, during a psychotherapy session; he is in treatment for depression following the success of the first volume, titled *My Father Bleeds History*. The therapist, himself a Holocaust survivor, says, "Anyway, the victims who died can never tell *their* side of the story, so maybe it's better not to have any more stories." Spiegelman's character replies, "Uh-huh. Samuel Beckett once said: 'Every word is like an unnecessary stain on silence and nothingness.'" The next image *is* "silent," with wisps of smoke from two cigarettes winding around the little mouse figures instead of speech bubbles; indeed, this is the only entirely silent panel in the book. Yet, in the next picture, Art "links on" over the abyss of the wordless frame and remarks, "On the other hand, he *said* it."[28]

Toward a Feminist Ethics of Dissensus

POLEMOS, EMBODIMENT, OBLIGATION

Ewa Płonowska Ziarek

Partly because of the pivotal role *The Postmodern Condition* has played in the debates about postmodernity, Lyotard has had the bad or good luck to be interrogated within feminist theory as a representative of postmodernism as such. As a result of this "exemplary role," his work has been frequently read in terms of the cautionary tale about the possible misuses or dangers of postmodernism for feminism. Thus, the question posed most frequently to Lyotard is whether his work can be "compatible with the normative content of feminism, not just as a theoretical position but as a theory of women's struggle for emancipation."[1] What is symptomatic about this type of reading is that it usually focuses on Lyotard's critique of metanarratives but ignores its aftermath, the search for an alternative justice. This omission is perhaps a symptom of a reluctance to interrogate "the normative content" of feminism itself. Consequently, I will argue that a more productive rapprochement between Lyotard's work and feminist theories would occur in the context of the complex negotiations between antagonism and justice, between the agonistic politics of difference and the ethical responsibility grounded in embodiment.

From the outset, the feminist critiques of Lyotard are split according to different conceptions of feminism defined either as a continuation of the emancipatory promise of modernity or as the political project of postmodernity. Seyla Benhabib's works, "Epistemologies of Postmodernism: A Rejoinder to Jean-François Lyotard" and her *Gender, Community, and Postmodernism in Contemporary Ethics*, are powerful examples of the first position, whereas Nancy Fraser's and Linda Nicholson's essay, "Social

Criticism without Philosophy: An Encounter between Feminism and Postmodernism," is a compelling instance of the second. Reformulating Habermas's project of communicative ethics, Benhabib's criticism of Lyotard seeks to advance the emancipatory potential of feminist critical philosophy by preserving the universalizable validity claims. In contrast, Fraser's and Nicholson's critique is motivated by a vision of feminist social criticism "without philosophy," and thus without a need for a global theory of justice to validate "a politics of difference." Warning that a feminist alliance with Lyotard's "strong" version of postmodernism entails "the risk of incoherence,"[2] Benhabib claims that Lyotard's critique of metanarratives, autonomy, and philosophy fails to distinguish between operations of power and the normative criteria of justice and thus "is not only incompatible with but would undermine the very possibility of feminism as the theoretical articulation of the emancipatory aspirations of women."[3] Lyotard's "agonistic" politics can lead thus to two contradictory outcomes: either to the polytheism of values, which does not allow for a "practical-moral" critique of social inequalities, or to some unacknowledged criterion of justice, which creates an internal contradiction and blindness to validity claims in his work. The ambiguity Benhabib sees in Lyotard stems from her exclusive focus on one side of his thought—on the agonistic conception of language, which perpetuates the legacy of Nietzsche—to the glaring disregard of his work on justice and reflective judgment, which continues the legacy of Kant, Buber, Derrida, and Levinas, among others. This disregard is evident even in Benhabib's more mitigated recent work, in which she admits that "the task of philosophical politics today is the conceptualization of new forms of association which will let the 'differend' appear in their midst."[4] In place of the either/or choice she places before feminism—between the indifferent struggle of heterogeneous forces or the normative criteria of justice—Lyotard poses a different task of thinking justice within conflict, that is, the task of pursuing a just judgment in face of the contestation over the criteria of such judgment.

The force of Benhabib's critique is to pose the question of justice as a central issue for feminist political projects; its weakness is to reduce this question to universalizable validity claims. By contrast, Fraser and Nicholson reject universal validity for the sake of the politics of difference and, in so doing, disregard the problem of justice in their conception of postmodern feminism. As a consequence, their negotiation between feminist theories and Lyotard's work is reduced to the mutual correction of the global/local perspective of social criticism. They argue that Lyotard's project of social criticism is too localized and thus is incapable of diagnosing systemic inequalities of race, class, and gender. Yet, paradoxically, if the postmodern dissolution of metanarratives seems to rule out the possibility of "a critical analysis of large scale institutions and social structures" of oppression,[5] the persistence of such metanarratives within feminism forecloses the analysis of gender, race, and class differences among women. The feminist critiques of metanarratives are evident not only in the increasing contestation within feminism but also in the explicit attempts to fashion feminist theory in the 1990s on a model of dissensus, suggested, for instance, in such diverse works as bell hooks's *Yearning* and *Outlaw Culture*, Jane Flax's *Disputed Subjects*, Diane Elam and Robyn Wiegman's *Feminism Beside Itself*, or Patricia Hill Collins's *Fighting Words: Black Women and Search for Justice*. bell hooks, for instance, has repeatedly criticized white feminism not only for its incapacity to address the differences of race, class, or heterosexual privilege but also for its appropriation of the discussion of race to further marginalize the theoretical contributions made by women of color:

> An example which readily comes to mind from the feminist movement centers on efforts made by women of color to call attention to white racism in the struggle as well as talking about racial identity from a standpoint which deconstructs the category of "woman." Such discussions were part of the struggle by women of color to come to voice and also to assert new and different feminist narratives. Many white feminists responded by hearing only what was said about race and most specifically about racism. . . . White feminists could now centralize themselves by engaging in a discourse on race, "the Other," in a manner which further marginalized women of color, whose works were often relegated to the realm of the experiential.[6]

As hooks's argument makes clear, working class women, African-American women, women of different ethnic backgrounds and sexual orientations have been placed in the position of the differend within feminist theory even when their voices have been supposedly heard—they have been deprived of the means of signifying their oppression by the very discourse that claims to struggle for the emancipation of all women.

For Fraser and Nicholson the appropriate response to the accusations of white feminist theory is a project of postmodern feminism that "would replace unitary notions of woman and feminine gender identity with . . . complexly structured . . . social identity, treating gender as one relevant strand among others, attending also to class, race, ethnicity, age, and sexual orientation."[7] Although this version of postmodern feminism might seem to mirror Lyotard's analysis of the heterogeneity of the social bond, it unfortunately does not convey adequately the fact that his post-Wittgensteinian notion of relational and antagonistic language games would preclude, as Tina Chanter has pointed out, the approach to gender "as one relevant strand among others," as if it were possible to separate mutually constitutive historical relations of "gender, class, race, ethnicity, age, and sexual orientation" into distinct "strands" possessing identity prior to such relations.[8] Furthermore, feminist politics of difference disregards Lyotard's equally important emphasis on the limits of discursive constitution, the limits which correspond to the non-signifiable exclusions of the suffered wrongs within the dominant sociopolitical articulations of power and knowledge, including feminist articulations of gender oppression. And finally, it ignores the claim that the heterogeneity and the exclusions characteristic of antagonistic social relations call for ethical judgment. Thus, what is missing from postmodern feminism is a concept of justice that would correspond to a democratic politics of difference.

The fact that Lyotard's work can be criticized simultaneously on the contradictory grounds of universality and difference, philosophical and antiphilosophical social criticism, normative justice and antagonistic politics suggests that his work does not fit easily within either of these alternatives. Furthermore, I would argue that these either/or oppositions are too constrictive for feminism itself: in fact, neither the local, non-theoretical politics of difference without ethics nor the grand theory of normative justice transcending conflict is a viable option for feminist theory today. Perhaps the importance of Lyotard's work for feminism might be precisely in the way it enables us to move beyond these oppositions and to reformulate the very project of the feminist politics of difference. Such a reformulation of the feminist agonistic politics requires three interventions. First, it has to take into account how the limit cases of the antagonism that lack the means of expression and resolution problematize feminist conceptualizations of the historical race, gender, and class relations of power; second, it has to supplement the conceptualization of struggle and resistance with the necessity of justice based on indeterminate judgment; and third, it has to reconceptualize an ethical judgment in the context of embodiment and sexuality.

Consequently, to respond to differends within feminism requires not only a critique of unwarranted generalizations, which could be corrected by a better knowledge of historical and cultural differences, but an elaboration of ethics in the aftermath of a delegitimation of the practical collective subject—women—and its claim to speak for all women in the name of the common goal of emancipation. As bell hooks argues, if it does not claim responsibility for racial and class oppression, if it lacks a "fundamental attitude of vigilance," the knowledge of differences risks the denial of the racial and economic injustices, perpetuated this time by feminism itself. For hooks, the recognition of the injustice of racism and the commitment to political transformation contests the neutrality of knowledge and requires, in addition to historical specificity, persistent self-critique and a "fundamental attitude of vigilance rather than denial."[9] Similarly, for Lyotard, the description of cultural differences, no matter how precise, cannot respond to the demand of justice: "There is nothing to prove that if a statement describing a real situation is true, it follows that a prescriptive statement based upon it . . . will be just."[10]

To clarify the stakes of a feminist reformulation of the agonistic politics of difference in the context of the differend, I would like to compare Lyotard's work with Laclau and Mouffe's thesis, articulated in *Hegemony and Socialist Strategy*, that operations of power and antagonism are constitutive of all social relations and identities.[11] Lyotard concurs that antagonism does not take place between actors with already established identities, but rather constitutes both the social identities and the positions of actors themselves. What is important for feminist politics here is the fact that antagonism is no longer posited as an external relation that can be transcended through an appeal to moral norms, but rather is seen as constitutive of the social relations of race, gender, and class and the subjective identities formed within these relations. Since both the social subject and the dialectical notion of struggle are diffused along the heterogeneous and plural network of antagonistic relations, a collective identity—such as that of women—cannot be finalized by a determined judgment or consensus but remains an object of continual contestation: "The nature of the social . . . is immediately deferred. . . . The social is the referent . . . of a judgement [*sic*] to be always done over again."[12] Thus, one striking consequence of the internal role of conflict in the determination of the mutually constitutive relations of race, gender, and class is a temporal deferral of the collective social identities—the limit of their full determination—because the recurring threat of the *polemos* can put them back into question.

Despite Laclau and Mouffe's often dismissive critique of Lyotard's work, his inscription of antagonism into the formation of political identities does not dispense with "the necessity of articulation" of the constitutive contradictions between diversity and equivalence, equality and difference, conflict and consensus, but rather foregrounds the limit cases of antagonism, which lacks a means of expression within existing hegemonic arrangements. According to Lyotard, the differend represents not an instance of conflict between two well-articulated positions, but a case where the wrong is not signifiable, where the very capacity to testify is threatened with destruction:

> I would like to call a *differend* . . . the case where the plaintiff is divested of the means to argue and becomes for that reason a victim. If the addressor, the addressee, and the sense of testimony are neutralized, everything takes place as if there were no damages. . . . A case of differend between two parties takes place when the "regulation" of the conflict that opposes them is done in the idiom of one of the parties while the wrong suffered by the other is not signified in that idiom. (*D*, 9)

By analyzing numerous cases of such conflicts—from labor arbitration under capitalism and women's struggles against patriarchy to the contestation of Western imperialism by the movements of decolonization, Lyotard's agonistic politics intervenes into the situations of antagonism in which victims cannot signify their damages. The importance of such an intervention for feminist politics cannot be emphasized enough: consider, for instance, the critiques of feminism by queer theorists for its reliance on the patterns of normative heterosexuality or the indictment of white feminism by women of color for its failure to address racial and class oppression. These cases reveal differends within feminism, where the differences and inequalities among women have been obliterated by the very movement that purports to speak for all women.

There are two seemingly paradoxical consequences of the notion of the differend for feminist theories of power and oppression: first, the differend allows us to radicalize the role of antagonism in progressive democratic politics; yet, secondly, this radicalization of antagonism reveals the necessity of ethical judgment and obligation in political life. The case of the differend calls for supplementing the constitutive role of power, and the historical configurations of race, class, and gender it produces, by the notion of antagonism conceived as a disruptive event. This productive tension between constitution and disruption, between determination and dislocation, and between articulation and event in the very concept of antagonism is implied in many theories of modern power but never sufficiently developed: on the one hand, antagonism conceived as historical relations of power and knowledge constitutes political identities, historical relations of race and gender, and social objectivity; on the other hand, antagonism understood as a disruptive event reveals the limits of such constitution. Stemming from the relational character of discourse and power and reflecting the radical contingency of social relations in democracy, antagonism, as Laclau and Mouffe, Foucault, Judith Butler, and most of the social construction theorists argue, constitutes political identities and social relations of race, gender, and class. At the same time, antagonism conceived as rupture—for instance, as Fanon's "leap," Laclau's "dislocation," Foucault's "outside," Butler's abjection, and indeed, Lyotard's "differend"—shatters existing power relations and in so doing blocks the full constitution of historical objectivity and subjective identities. As Ernesto Laclau argues, "the crucial point is that antagonism is the *limit of all objectivity*."[13] That is to say, the unpredictable emergence of new antagonisms, which lack articulation, can disrupt sedimented hegemonic power structures and reveal their contingent character.[14] Insofar as this twofold conception of antagonism emphasizes both the formative effects of power and the limits of constitution, it reveals radical alterity in political life. Since a disruptive force of antagonism cannot be integrated into discursive formations, it cannot be immanent to historical objectivity, but instead forms, as Lyotard, Laclau, and Foucault in different ways argue, a permanent outside or exteriority of history.

For Lyotard, however, the dislocating force of antagonism not only shows the limit of social objectivity, but also calls for the supplementation of agonistic politics with a notion of justice based on indeterminate judgment. Although Lyotard, like many other contemporary political theorists—Foucault, Lacoue-Labarthe, Mouffe, and Laclau, to name only a few—protests the reduction of the political premised on the elimination of conflict as the goal of social justice, he also argues that the problem of justice is not thereby solved with the deployment of the agonistic model of power. On the one hand, Lyotard's conception of agonistic politics rejects the utopian conception of justice, which precludes contestation, dispute, or conflict over the constitution of the political identities or over the demands of justice itself. For Lyotard, the question of justice not only arises out of conflict but is itself submitted to dispute. Yet, on the other hand, Lyotard argues that the question of justice does not disappear in the aftermath of the crisis of legitimation, but remains more urgent than ever because its criteria cannot be established on the basis of either knowledge or the emancipation of the universal subject. Like Derrida's emphasis on the futurity of democracy, Lyotard's refusal of the final determination of the social opens a horizon of justice as the incessant necessity of judging without fixed criteria or law, where the outcome of this judgment provokes further contestation.

Because of his unwillingness to let go of the problem of justice, Lyotard, as Emilia Steuerman suggests, persistently returns to Kant and to Levinas despite his closeness to Nietzsche.[15] According to Lyotard, neither Levinas's separation of the infinity of ethics from the totality of war nor Nietzsche's and Foucault's demystification of morality as the expression of the will to power "do justice" to the necessity of judging social and political conflicts. Rather, for Lyotard the central ethical problem of the politics of difference lies in the way we judge that the differend takes place if the wrong lacks the means of expression/articulation and thus cannot be the object of cognition but is signaled merely by the "alarm" of feeling:

> The differend is the unstable state and instant of language wherein something which must be able to be put into phrases cannot yet be. This state includes silence, which is a negative phrase, but it also calls upon phrases which are in principle possible. This state is signaled by what one ordinarily calls a feeling: "One cannot find words," etc. (*D*, 13)

If the differend cannot be resolved by the appeal to the legal tribunal or the tribunal of history (*D*, 31), then what kind of judgment can do justice to this "unstable instance of language"? To solve this dilemma, Lyotard reformulates Levinas's eschatological judgment in the context of the Kantian concept of the sign of history. As Levinas writes in his preface to *Totality and Infinity*, an eschatological judgment calls for an evaluation of each particular case without a rule or without a reference to the totality of history:

> the eschatological, as the 'beyond' of history, draws beings out of the jurisdiction of history and the future. . . . Submitting history as a whole to judgment, exterior

to the very wars that mark its end, it restores to each instant its full signification in that very instant: all the causes are ready to be heard. It is not the last judgment that is decisive, but the judgment of all the instants in time.[16]

Yet, although Lyotard concurs with Levinas that the totality of history cannot be appealed to as the tribunal of ethical or political judgment, he argues that such a judgment cannot be situated "beyond history" since it has to respond to the historicity of the differend. Furthermore, such a judgment has to grapple with the crisis of the presentation of the particular, where the very ability to say "this is the case" is put into question—for example, when the instances of sexist or racist oppression are rendered non-signifiable by color- and gender-blind justice.

To formulate the possibility of such a judgment, Lyotard turns not only to the aesthetics of the sublime, as is frequently claimed, but, more important, to the Kantian concept of the sign of history. Since the differend presents the problem of judging the wrong that cannot be the referent of the cognitive/descriptive discourse, it necessitates a rethinking of the ways in which "the datum of history" is given. One of the crucial ways in which Lyotard wants to restore the possibility of judging the differend is by maintaining the distinction between historical fact, established through the procedures of verification and evidence, and the Kantian "sign of history,"[17] which functions as the negative presentation of what is not presentable under this regimen of verification. Although judgment in the empirical/descriptive discourse treats the object as an example validating cognition, in the dialectical discourse dealing with Ideas—for instance, the ideas of historical progress—such a presentation of the object corresponding to the idea is by definition not possible. In his inquiry into the possibility of judging the progress of human history, Kant claims that such a judgment cannot be made on the basis of historical evidence; at the very most, it can be formulated in response to an event taken as a commemorative or prognostic sign: "the event would have to be considered not itself as the cause of history, but only as an intimation, a historical sign (signum rememorativum, demonstrativum, prognostikon)."[18] In that case, judgment proceeds analogically, presenting merely an "as if referent"—that is, an analogical object "which would be its referent if the phrase were cognitive" but which can never function as an example. This analogical substitution saves the possibility of "judging a phrase, even when there is no empirical case directly presentable for its validation."[19]

In Lyotard's interpretation, however, the sign of history points to the formless and "figureless" event "refractory to all functions of presentation," even by *analoga*. Judgment in such a case is based on affect, on "the alarm of feeling," or the feeling of pain: "That, in a phrase universe, the referent be situated as a sign has a corollary that in this same universe the addressee is situated like someone who is affected" (*D*, 57). What functions for Kant as a sign of history—the spectators' enthusiasm for the French Revolution—is the extreme version of the sublime feeling, which underscores the failure of the presentation of an object that could possibly correspond to the Idea of the Republic or to the Idea of progress. Thus, the affective paradox of enthusiasm implies that even the "as if" presentation for the idea of the civil society is not forthcoming. Based on the feeling of pain, it remains entirely negative, without the support of *analoga* or symbols: "The *dementia* of enthusiasm . . . bears witness to the extreme tension felt by the spectating mankind—a tension between the 'nullity' of what is presented to it and the Ideas of reason" (*SH*, 174). In contrast to the transcendental illusion, which claims to see beyond the limits of experience, and thus confuses *analoga* with exempla, the Kantian enthusiasm "sees nothing, or rather sees *the* nothing and refers it to the unpresentable" (*SH*, 173). Consequently, for Lyotard the sign of history problematizes even the analogy at the basis of analogical judgment (*D*, 131).

Lyotard retrieves the Kantian "sign of history" in order to respond to the predicament of the differend—the "derealization of objects" corresponding to the "proper names" of our catastrophic history, which, like Auschwitz, throw the historical and political knowledge into a crisis (*SH*, 163). Yet, what functions for us as a sign is no longer a painful enthusiasm for great historical upheavals like the French Revolution, but the overwhelming silence surrounding the suspension of the historical/political commentary in the aftermath of the catastrophic event of the Holocaust:

> The scholar claims to know nothing about it, but the common person has a complex feeling, the one aroused by the negative presentation of the indeterminate . . . the silence that the crime of Auschwitz imposes upon the historian is a sign for a common person. Signs . . . are not referents to which are attached significations validatable under the cognitive regimen, they indicate that something which should be able to be put into phrases cannot be phrased in the acceptable idioms. . . . The silence which surrounds the phrase, *Auschwitz was the extermination camp* is not a state of mind . . . it is the sign that something remains to be phrased which is not. (*D*, 56–57)

By judging the painful silence surrounding the unpresentable as a sign of the victim's wrong, the critical subject at the same time testifies that "every wrong ought to be able to be expressed" even though it cannot be phrased in the available idiom (*D*, 13).[20] Through the silence and the feeling of pain that accompanies it, the differend confronts the subject with an obligation not only to testify and redress the wrong, but also to institute a new sense of addressee, addressor, and testimony.

What is striking in Lyotard's formulation of judgment in the context of the sign of history is such explicitly ethical formulations as "every wrong ought to be able to be expressed." The recurrence of such prescriptive phrases requires a further reflection on the place of ethics in the process of judging the historical-political reality. Yet, to elaborate a radical sense of responsibility in political life, which obligates the political subject to find the means of expression and compensation for obliterated wrongs, Lyotard can no longer remain within orbit of Kantian thought but has to return to Levinas's ethics. Unlike Kant, for whom enthusiasm verging on pathological pathos is ethically suspect and thus retains only aesthetic validity, Lyotard subjects the judging spectator to the burden of ethical obligation. To underscore the anarchic force of this obligation, Lyotard consistently deploys Levinas's ethics with and against Kant's moral law. As is the case with Levinas, for Kant, too, morality is irreducible to theoretical cognition. In contrast to hypothetical obligations, which are like strategies leading toward a goal and thus depend on the clearly prescribed stakes and conditions, the categorical obligation remains for Kant unconditional and unlegitimated. The impossibility of deducing the moral law (or its reversed deduction—the moral law taken as a premise for the negative deduction of freedom) in Kant's *Critique of Practical Reason* shows that the prescriptive force of categorical obligation cannot be deduced from cognition or from the political calculation of stakes. The failure of deduction, which is concomitant with the failure of theoretical discourse, suggests that obligation happens like an event—it precedes commentary and cognition, and thus remains anarchic and unlegitimated.[21] Kant, however, curtails the anarchic force of the categorical obligation by maintaining the interchangeability between obligation and freedom, on the one hand, and obligation and norm, on the other.

Lyotard's logical and pragmatic critique of the Kantian moral law underscores the decisive character of the Levinasian intervention, which precisely destroys the series of equivalences set up by the categorical imperative: between the descriptives and prescriptives, obligation and norm, obligation and freedom, and finally, between the addressee of prescriptives and the subject of enunciation. For Levinas the scandal of these equivalences betrays "the ego's infatuation with knowledge" and with the free spontaneity of speech. Following Levinas, Lyotard argues that neither the symmetry between the self and the other nor the reversibility between the obligated self and the subject of enunciation can be maintained. As Lyotard claims, "to find oneself placed in the pragmatic position of being obligated is incommensurable with the position of enunciation, even of enunciating prescriptives."[22] The violence of obligation lies precisely in the deprivation of the free use of oneself, in the dispossession not only of one's narcissistic image and enjoyment but also of the power of enunciation. As Lyotard writes, "It happens like a scrambling of the universe in which I am I" (*D*, 112). Or, to evoke Derrida's argument in "The Force of Law," we can say that obligation can be experienced only as an aporia of experience—as that which is not given to experience.[23]

Confronted with the performative force of obligation, with the prescriptive that every wrong ought to be expressed, the judging "I" forgoes the spontaneity of enunciation and becomes displaced instead onto the addressee of a prescription, onto a "you," as in the phrase "you ought to." By displacing the judging subject into an accusative position, the performative effect of obligation restores a paradoxical possibility of an address for a victim. A victim who, in the situation of the differend, lacks the means of expression for the suffered wrong becomes, in the ethical encounter, an other who imposes obligation to institute the new modalities of discourse. In other words, to be situated as an obligated self is an asymmetrical correlative of the other who calls the subject to responsibility for the social wrongs. Unlike the erosion of the testimony, the pragmatics of the ethical situation posits obligation as an ethical response to the call of the other, even if this call does not amount to the fullness of speech but manifests itself as a trace or a negative phrase of silence.

From the outset, Lyotard compares the call of the other to the ethical summons experienced in the situation of the differend:

> In the differend, something "asks" to be put into phrases, and suffers from the wrong of not being able to be put into phrases right away. This is when the human beings who thought they could use language as an instrument of communication learn through the feeling of pain which accompanies silence . . . that they are summoned by language . . . to recognize that what remains to be phrased exceeds

what they can presently phrase, and that they must be allowed to institute idioms which do not yet exist. (*D*, 13)

As this comparison between the differend and ethical obligation suggests, the other, whose infinite alterity is refractory to thematization, obligates the subject to testify to the obliterated damages and to restore the capacity to signify them. It is a minimal but categorical responsibility to testify to the differends, to find "the (impossible) idiom for phrasing them" and the means of restitution (*D*, 143).

Although in *The Differend*, there is no direct passage between the notices about obligation and the notices about the sign of history, the "guiding thread" between these notifications, which I've tried to reconstruct here, is nonetheless crucial for the ethical supplementation of agonistic politics: it uncovers a peculiar displacement of the political subject in the process of judging a "derealized" historical object. If we wish to preserve for this displacement the ethical name of obligation, we risk contaminating what Levinas calls the eschatological dimension of ethics by the "pagan" historicity of the *polemos*. Yet, this risk is worth taking; indeed, to use Levinas's words, it is "a very fine risk," which enables us to exit the philosophical discussion of the history of war, aptly characterized by Levinas as "the ontology of totality," and to confront instead the ethical necessity of judging the differends of history. In place of the opposition between the historicity of war and the eschatological dimension of ethics beyond conflict, deployed in different ways not only in Levinas's ethics but also in Laclau and Mouffe's radical democracy and in the feminist politics of difference, my reading of Lyotard stresses the necessity of assuming responsibility for a just judgment within agonistic politics. It is this difficult negotiation between ethical obligation and political conflict indicating two different forms of alterity in political life that I see as the crucial task for feminist theory today.

However, the encounter between feminist politics and Lyotard's philosophy is not a one-sided negotiation—on the contrary, this encounter poses new questions and new tasks, which were not previously legible within these separate fields of inquiry. Thus, if feminist political theory, necessarily focused on reclaiming the possibility of enunciation for those who have been objectified or excluded from the domain of legitimate political subjects, has yet to elaborate the aporetic experience of the ethical displacement of subjectivity into the accusative "me" of obligation, feminist analyses of racial, class, and gender oppression pose a crucial question about the extent to which ethical theories of obligation, including Lyotard's own work, always already presuppose the capacity and the privilege of the subject to occupy the position of enunciation. To what extent do they indeed presuppose, to recall Lyotard's telling words, "the universe in which I am I," which is subsequently "scrambled" by ethical responsibility? Can the abject beings excluded from the political universe of subjects be called into responsibility? And if so, how can we begin to theorize the displacement from the non-position of the differend to the accusative position of the obligated subject?

Furthermore, the encounter between Lyotard's work and feminist politics should also elucidate Lyotard's own debts to feminism. On many occasions, Lyotard himself credits feminism for posing the question of the sexed body and for diagnosing its erasure in the legitimations of the patriarchal power. Written at the same time period as *The Postmodern Condition* (1979), Lyotard's essay, entitled "One of the Things at Stake in Women's Struggles" (1978), provides an important addition to his analysis of the crisis of legitimation—a supplement in which Lyotard returns to the problem of the sexed body in order to outline "a politics that would respect both the desire for justice and the desire for the unknown" (*PC*, 67). Lyotard's turn to the problematics of the sexed body in feminism is at the same time a return to his earlier interest in reworking the phenomenological problematic of the sensible and intelligible in the Freudian perspective of the unconscious, which dramatized the abyss between the libidinal intensities of the body and the intentionality of consciousness. Although Lyotard abandons this line of research in the middle of his career because he suspects that libidinal politics alone cannot come to terms with the problem of injustice and thus risks indifference or even "violence and terror,"[24] in his engagements with feminism he argues that the question of justice could not be adequately posed without rethinking the sexed body.[25]

In both of his essays, "One of the Things at Stake in Women's Struggles" and "Can Thought Go On without a Body?" (1987), Lyotard contests the erasure of the sexed body from the metanarratives of sociopolitical legitimation. As he points out, the metadiscourse of norms aims to transcend not only the agonistic relations but also the body and its relations with the world. The only limit to the recursiveness of the symbolic—its necessary rootedness in immanence—that technoscience or philosophy recognize is the concern with the survival of the body: "The opposite limit of this symbolic recursiveness resides in the necessity by which it is bound . . . to maintain regulations that guarantee its survival."[26] Yet, to pose the limit to abstraction exclusively in terms of survival suggests that a certain unacknowledged abstraction of the body from sexual difference has already taken place.

The abstraction of metadiscourse from the sexed body posits language as the active principle constituting the meaning of objects and reduces bodies to the passive surface of inscription. Lyotard's critique of metalanguage is analogous here to recent feminist attempts to rethink the significance of the body apart from the sex/gender distinction, which, as Elizabeth Grosz points out, associates gender with the process of socialization operating on the level of cultural consciousness/discourse and treats the sexed body as the material ground of social inscription. Like Luce Irigaray in her critique of the culture of death, Lyotard argues that this disembodied character of language manifests itself in the persistent relation between embodiment, death, and the political authority in the Western tradition running from Hegel and Freud to the contemporary scientific dream of artificial intelligence without a body: "What is pertinent for distinguishing the sexes is the relation to death: a body that can die, whatever its sexual anatomy, is masculine; a body that does not know that it must disappear is feminine. Men teach women of death, the impossible, the presence of absence."[27]

The dual determination of metalanguage as the abstraction from the sexed body and the active principle of meaning is crucial, Lyotard argues, to the patriarchal model of legitimation of political authority, the origins of which he sees in the conception of Greek democracy. For Lyotard, the formation of patriarchal authority exposes a certain parallelism between the symbolic agency of language constituting the meaning of the body and the power of the normative discourse constituting the order of the social corpus. This analogy is based on the principle of active determination of meaning—on the power of unlimited initiative and decision: in both cases the transcendent metalanguage abstracted from embodiment and antagonism claims to form the "corpus in its entirety." Reduced to the passive surface of inscription, the corpus is no longer legible as the locus where the struggle over meaning takes place. The complicity "between political phallocracy and philosophical metalanguage" depends, therefore, on "the line of demarcation," which is at the same time the line of sexual division, "between an empirical given, women, the great unknown and a transcendent or transcendental order that would give them meaning" (*TSWS*, 119).

As Lyotard's critique of the metadiscourse of norm in *The Differend* makes clear, the principle of the active determination of meaning—the power of initiative and decision—is localized in the position of enunciation, in the performative authority of the tribunal proclaiming norms. Lyotard makes a similar argument in his earlier analysis of the patriarchal power: "The activity men reserve for themselves arbitrarily as *fact* is posited legally as the *right* to decide meaning" (*TSWS*, 119). Together with the right to constitute meaning, groups of free men in Ancient Greece claim the political right to constitute and represent the whole social order—they "allocate the responsibilities of the *corpus socians* for themselves." By contrast, women, foreigners, and slaves, relegated to the place of the constituent, are identified with those passive parts of the social body that remain to be formed and governed. Influenced by Irigaray, Lyotard associates disembodied philosophical metalanguage with the emergence of the homosocial order in which women and slaves are either figured as objects of exchange or expelled beyond the borders of the intelligible—in other words, expelled from the positions of political subjects:

> An empty center where the Voice is heard (God's, the People's—the difference is not important, just the Capital letters), the circle of homosexual warriors in dialogue around the center, the feminine (women, children, foreigners, slaves) banished outside the confines of the *corpus socians* and attributed only those properties this *corpus* will have nothing to do with: savagery, sensitivity, matter . . . hysteria, silence. (*TSWS*, 114)

This intrinsic relation between disembodied language and political authority inscribes the sexed body in the network of other differences constitutive of the *polis*, in particular, racial differences: in the Greek *polis*, the differences between men and women are determined in the context of the relations of citizens and its others—barbarians, foreigners, children, and slaves.

What this early essay "One Thing at Stake in Women's Struggle" adds to the critique of the normative discourse in *The Differend* is an important insight that the transformation of the particular strategies of winning into norms transcending political conflict occurs at the price of effacing embodiment as the site of historical struggles. Consequently, the "normative we" is a "disembodied we," and those who occupy that position and thus claim its performative power know how, in good Hegelian fashion, to make use of death, how to risk life in order to gain mastery, the ultimate expression of which is the capacity of thinking death itself. As Lyotard writes, "Thought without a body is the prerequisite for thinking of the death of all bodies . . . and of the death of thoughts that are inseparable from those bodies" (*CTGWB*, 14). Given this analysis, what is at stake in the women's movement and in the struggles for decolonization is not just an attempt, as Seyla Benhabib suggests, to close the gap between the normative and the declarative we, between those who enunciate the norms and those who are subjected to them. More fundamentally, it is the contestation of the disembodied character of the normative discourse from the embattled position of the sexed and racial bodies. As Lyotard writes, "If the women's movement has an immense impact equal to that of slaves, colonized peoples, and other 'under-developed' groups, it is that this movement solicits and destroys the (masculine) belief in meta-statements independent of ordinary statements," sensibility, and perception (*TSWS*, 119–20). Ultimately, I would add, at stake in women's struggles is a search for a different model of justice and citizenship, no longer predicated on the universalizable norms transcending conflict and embodiment.

If Lyotard contests the normative discourse transcending embodiment and struggle, how can we imagine the relation between the body and the "justice of multiplicities"? In Lyotard's essay "Can Thought Go On without a Body?," a feminist philosopher, in the figure of which I am tempted to see Luce Irigaray, argues that the sexed body functions as the limit to both abstraction and the language of decision or constitution. In contrast to the normative discourse that posits metalanguage as the transcendence of the power relations inscribed in the body and in contrast to the technoscience that produces the phantasm of the artificial intelligence without a body, Lyotard's feminist philosopher approaches the sexed body as the model of the fundamental incompleteness of thinking, as the suspension of determination manifesting itself in the receptivity to what is not yet. By rejecting the paradigm of metalanguage that treats the body as the passive surface and language as the active constitution of sexuality, the feminist project of rethinking embodiment not only builds on the Foucauldian notion of the body as the materialization of the relations of power, but also recovers the sexed body as the unthought, or the unconscious of thought. Conceived as the limit of separability of language from embodiment, sexed bodies also obstruct the complete determination of the racial and gender norms in the symbolic. This means that sexual difference is itself marked by incompleteness, or, as Lacan suggests, by the failure of sense,[28] and thus cannot be determined by the symbolic without a remainder. Exceeding symbolic/political determination and regulation of bodies, this remainder of sex "makes thought go on endlessly and won't allow itself to be thought" (*CTGWB*, 23). In contrast to the abstraction of thought from the body characteristic of the language of constitution and determination, the withdrawal of sexual difference from the realm of sense marks a certain transcendence within immanence. In other words, Lyotard's contestation of the disembodied metalanguage allows not only for a discussion of bodies as the sites of regulation and materialization of power, but also for the analysis of the sexed body as the limit, or the remainder, of that regulation.

One consequence of such a formulation of the sexed body in excess of its symbolic and political constitution/regulation is the implicit relation between the embodiment and the process of judging the differend. In a manner evocative of Levinas's discussion of the chiasmic ambiguity of the constituted and the constituting character of "the original incarnation of thought,"[29] where thought, in an attempt to constitute the body, finds itself always already dependent on embodiment, Lyotard calls our attention to the other side of this paradox: thought (and language) is inseparable from the phenomenological body, but the sexed body is always already irretrievably separated from thought. To expose this paradoxical logic of the bodily remainder, Lyotard refers to the discontinuous temporality of Freud's deferred action: "It inscribes the effects without the inscription being 'memorized' in the form of recollection" (*CTGWB*, 21).[30] This paradox situates the sexed body not only as the limit of thinking and "the only available *analogon*" of its complexity, but also as the *analogon* of ethical judgment. Rather than being entirely constituted by language, the sexed body "is what initially sets up fields of perception and thought as functions of waiting and equivocation" (*CTGWB*, 21). Like a historical sign indicating a derealized historical object, the sexed body can be approached as a sign of radical exteriority enabling the negative presentation of the unpresentable and the unthought:

> We think in a world of inscriptions already there. Call this culture if you like. And if we think, this is because there's still something missing in this plenitude and room has to be made for this lack by making the mind a blank, which allows the something else remaining to be thought to happen. But this can only "emerge" as already "inscribed" in its turn. . . . The unthought hurts because we're comfortable in what's already thought. (*CTGWB*, 20)

By marking the limit of the linguistic constitution of objects, sexed bodies allow us to register, therefore, what is missing, what is still unthought, not only in the sphere of sense perception but also in culture at large. Through the overlapping of thinking, sexuality, and suffering, this carnal receptivity to what is lacking in the world of available articulations bears a striking resemblance to the process of judging the differend, which is also characterized by the painful attentiveness to the limits of the presentable. Let us recall that the necessity of judging the differend entails responding to what is not signifiable in the idiom of the tribunal in which the regulation of conflict takes place. Since such a judgment is often based on "the alarm of feeling," or the affect of pain, it itself bears a necessary relation to carnal sensibility, which Levinas defines as the capacity for being affected, and Lyotard, as the patient awaiting of what is not yet. Perhaps the very possibility of an ethical judgment depends on the often unthematized "debt" to embodiment, to what Levinas calls the irreducible condition of "being in one's skin." We can, therefore, extend Lyotard's analogy and say that the sexed body is the *analogon* of the complexity of justice occluded by the disembodied metanarratives of legitimation.

In this essay, I have proposed to shift feminist engagements with Lyotard from an almost exclusive focus on the critique of metanarratives to a more complex negotiation between antagonism and justice, between the agonistic politics of difference and the ethical responsibility grounded in embodiment. The outcome of this negotiation is neither nontheoretical politics of difference without ethics—that is, a politics reduced to the indifferent struggle of the heterogeneous forces—nor a utopian theory of justice transcending conflict. Rather, as I have proposed in my theory of a feminist ethics of dissensus,[31] at stake here is a decisive reformulation of the politics of difference so that it not only strives to contest the mutually constitutive forms of racist, sexist, and class domination but also bears an obligation to redress differends—those limit cases of antagonism in which victims cannot signify their damages. Finally, I have suggested that such a politics has a necessary relation to embodiment, conceived not only as a site of struggle and normalization but also as a condition of ethical judgment. By exposing what is missing in the antagonistic articulations of racial and gender differences, sexed bodies mark, therefore, a point where the feminist politics of difference crosses the path with the feminist ethics of dissensus in an infinite pursuit of justice.

The Writings of the Differend

Gérald Sfez

Give the differend its due, bear witness to the differend. The thought of Jean-François Lyotard will have multiplied its testimonies. Taking on all tones, using all forms, from argumentation to reflexive writing to the poetic, it inscribes itself in genres such as commentary or biography, each time inscribing itself in such a way that the resistance posed to it by these genres is detoured. Each time it must seek the necessary obliquity, the form of the essay,[1] the diagonal susceptible of bearing the trace of, or of presenting, what he calls "differend"—in a new and bizarre sense, juridical and extrajuridical, the very definitions of which do not escape the instability of its occurrences.

It is a concept or essential category of his thought, but one which refers more to a tune, an immemorial music, for which he never gives the date of origin—an "I began to write it at such and such a moment"—without adding immediately a reservation—an "and even before." This tune touches the navel of the unknown. And this tune, whose trace all of his work seeks to rediscover, always in appeal of another trace that might approach it, is the balancing wire of his writing. Here, on this tightrope, the dancer is the witness. He is the keeper of the vigil. Devoted to the writings and to the arabesques of the differend. "For us, to philosophize," he declared in a discussion about *The Differend*, "it is nothing other than to write, and that which is interesting for us in 'to write' is not to reconcile but to inscribe that which does not let itself be inscribed."[2] It is a cutting formulation, clearly provocative, and which speaks the profound vow for which he is called, *vocatur*.[3]

How can the differend give itself to writing? Its mode of presentation adheres to the difficulty posed by the differend itself, to its very consistency. "As distinguished from a litigation, a differend would be a case of conflict, between (at least) two parties, that cannot be equitably resolved for lack of a rule of judgment applicable to both arguments. One side's legitimacy does not imply the other's lack of legitimacy. However, applying a single rule of judgment to both in order to settle their differend as though it were merely a litigation would wrong (at least) one of them (and both of them if neither side admits this rule)."[4] Further: "A wrong results from the fact that the rules of the genre of discourse by which one rules are not those of the judged genre or genres of discourse" (*LD*, 9; *D*, xi). From the very start, it is apparent that to present the differend—which necessarily must be done according to one rule of judgment or in one genre of discourse, one language, one idiom—is already to risk doing a wrong to one of the parties involved, if not both, and hence to disregard the differend. How to voice the differend [*Comment dire le différend*]? This formulation, in its proximity to and its distance from that of the expression of "giving each his due" [*dire le droit*], immediately reveals itself in its paradox: giving the differend its due cannot be brought to pass through a relation of arbitration according to the rule of one genre of discourse, because it is all but impossible to judge the conflict and present the discord in a genre of discourse or a language that would not be that of either one or the other of the two parties involved, or of a third. In any case, one argumentation or idiom is doomed to suffer a wrong, if not both. The third party cannot legitimately arbitrate. Should we say, then, that the legitimate presentation of the differend is to be taken from the argumentative case or testimony of the injured party? In this case, would "saying the differend" [*dire le différend*] coincide with the plaintiff "voicing his or her complaint" [*dire son désaccord*]? But the complaint [*ce dit du désaccord*] of the purportedly injured party (the plaintiff) has meaning only if there is someone or something to confirm it, that is to say, if it is corroborated through the testimonies of witnesses, the rulings of judges, and so on. All of which brings us back to the previous question. This difficulty signifies that "saying the differend" must find an indirect and problematic route: "Given . . . the absence of a universal genre of discourse to regulate them (or, if you prefer, the inevitable partiality of the judge): to find, if not what can legitimate judgment (the 'good' linkage), then at least how to save the honor of thinking" (*LD*, 10; *D*, xii).

The indirect presentation of the differend must circumvent the impossibility of a third party that would give the concluding and decisive proof; it must do so, however, without validating partiality. The discontinuous form of the essay must occupy a place situated between that of the third party and that of the plaintiff, in full knowledge of the arguments and languages that are in opposition; that is to say, in playing, at the same time, the role of the double agent for a third party all the more essential or constitutive of the field because it is to be found on its borders, a third party appearing and disappearing. Lyotard's writings of the differend are always the invention of diagonals for responding to this indirect and oblique discourse; each time this necessarily requires the invention of different styles of reflexive writing.

The Differend is itself an exemplary presentation of this. In the moment at which it sorts out certain genres of discourse and modes of being of phrases (presentation, obligation, historical-political, narrative, etc.) and describes the differends internal to each, the book, in its singular character, opens a polemical space of definitional occurrences. As at once both arbitration and dissension, both invention and infringement, the book, through its invention of idioms and their faculty of prevailing, attests to the differend itself. The argumentative *modus* deploys itself in the form of an incessant dialogue and constant rapport between the objection and its refutation so that the dispute, at the same time it appears to wrap things up in a coherent manner, does not come to an end. The play of referrals between paragraphs, which are separated by the distance between them, represents an inscription, which essays to evade the defeat and pretense of the book form. It does not so much seek to facilitate passages or resolve contradictions as to multiply the crossroads and thresholds of writing: the overlapping and infringement between the paragraphs leave the phrase in remainder. Between the paragraphs, there is always an inadequation; each paragraph retains an edge that does not allow the other paragraphs to be superimposed upon it. The argumentative *modus* deploys the inconclusive character of the book and gives itself in micrologies. This is precisely how the differend renders itself to writing: not only as the writing of dissimulation and of dissimilation, but as the implication of the phrase.[5] Contradiction is not a mark of falsity, nor is the syncopation of speech the mark of the absence of a phrase. Between the watch guards of coherence and those of dissension, the promise of ambiguity is kept.

The precision [*justesse*] of writing belongs to the *idea of the differend*, which allows only an oblique approach. Lyotard's thought writes itself as the site of tension between the phrases, phrases between which it would be wrong to decide. If the wrong defines the differend, the wrong also exceeds it: there is a victim beyond the wrong, in spite of what certain passages say. But if the differend defines the wrong, in return the differend exceeds the wrong: for the differend refers as much to the undecidability between two equally legitimate argumentations or two heterogeneous idioms of argumentation, which require that one suspend one's judgment as to the irreparable wrong done to an idiom by the tyrannical inroads of another—to a mistreated idiom or one that never even had the right to exist. Moreover, the wrong signals the differend; it does not coincide with it. If the wrong and the differend appear to concern specific cases, it is at the same time a matter of the universality of phrases. And if the arbitration respects heterogeneity by restituting this or that phrase to one heterogeneous faculty or another (as in the Kantian analysis of that which belongs to each faculty), the faculty of the phrase undoes all economies of faculties.

The thought of the differend undergoes a major inflexion—in which the reading of the Kant of the Third *Critique* and in particular the *Lessons on the Analytic of the Sublime* plays a decisive role, along with a consciousness [*une conscience*] of postmodernity that becomes more and more critical. One can almost speak of a second philosophy of the differend, whose role is not to resolve the contradictions, the aporias, and the already existing dissonant voices involved in the use of the term—it was never designed for this—but to encounter them again otherwise. One witnesses a shift in accent that neither resolves nor discredits the previous thought. The differend undergoes a change of aspect. The question of writing is accentuated differently, and a chasm opens between inscription and writing as such. The witness to the differend does not speak in the same manner nor from the same place.

The distance between the two formulations of the question is quite clear. In *The Differend*, Lyotard wrote: "What is at stake in a literature, in a philosophy, in a politics perhaps, is to bear witness to differends by finding idioms for them" (*LD, 30; D*, 22). By 1988, the stakes undergo a change of aspect. Thus he writes, for example, in *The Inhuman*: "But it is enough not to forget it in order to resist it and perhaps not to be unjust. It is the task of writing, thinking, literature, arts, to venture to bear witness to it."[6] One notes the eclipse of the political, the substitution of thought for philosophy, and the sudden appearance of writing as that which commands all the forms of bearing witness to the differend. To bear witness to the differend is to venture into writing. One is very far from the earlier conjunction—very far from the previous encounter—between philosophy and politics. How does it happen that the writing of the differend has changed? That it is subsequently more integral to writing itself? And that Lyotard himself, in order to speak of this, becomes more and more of a writer?

The new conjunction that is born here does not let itself be broken down simply into historical circumstances or thoughts. It carries with it another world. It is born from the encounter between inextricably blended concomitances. The three registers—the eclipse of the political, the *mise en relief* of thought, the adventures of writing—define, with the modifications of its transcriptions, another configuration of the concept of differend. Between the three, to search for one to predominate would be in vain.

The eclipse of the political differend is, without doubt, the most perceptible trait. The political loses its value as witness. Whereas during the period of *The Differend* Lyotard left the door open to a "perhaps," by 1986 testifying to the differend no longer passes through politics. The increasingly critical attention to postmodernity leads to the thought that, in social and political struggles, where it once made itself heard, the differend is now silent. It is not simply a question of the decline of politics as an ambition to resolve conflicts, a question of sublation, a question of the true site of the intrigues of the narrative of humanity (be it tragedy or epic). Rather, it is a question of the decline of inscription as the ambition of politics. The differend and its inscription—this is no longer the major stake of the political. To be sure, there is always some differend at work in the specific conflicts of our societies (such as identifying who is a citizen and who is not, who is a foreigner and who is not, questions concerning immigration, women's struggles, education, etc.); however, "their status as *differends* is much smaller than their status as *litigations*."[7] This is the case, notwithstanding the extreme violence of this litigation and the necessity of intervening as citizens in order to say what must be said.

The historical dimension of the event is tied to the all-encompassing power of that which Lyotard calls the System—to which one would do too great an honor in naming capitalism. The System repairs, redresses, makes amends. Or rather, it repairs itself, redresses itself, and makes amends to itself. The System "arouses disparities, it solicits divergences, multiculturalism is agreeable to it but under the condition of an agreement concerning the rules of disagreement."[8] If the differend disappears as a major stake, if politics is no longer a medium for testifying to a radical wrong, if there is no collective inscription of the differend simultaneously with litigation, it is because the complaint finds its expression within transactions, precisely where it cannot sign its resistance. What prevents it from doing so? How is it that the political inscription of the differend comes to be a thing of the past and that one can no longer constitute oneself as a civil party on the scene of History? It is because the System divides the world into two regimes: on the one hand, there is the regime of calculation without subjects, a regime of the infinite flight of development; on the other hand, there is the regime of the countries unaccounted for in any calculation, abandoned there, in a space without place. There is no political writing capable of writing this disaster. This space divides itself in the nonrelation between the damage without sign of a wrong and a wrong without any sign of damage, below or beyond the differend. The whole correlation between wrong and damage, which is the trait of the differend, and which is not sublated in a negative dialectic, here finds itself disjointed. No struggle can claim to appeal for—or be the sign of—the emancipation of Humanity faced with the System of a triumphant and frozen postmodernity, a System without author or project. In a universe where our horizon is happily that of liberal democracy but where the System always has the last word—and where the last word is always that of performance—the writing of the political leaves no trace.

There is of course a paradox here. It is at the very moment when the political differend appears in full light, freed from the illusions of its sublation in the staging of a project for social revolution, that it erases itself as a major dimension, leaves the stage. There was a political inscription of the differend only to the extent that the incommensurable made a *sign*.[9] One does not understand the differend without *thinking the gesture*. The differend could only be addressed in this gesture (the gesture that signals a potential promise of emancipation for Humanity, the gesture that is a sign of a possible threat of destruction to the System), in the in-between of a suspended gesture. Such a suspended gesture could not be actualized but made a sign toward this actualization as its horizon. If the differend no longer finds a surface of inscription for a writing, it is because, on this stage or in this public theater, it can no longer make a gesture.[10] The end of the differend in politics: the suspended gesture itself is suspended. In fact, this suspended gesture only gained meaning through the equivocation between its destination and its actualization, so that the differend could only appear in its truth enveloped by the illusion of its sublation. The exactitude of the phrase of the differend will not take place in politics.

The age in which we would have thus entered—and which, at the same time, defines an attitude toward the differend—could be titled: "The Political Differend and Afterward." The expression would designate this parachronic time where the news of the political differend arrives belatedly. And it brings with it more news still: that of its own erasure. We would learn at the same instant that there has been a political differend and that there can no longer be one. That there has been a differend: testimony without sublation, political writing. And that there can no longer be one: that with both the end of the promise of resolution and the end of the illusion of sublation comes also the end of the promise of inscription and of the truth of the differend. This "Differend and Afterward" would mark the encounter with the abutment of politics: What good is politics as a major stake of thought? In this time of "in vain" and of "what's the use?," this time of vanity, this frightening time in which we are seized by the vanity of it all, this time of futile or informed nihilism, is not the political incapable not merely of resolving the differend, but also of even inscribing the differend?

Should we regret the old state of things, with its promising and terrifying ambiguity, or should we instead congratulate ourselves on its erasure? What should we think of the end of the political writing of the differend? It's for the better! It's a shame! Praise or blame? Lyotard hesitates. It's for the better! It is better, if we think of the perils that we incurred in the pursuit of this stake, two centuries of unparalleled massacres, inextricably binding within history the hidden face of the light of the differend apparent in the face of its dark illusions. It's a shame! It is a shame, if one thinks of the now incontestable victory of the System of global development, now on automatic pilot and at top speed, incessantly pushing ever further back, on the one hand, the limits of development, and, on the other hand, the obstacles to the abandonment of entire populations. The postmodern event can only inspire relief and revulsion.

Our epoch evokes a dark daydream. The way totalitarianism collapsed—by implosion, dismantled from within—tolled the death knell of the inscription of the differend in the political. Already, in the thought of the struggle against totalitarianism, the line of resistance situated itself at the frontier between the political and its outside, as in the case of the journal of Winston in Orwell's *1984*. The line of writing is the last and the least breachable resistance, the place where sensibility touches the insensible, where it touches the speech of fear. Totalitarian power would have had to look for the subject there, if it wanted to find it—at the point where the extreme real gives itself to writing. With the new despotism of postmodernity, that of the System, which solicits divergences, which forces back into order the dysfunctionings and repairs itself, resistance is solely in writing. It is a writing which is not even political. *Pâtir*,[11] affect, the passibility to the event—this no longer belongs to this world nor to the appeals court of its phrase. Affect no longer finds its masks in the round of political passions, nor does it find a place in a political writing of resistance. In an interview for the journal *Rue Descartes*,[12] Lyotard wrote, "Politics is one of the corrective channels of the System. The sacrificial deployments, holocausts perhaps, genocide certainly, to which the retreat of empires gives rise in the abandoned zones, manifest the violence of affect. But what happens to it in the aseptic politics of wealthy countries? A diffuse anguish, which does not take the stage in the public theater. Where does the extreme real *go*?" (*ER*, 204).

There is, in Lyotard's thought, a sober wake-up call for the event, as well as a profound stoicism (a Hellenistic philosophy, at least, in any case) that accompanies the new thought of the differend. It is a thought that only Hegel would call an unhappy consciousness and a spiritual nihilism, for it is mind out of joint with itself, the soul. It is a new light from the night, since to this major change corresponds a change of aspect of the phrase of the differend. With the end of politics as a major stake, the political instantiation of arbitration disappears. Lyotard no longer says that "politics means linking" or "knowing how to link correctly." He henceforth keeps silent concerning the political occurrence and no longer poses the question in the terms of the obligation to link.

The thought of the differend that emerges is more extreme. The complete opposite, he says, of extremism. For it is now henceforth a matter of taking the intractable into account. Tautening further still the canvas of the incommensurable, the unpresentable, the unacquittable, Lyotard bears witness to a complaint that is all the more vehement because it cannot even claim the right to lodge itself in court. It is a complaint against nothing, against everything, "the mute lament of what the absolute lacks"

(*MP*, 36; *PF*, 31). And when the Marxist phrase returns, it is in order to voice a higher regime of the differend over this extreme affect without opposition. When the Marx of 1843 appears in court, confronted with Hegel's philosophy of right, we find a Marx, he tells us, "more brazen than brave, searching to break asunder the binary passion principle of the intrigue" (*ER*, 202). Lyotard cites Marx, he rewrites him in this sense: "I like this text: 'Extreme reals cannot be mediated one with the other, precisely because they are extreme reals. . . . The North and the South are the opposite determinations of the same being . . . , they are both poles. Likewise the masculine sex and the feminine sex are both species. . . . The true extreme reals would be the pole and the nonpole, the human sex and the nonhuman sex" (*ER*, 202). The extreme real of *pâtir*, the extreme real of affect, says itself in the phrase of Marx. It makes a sign toward the differend which is much more at the bottom of things, which is, for that matter, even at the surface of things. It makes a sign toward the affect differend, which traverses the political differend and even the sexual differend itself, and which touches upon the absolute intractable. The intractable here no longer designates what would be manageable by another phrase, that for which a phrase to be found can give—if not a reason or an account—at least an appropriate testimony. It no longer is that which gives itself to linking elsewhere, otherwise. It escapes definitively the political *modus* as well as its exercise of judgment: "*Polemos* is not the father of all things, he is the infant of the relation of the mind to the thing which has no relation to the mind" (*MP*, 165; *PF*, 190). Inversion of roles: *Polemos* is no longer the father. It arrives at its maturity of childhood, and its voice changes. It has abandoned linkage. The change of aspect of the differend is beyond the principle of conflict or even heterogeneity. It is the thought of the relationship with that which is without relation, the thought of the intractable. It is the relation of the mind to that which escapes it, now and forever.

At the same time, this relationship is no longer philosophical. It is a relationship of thought to that which exceeds the measure of thought. For this reason, this relation does not allow itself to be returned to—subsumed under—the critical experience. It is rather the extreme point of this experience, the abrupt rupture it encounters. The *Lessons on the Analytic of the Sublime* have been decisive. The Kant of the Third *Critique* is the watchman over the correct distribution of faculties, the one who declares for each faculty the phrase that belongs to it and who reflects the way the mind links. He speaks of this place which has no place, the place of judgment from which is distributed the partitioning of the faculties and the linkage of phrases. He is the one who can say that the Inhuman signifies in a manner incompatible with the phrase of the Idea, the phrase of Humanity, and who can thus arbitrate the differends that inhabit the war between phrases. The legitimate linkage of phrases reflects itself here. This relationship is from now on also a completely other relationship: the differend of the faculties only covers over the differend of thought with that which has no relation to it. The Kantian critique has a false bottom. It transcribes the differend of the sublime in terms of a differend between the faculties of imagination and of reason: where each faculty remains absolute and continues to be for itself its own court of appeals, without the possibility of any third party, in this relationship of misrecognition in recognition according to a disconcerting relationship between two absolutes, a relationship that produces feeling. And, in the same gesture, this critique describes the line of this relationship, where thought feels itself to be beyond partition, in a way that is immanent to it and that touches upon the absolute; the relation touches that which has no relation. This time, the Inhuman takes on another tone. Within the differend of the faculties, there is at play a differend that is no longer one between faculties, one that gives a glimpse and a murmur of the mind's resistance to that which has no relationship with the mind—resistance without opposition, the soul. The experience of the feeling of the sublime is encountered otherwise in the Analytic of the Beautiful. In *Que peindre?*, Lyotard writes: "The analysis of taste leads criticism to go beyond the dis-articulation of the 'I think' into different faculties (I think of the true like this; I think of the just like that; each time according to heterogeneous rules) until it exhumes a state of thought which is plural, a 'faculty' perhaps still in some sense but one which is the infancy of all the others, and which remains their creditor" (*QP*, 62). It is to return to the faculty of the infancy of all faculties, to the essential non-economy that subtends the economy of faculties, to the intimate differend of thought and the real that sustains all of the differends between the faculties. Within thought itself, it is a question of anamnesis, of the resurgence and of the perlaboration of the infancy of thought and of its relationship—this time without any relationship and without any recognition of cause—with the absolute. It is the faculty of the infancy of thought, whose touch would have engendered thought, in all its states of enlightenment and blindness. It is necessary to do an anamnesis of reflection, or a completely different anabasis.

The soul does not orient itself in the same way as the mind links. The orientation of the soul undoes the interests of the faculties and enters into a relationship with those poles which are no longer north and south, but pole and nonpole. Its orientation is disorientation. The soul is that poverty of the mind, the opposite of its misery; it is an enlightenment withdrawn from the evidence: "I am not talking about evidence (not at all), let's say that it is a question of the soul. The soul is the poverty of the mind. Zero degree of reflexivity, an aptitude for presence" (*QP*, 18). It is the humility of art, in which one cannot fail to hear the Pascalian formula: "Wisdom sends us to childhood."[13] The gesture of the writing of art is a strange and negative reflexivity of this humility, of this childhood.

The soul makes itself felt in the writings of art. The differend of the soul is suspense, stupor even, which marks itself in this phrase where the art of presence says itself, and where it undoes the art of deferral, this time, and not elsewhere: "Space-time unravels in its entirety" (*QP*, 18). Painting transports us beyond negative presentation or the presentation that there is some unrepresentable. In *Que peindre?*, Lyotard pleads for the blue event of Adami: "The blue will have preceded you. Such is presence" (*QP*, 11). The phrase of the blue is stripped of deictics: "You forget, Kant forgets the blue event. Which is not an object" (*QP*, 31). It is a phrase of presence that is neither one of presentation nor one of parousia. Without abandoning critical philosophy entirely, while at the same time making its walls come tumbling down, Lyotard finds again the very letter of phenomenology: the carnal formula of "I think in painting" (Cézanne),[14] the formula of line or "to go line" (Michaux),[15] or further still the Merleau-Pontian notion that the gaze of the things is indistinguishable from our own gaze: "The landscape thinks itself in me and I am its consciousness."[16] When the mind is touched by this, it is soul. This soul is indistinct: it is at the frontier between the subject and the object in a community of the affect of thought. Lyotard: "The landscape does not expose itself, it poses itself as a state of the soul" (*QP*, 62). It is a state beyond the ciphered writing that is described in Kantian thought, in its virtuosity of sober presence, without the support of the partition between faculties; it is a state beyond all prose, beyond any voice that may have lent itself to silence, beyond the peaceful chiasmus of active and passive. The blue, poised on its dove's feet, gives itself as an event only if it is not expected by the forms. To catch it, it will not suffice, as Merleau-Ponty thought, for the body to "find the attitude which will allow it to determine itself and to become part of the blue."[17] All posture is imposture; to mark out a trail is to forfeit the game. The faculty arrives with the phrase, and the welcoming arrives with the event. Presence outside of forms—it is a phrase without its reference points. The phrase that is said there remains interdicted. It is a phrase that forbids itself cardinal points, one or several of them, or all of them at once. It is a phrase bled white of references, luminous. Forbidden, muted, impenetrable: "its green light is a red light."[18] This inarticulated phrase forbids itself those minimal instances by which a phrase attributes a sense to a referent, by which it authorizes itself to have an addressor and by which it addresses itself to an addressee. In *Flora Danica*, accompanying the secession of gesture in the paintings of Stig Brøgger, Lyotard speaks of these "phrases that do not refer to anything identifiable, do not signify anything conceivable, phrases that emanate from nobody and address no one. But phrases still. Their negative properties, their inarticulation, make them like feelings" (*FD*, 11). They are phrases which suscitate a susceptibility to the impossible, the feeling. And they are phrases for which no logos, not even the logos of lines so dear to Merleau-Ponty, can account. The suspense of the unarticulated phrase, stripped of the valences of the phrase, is what touches. The *virtù* of the pictorial phrase is without cardinal points or deictics.[19] The pincers of articulation are not blunt enough for the art of presence.

The presence that comes to the surface here, sensible presence, a trait of the soul,[20] which is neither of form nor of matter, is an infraction; you could say that it was an effraction of being were it not an effraction of the Other. The intrigue of the touching-touched borders upon the untouchable, the enigma. In a dialogue with Rouan,[21] Lyotard speaks of this "presence that escapes all grasps, said otherwise: 'that which of the other I will never touch' . . . and not even of myself. This absolute untouchable, it is what one calls the real." And he continues: "I therefore awaited the real, you say beauty" (*VT*, 225).

The sensible presence touches upon the extreme real, but in the writing of art, it touches writing only. It is the point most susceptible to making appearance and disappearance meet, like two extremes that touch one another; it is a sensibility outside itself, outside of the "that which it is" of sensibility, and in this, at the frontier of the intimacy of terror and of phobia, the last line of resistance. "Aesthetics is phobic, it arises from anaesthesia, belonging to it, recovering from it. You sing *for* not hearing, you paint *for* not seeing, you dance *for* being paralyzed" (*MP*, 197; *PF*, 232). The absolute, in the manner in which it retracts itself, lets itself be felt as a haunting. The visible frequents the invisible, the infancy of vision is brushed by blindness. The art of presence reaches beauty only in the silent promiscuity with an opaque thing, named the extreme real, which comes from the inarticulation of an undecidable affect. In *Que peindre?*, Lyotard already writes, "And is not the purpose of painting—even when it is withdrawn, even at its haughtiest, its most reserved or its most modest—to tame the savagery of the thing, to make it submit to the visible, and at the same time to make our usual gaze submit to its savagery?"[22]

The accent of the differend has displaced itself: it no longer lies so much in the obligation to link, as in the obedience of writing. The gesture of the thinker accompanies that of the painter, of the musician, of the writer. It reiterates the gesture which is outside commentary. The complaint no longer concerns some wrong suffered but an occluded passibility. The gesture of the thinker accompanies the artist in a duet; this duet is a duel: "One clearly sees that Diderot's pen strives to rival the brush of a Chardin, of a Vernet, of a Greuze. Will I force my talent? I will not succeed" (*QP*, 72). Pleading painting, lodging a complaint with it, and writing with the painter, composing a dialogue between commentary and that which effracts commentary, one hand fighting the other, the hand of the thinker pursues the gesture of the painter. The thinker is jealous, competitive, and an intimate friend. The thinker measures his- or herself against the impossible; the thinker writes, surrendering the weapons of discourse in front of that which has no voice. The arbitrator is off the field and can very well be. The scenography of the differend has changed.

The reflexivity of thought is no longer one of judgment. It is one of writing. Reflexive writing multiplies its styles. From *Que peindre?*, which is like the *Rameau's Nephew* of beauty, to *Signed, Malraux*, one life, one oeuvre, what is literature? What is thinking in literature? When art itself is tinted in the pastels of night and is under the cape of shadow? When we push back further the frontiers of the differend? After aesthetics, after art and anti-aesthetics? When, from the abruptness of *Signed, Malraux* and then on to *The Confession of Augustine*, we must go back there to where grace springs forth? When, after that, going by way of *Soundproof Room*, which is like the vocal cavern and the sensible negative of the thinker's writing, we must suffer the paradoxes of the voice and of writing? Essaying—in so many ways—to retract the foot bridges of argumentation and to pull up its landing gear, thought strives to reach that which exceeds it.

Henceforth the truly serious philosophical problem is no longer that of linking but that of writing. In the first deal of the thought of the differend, Lyotard maintained that "the linking of one phrase with another was problematic and that this problem is the problem of politics" (*LD*, 11; *D*, xiii). The problem has changed. It is not that the question of linking has disappeared. Nor is it that this eclipse says itself in a univocal manner, or only in the terms of sensible presence: "What he wants, from presence, no linkage" (*QP*, 27). Linkage becomes secondary. Writing precedes it, and the obedience to writing reminds one of the trait of the intractable. The double path of the differend—the call of the heterogeneous and of the intractable—inflects the paradigm of the obligation to link and unclasses the paradigm of argumentation. On many occasions, Lyotard renews the interrogation: Nothing says that the stake of thought should be consensus rather than differend, the order of litigation rather than pragmatic disorder, the partaking of speech rather than passibility to the event. Nothing says that "health" (*LD, 142; D,* 146), if one can call it that, or the "reasonable" (*MP*, 130; *PF*, 146) should be on one side rather than the other. From one formulation to the other, the variation of occurrence attests to a double and simultaneous stake of the differend: on the one hand, that which is bet on the divergence from and the listening to the other, and, on the other hand, that which is bet on the intractable and the absolute other, that which Lyotard names the nothing, the Thing, and the extreme. *Alter* and *aliud*. These two ends of testimony are interlaced. The differend is a relation to an enigma more disarticulated than the one posed by the deformity of the female Sphinx, it is a relation to the question of the Thing that does not even interrogate. Borrowing the term from Lacan, Lyotard gives it another meaning. If the Thing can suscitate attraction and horror, it will be less tormented by abjection. Thing-nothing—this would be a way of hailing it. The extreme real is *nihil*. It is in the relation between these two ends of listening to the differend that linkage loses its ethical consonance, unless it belongs to an order of ethics that mocks itself. The two others, that of the voice of obligation and that of the Thing and its demands, represent not only two domains or two territories of the differend, nor even two modalities, but two tangled paths of its mode of arrival, of the very occurrence of the differend. This is the reason why writing—which par excellence puts itself in relation to the Thing, and does so in a sovereign manner—represents the privileged mode of bearing witness to the differend. This preferred *modus* of transcription is not just aesthetic; rather, it is accompanied by the beyond of art.

In "A Bizarre Partner," Lyotard writes: "I believe we sincerely think that the real questions are not subject to argumentation and that writing is the only thing that can *embrace* them" (*MP*, 118; *PF*, 123). Writing bears witness to that which escapes the argumentative interlocution (as it is the case, for example, in the phrase of obligation) and represents any other phrase than that of argumentation. Only writing can respond to and be responsible for the plurality of phrases. It is at the same time one of the modes (the one that relates to the intractable of the real) and the sovereign mode, the only one capable of saying all the differend. It is both an inscription and inherent in all inscriptions. It is the mode, while it itself is plural. There exist writings and between them no system of equivalence or of correspondence, no honorable translation, no logos of the writings.

The argumentative *modus* finds itself unclassed. What challenges it is its inveterate pretension to hegemony. Its rationality is not reasonable, for it does not admit the multiplicity of reason and does not recognize the diversity of phrasing. The argumentative temptation is to admit but one stake, that of veracity. For example, it proceeds as if the procedure by which I seek to persuade my interlocutor that something is beautiful could be translated into the procedure by which I try to persuade him or her that something is true. The subordination of all stakes to that of veracity is accompanied by a superposition of gestures. More still: the hegemonic operation proceeds from the fact that it admits but one procedure, that of persuasion in general. The argumentative aim leads any encounter of phrases back to the closed field of the contest of persuasion and, by this, to the unique stake of this binarity of true and false according to the discourse of proof. Lyotard does not only situate argumentation as one mode among others of phrasing. He gives us to think how much argumentation itself owes its idiomatic singularity to an indisputable turn of phrase: a relation kept secret from interlocution, which is a relation to an intractable alterity, unbeknownst to the one who speaks as well as to the one who is addressed, a kind of situated unconscious within the argumentative phrase.

Thus, for example, in his "American discussion" with Rorty (in "A Bizarre Partner"), he writes: "I think if Rorty himself, to deal only with him, writes and thinks, even just to signify that discussion is the only important thing, it is because he too is taken hold of by a duty that was never the object of a discussion nor of a contract, or to put it otherwise, because he is held hostage by an other who is not his interlocutor" (*MP*, 125; *PF*, 140). A formula to be heard radically: the one who is smitten with argumentative interlocution is the hostage of an other who is not an interlocutor, not even an absent one, and of whom we cannot even speak in terms of a profound address. There is an unacquittable other who destines this argumentative phrase, who is the alterity in its singular actuality that makes you speak and requests the sharing of argumentation. The continuous bass of a *loneliness*.[23] For such an argumentative phrase, the turn of phrase or the figure of the other, or the very being of the other "who haunts me," is that which exercises a silently absolute right, which gives to the right to argue its right, and to the duty to argue its duty, but which simultaneously escapes this right, in a no-man's land or an amnesty. The entire interlocutory relation depends upon this other, whom the interlocution occludes, even though it seems to take place right in front of him or her; this other is unnamable. In interlocution can be heard the mute debt to the other. It is a lateral relation, which is not one of communication but which presides over every form of communication. Argumentation would be one case of this.

But the *sensus communis* of aesthetics is another case as well. Kant, as reread by Lyotard, brings to light the shattered origin of the *sensus communis* of sensible presence. It is a voice which is not of a shareable meaning, a supersensible which hides itself, but which requires that we share the aesthetic sense. One can multiply its names: it is the real which puts us in debt; a debt of thought, one owed by those on this side of the hinge of what the real offers up for symbolization; it is the unconditional supersensible of the *sensus communis*. There are so many openings from the unknowns, so many multiple unknowns, that cannot be unified amongst themselves. Everything would find its source again in intimate differends. And they would be recognized as differends only to the extent to which one could manage the unmanageable task of recognizing the differend with that which has no relation. The affect phrase paralyzes all phrases. This is the outline of this second and more encrypted differend, which imprints its mark upon the first. Only writing can testify to this. Each writing in its singular actuality is like a susceptibility to return to the navel of such an unknown. Through such a susceptibility, writing might give its letters of nobility to this sequestered unknown, perhaps thereby exhuming the debt owed to this unknown, the unknown that haunts, to cite but one example, argumentation.

Is this to say that argumentation experiences a decline? Rather, it is to say the inverse. The disavowed writing of argumentation—the writing that argumentation disavows, the writing that argumentation has rendered highly implicit, so to speak—can be accounted for only by an avowed writing. Moreover, argumentation itself bears the traits of a particular writing, *sui generis*. The argumentative *modus* is at once both the effacement of style in the philosophical and a philosophical style. Disavowed writing is, at the same time, a stylization of writing. As such, argumentation is not reducible to writing, since writing could not unify everything under a single emblem without reducing itself to a mere being of reason. In doing so, writing would thereby turn itself into an idol.

Is this to say that, with the thought of writing, philosophy begins to fade away? If it is the case that, with writing, the philosophical pen calls out to the dust—the *nihil*—and inscribes the nothingness, this nothingness "requires its inscription by thought not as a product of its critical argument but as a style of its reflexive writing" (*MP*, 30; *PF*, 24). Philosophy has become clearly a question of style; in truth, it has never ceased to be so. With the new occurrence of the differend, the thought of style exposes itself. The philosophical style that inscribes itself in the interstice of vanity—between the "What's the use?" and the "And so what?"—demands from the philosopher more than the recognition of an amnesia of writing. It demands the secession of a gesture: "[Philosophy] must work through the resistance that, in its own articulation, puts *animus* in opposition to *anima*" (*MP*, 209; *PF*, 248). It demands that the thought-body work on philosophy otherwise than in spite of itself.

Does this mean the effacement of any sharing? Is it a question of dying to the philosophical spirit to be born to the poet-soul? This would be quickly and badly said. It matters that the philosopher does not turn himself entirely into an artist, that he does not revoke himself as he works on his resistance. "[A] reflective writing insists," writes Lyotard, "on questioning its propriety, and on that very account, to expropriate itself endlessly" (*MP*, 209; *PF*, 248). Philosophical writing lodges a complaint. The philosopher lodges a complaint about "the mute lament of what the absolute lacks" (*MP*, 36; *PF*, 31). It is a singular and idiomatic complaint. In recognizing itself as such, in recognizing itself as a matter of style, philosophical writing does not dissolve into the writing of writers, regardless of the extent to which they may overlap. Whatever his writing might be, it is singular to him. We may put it to the criterion developed in Lyotard's reading of Valéry: if the vocation of style is to transmit the feeling that not only engendered the oeuvre but that also calls for more work yet to come, then philosophical style transmits the feeling that calls for more thought in philosophy, as pictorial style passes on the feeling that prompts more thinking in painting.[24] It engenders another such gesture.

But to trace this gesture back to the affect transmitted by the writing of art exclusively, to say that it is exclusively to this that we owe this gesture, would be mistaken. There are several others that escape interlocution, show it out, and send it on its way. As long as there is some incommunicable imperative present at the very birth of communication, there will be a transfer of writing. There are several others and several writings of the differend, like so many warnings that "the time has come," so many proddings.

The one with whom we play and write, the bizarre partner or the unnamable addressee (who is never the same), answers according to a different game. At the opposite extreme of this uncommon ground, he or she stands in silence, at the edge of a cliff, where trajectories and lines are not visible. Whether real or phantom, as long as he or she stands there, we will be *as if we were saved*. All that will be left for us to do is to worry. *Misreading*—it is the threat that nothing will henceforth arrive, and the memory of suspense. The relation of thought with that which has no relation with it will remain insistent. It will resist, in its permanent tension with the differends diverging amongst themselves and dividing our interior and exterior space. Better than any other transcription, writing provides the support for this and bears witness to it. Writing is the frequency of resistance. For this, writing is even better than argumentation. To be sure, argumentation is itself a writing, but it is a disavowed writing. One must loosen the fist of argumentation. Writing takes more of a risk, makes more of a gesture. It does so by not denying that which it cannot inscribe, that which it will never be able to inscribe, however much it may try. No matter how eloquent it is, it is still too eloquent, still within the space of discourse that one must, in the dark, undo. This is because the mind also haunts the places of the soul, prowls there eloquently. Hence a conflict of hauntings. Augustine and Pascal knew this: the art of persuasion—in this case, the art of writing—circumvents writing. Writing is without a name. Even calling it "an art" does not fit it. Any art is in a relation of obedience to a writing, a type of obedience that is unique to the art in question. The routes taken by the perlaboration of resistance are multiple. Arts and literature are some of them. Between writings, family resemblances leave intact the very fact of writing, which itself is without family. It is there that we find points of soul, which are signs. But these signs are isolated ones, outside the world of signs and outside semiotic and phenomenological apprehension. These signs, which are almost without reiteration, are the only ones to go against any such semiotic or phenomenological world of signs and their meanings. Through them, writing takes place. The nothing gives rise and place to the countersign.

Can the relation of the mind with that which has no relation to it, the point of soul, be annihilated? If the philosopher is affected by this "mute complaint," which the seductions of the megalopolis hide at same time as they manifest it, "Is it true," asks Lyotard, "that the climate-controlled aesthetics, which is the mode of existence in the megalopolis, 'displays and conceals,' the suffering over the lack of the absolute?" (*MP*, 36; *PF*, 31). This is the question posed to this space where the insensible has circumscribed the city, to "the frozen time of the oppressive postmodernity" (*QP*, 47), when indifference is a competitive performativity, when experimentation is without anamnesis. This question is posed and remains suspended, which is not the case with the phrase that follows: "Is this suffering not the construction of a fable that philosophy needs to legitimate the role that it attributes to itself?" (*MP*, 36; *PF*, 31). This formulation can easily be discarded. And Lyotard can resume: "The megalopolis, in any case, is perfectly well organized to ignore or forget these questions, this question. And nevertheless, the forgetting of forgetting still makes enough of a sign for writing—art, literature, and philosophy all mixed together—to insist on bearing witness to the fact that there is something left behind" (*MP*, 36; *PF*, 32). Still it makes enough of a sign, and time does not count. Writing will always make enough of a sign. The soul is interminable and cannot die. Such is the absent phrase. The shadow of a doubt has passed. But no matter how lightning fast it passed, does it not bear witness to a great fear, the fear that with the eclipse of the writing of the political differend, the differend itself, which links us to its writings, would be more than threatened? How can we know? Will we ever know? Lyotard often repeats these questions.

The Lyotardian inconclusiveness is clear. It is a refusal to claim to have recovered the tables of the trace. There are only sketches of the differend, all of them worked by an ineluctable tension. But they are not merely paths leading nowhere. So pathetic! Rather, Lyotard insists, they are something else entirely: passages that do not pass. The oeuvre is made of such passages, such impasses. These are the thresholds. Asceticism itself is a threshold, one of them. It does not resolve, no more than does the gesture that accompanies the brush of the painter and writes with him, no more than the argumentative harassment or the ruminated meditations. Each one of these gestures is a way of inscribing the "in vain," which finds no reprieve from vanity. It is a wisdom that sends us to infancy. The inconclusiveness of the Lyotardian oeuvre is the writing of thresholds. Lyotard ceaselessly writes by cutting out: method *per via di levare*:[25] "It is a form of language: less for more."[26] But whether he speaks with or without the cardinal points of the phrase, he adds on. The writings of the differend do not cancel each other out. They overlap each other. Without glossing, Lyotard writes ceaselessly alongside. He stands on the threshold, at the point of the soul, at the very instant. One of the figures that is suitable here is that figure, that sculptural snapshot, dancing and striving, which Giacometti wanted honorably inhuman: *The Capsizing Man*. "I mean also: soul-full" (*QP*, 28).[27]

Translated by Kent Still with assistance from
Scott Shinabargar and Anne Kelly

The Inarticulate Affect

LYOTARD AND PSYCHOANALYTIC TESTIMONY

Claire Nouvet

Philosophy rarely, if ever, engages psychoanalysis. It is then all the more noteworthy when a philosopher takes the risk of such an engagement. Jean-François Lyotard took this chance repeatedly and in different modes. While his American fame is largely based on his popularization of the term "postmodern," his early works were devoted to Freud's "libidinal economy," the title of one of his books. In the texts that appeared after *The Differend*—"[his] book of philosophy,"[1] as he called it—the task of philosophical thinking nevertheless changed. Philosophical thought was now asked to confront that monster which scandalizes the very rules of philosophical cognition: not libido, but affect.

What happens when philosophy encounters psychoanalysis at this specific site: the affect? How does this encounter affect both philosophy and psychoanalysis? And psychoanalysis in its clinical dimension?

While one can find in Lyotard a precise description of the impact of psychoanalysis on philosophy, the impact of philosophy on psychoanalysis is strangely downplayed. At the end of "Emma,"[2] Lyotard's reading of Freud's famous case study,[3] he bluntly asserts: "I am convinced that the 'phraseology' you just read does not bring anything to the psychoanalyst that he does not already know or that he can use. Its interest, if it has one, is philosophical" (*E*, 44; translation modified). Here is a philosopher who, for once, lets go of the typical philosophical arrogance. Philosophy renounces its claim to hegemony and bows, as it were, in front of the analyst. It has nothing to teach the psychoanalyst.

Modestly, then, philosophy claims to echo psychoanalysis. This is a modest echo indeed, since it does not even claim to echo psychoanalysis back to itself, but merely to propagate the turbulence of the psychoanalytic insight within the philosophical field. And still, I will argue, something worth listening to might be sent back to psychoanalysis by the philosophical echo. Philosophy reiterates psychoanalysis, but with a different inflection which underlines with a specific intensity some aspects of the well-known psychoanalytic material. This intensification gives rise to questions that are addressed not only to the clinic and to the specific *art* that, for Lyotard, analytic listening is, and must acknowledge itself to be, but also to analytical writing.

Lyotard's emphasis on analytical listening as an art is not, of course, a repudiation of psychoanalysis as fiction, although a third discipline no doubt makes itself heard at this point: literature. Paradoxically enough, it may have taken a philosopher to open psychoanalysis to literature, to offer a positive evaluation of the proximity of psychoanalysis to literature, and a reading of psychoanalytic literature precisely as literature. All of which occurs through a philosopher's attempt to think what philosophy has long resisted thinking, but with which psychoanalysis and literature must constantly deal: affect. It is, therefore, through this philosophical articulation of the affect that I will attempt to address some literary questions to psychoanalysis. They will focus on the muteness of affect, its radical heterogeneity to articulation, its tonal imprint on articulated discourse, and its transmission. Through these different problems, one overarching question in fact tries to articulate itself: what is owed to the testimony that the affect is according to Lyotard? And how does one acquit oneself of this debt: in a tone, a susceptibility to transmission, an intractable resistance, a work, be it analytical or literary?

As he listens to the psychoanalytical affect that comes to him from Freud, Lyotard claims to speak "as a philosopher," that is, "with no (clinical) authority on the question of excitation" (*E*, 25). To speak "as a philosopher" also means that one does not relinquish the philosophical pretension "to articulate in an intelligible fashion." What, paradoxically enough, will be rigorously articulated is the radical inarticulateness of the affect.

First, the affect is reframed within the pragmatic of phrases that Lyotard elaborated in *The Differend*. Lyotard's reading of Emma is indeed directed by the "philosophical intuition" that the affect must and can be thought as a phrase, without having recourse to the metaphor of physics that Freud deploys in "Project for a Scientific Psychology." A "phrase" for Lyotard presents a universe composed of four poles: referent, meaning, addressor, and addressee. The universe of the phrase can be thus summarized: someone (addressor) says something (meaning) about something (referent) to someone (addressee). A phrase is articulated to the extent that it presents this quadrangulated universe. It should be noted that a "phrase" is not necessarily linguistic and cannot simply be equated with the linguistic sentence. A gesture can also be a "phrase." If this is the definition of the articulated phrase, then the Freudian affect is of the order of the inarticulate in the very precise sense that it negates the poles of the articulated phrase. Lyotard highlights the following negative traits of the "Freudian lesson" (*E*, 25): the affect is not addressed, not referencing, and not signifying.

Where does Lyotard read this Freudian lesson? In Freud's study of Emma, certainly, but also in later texts, such as the *Three Essays on Infantile Sexuality* and *On Narcissism: An Introduction*, where Freud elaborates a theory of infantile sexuality which, according to Lyotard, concerns the referentiality as well as the addressor/addressee polarization of the infantile affect. It is in these later texts that Lyotard reads a definition of the infantile affect as neither referential nor addressed.

The infantile affect has no addressor. This lesson is supposedly derived from the hypothesis of primary narcissism. Sexuality (or rather "affectivity" according to the Lyotardian inflexion) is originally ignorant of the instance "I," since primary narcissism (which refers to a state prior to both the formation of an ego and the split between subject and external world) is, paradoxically, pre-egoic. Affectivity irrupts in the absence of an ego, "before" its emergence. The strike of pleasure and/or pain does not therefore "deceive" the ego, as Freud claims, since there was no ego capable of fending off the strike of affect to begin with. The ego that claims to have been deceived by an affect that somehow avoided its defenses in fact deceives itself as to its primacy. The infantile affect does not happen to "I." Strictly speaking, then, the child is not an "I" who can address an affect. "I" cannot address an affect that happens before "I" comes on the scene. The affect that seizes and cripples the "grown-up" sends this grown-up back to this condition of infancy, of non-addressedness. The adult in the grip of affect can no more address it than the child could. S/he reverts to the pre-egoic infant.

Ron Katwan spells out some of the consequences of this reformulation. If the affect "brings about the disappearance of the addressor, that is, of what is commonly and misleadingly called the subject," if affects are "experiences without a subject, that is, phrases without an addressor," then "the idea that affects are private mental experiences taking place within the mental space of the subject is not available to Lyotard," and "we have to face the threat of rendering incoherent the idea that such feelings are *our* experiences."[4] With the notion of an inarticulate affect, Lyotard indeed, and in proximity with some of the most puzzling insights of psychoanalysis, calls us to think the unthinkable: an experience that is not lived by the conscious "I." There can be feelings that "I" do not feel, experience, or live, at least consciously, feelings that exceed the feeling ability of the conscious subject, and that can therefore only be experienced in the absences of this subject. In that sense, the affect is not a "lived experience," since it entails a kind of death of the "mind" that claims to be the only subject of experience. It provokes its eclipse and inscribes itself, unnoticed, in its absences to itself. The affect: a feeling felt by no "I" and no "one."

The infantile affect has no addressee. "I" do not communicate to "you" the affect that seizes me. In making this claim, Lyotard points to Freud's objection to Rank's thesis on birth trauma. Birth cannot be the first trauma, since the child does not suffer the loss of an object. The maternal womb is not an object. This objection can be extended, according to Lyotard, to all primary relation of infant to mother: "this relation is not that of addressor to addressee nor the reverse" (*E*, 39). The mother's body is not a "you." Deprived of an "I," an ego or subject position, the affect or excitation is also deprived of a "you" or object in the sense of objectality. An affect, an excitation, does not address a "you": it does not demand anything, an affect for instance, from any "you." By the same token, it ignores the permutation of places that defines articulation: the "I" who addresses "you" can in principle become the addressee, the "you" of the next sentence addressed by "I."

The infantile affect has no referent. It "'speaks of' nothing" (E, 39). Pain and/or pleasure are not related to any object. Here the reader is sent to the Freudian notion of "polymorphic perversity," which, for Lyotard, means that any object can be made to serve as an "occasion" for the infantile affect: "every 'object' can be used as an occasion for the pleasure or displeasure of the ('pure') infantile affect-phrase" (*E*, 39; translation modified). The object provides only an opportunity or rather an "occasion" for an infantile affectability or excitability—described as "constant" (*E*, 40) but "vague" and "errant" (*E*, 43)—to get excited. In his *Three Essays on Infantile Sexuality*, Freud already signaled toward this "occasion," when he proclaimed the radical contingency of the object. If the object is merely an occasion for the affect, then the affect ignores referentiality: it cannot be said to be "about" any specific object. The object is only the contingent occasion for excitability to get excited.

But the affect may also ignore referentiality in still another way. The referent is not reality, but that which is established as reality through discursive procedures. Referentiality therefore presupposes interlocution: it is first and foremost that which we talk about. Since the affect ignores the dimension of interlocution, it follows that it ignores the dimension of referentiality. The affect means that there is no "I" to talk to "you" about "something." The infant feels pleasure and pain but cannot refer these feelings to an object, since it does not yet have any conception of objects as being precisely referents of a phrase to be exchanged between interlocutors. While the grown-up—Freud, for instance, when he writes the *Three Essays on Infantile Sexuality*—can know that the infant's feelings of pain and pleasure proceed from the excitation of various erotogenic zones of the body, the infant cannot refer these feelings to anything that s/he can call or conceive as a "body." The very notion of "body" or "organism" can only be elaborated as the referent of a cognitive phrase that is here missing. In "La phrase-affect (D'un supplément au *Différend*)," which, like "Emma," is collected in *Misère de la philosophie*,[5] Lyotard writes:

> There is a body only as the referent of one or many cognitive phrases, and as that which is established through procedures for the establishment of reality. There are different kinds of body according to the nature of the knowledge being sought. The body as existence therefore presupposes logos. Only the logical animal has a body. (*MPH*, 54)

In "La peinture, anamnèse du visible"[6] (another essay from *Misère de la philosophie*), Lyotard enumerates some of the bodies that logos constitutes: "the body of the doctor, the jurist, the sergeant recruiter, the manager, and the sociologist," as well as the "sensorimotor body of the psychologist" or the "accultured body of the anthropologist" (*MPH*, 107). In contradistinction to all of these "logical" bodies, the affect is not a body but rather an "incorporeal chaos" that cannot be "talked about" or referenced.

Affectivity ignores referentiality. The very strength of the affect resides in the fact that it prevents logos from referring it to any object. This affective ignorance of referentiality can be reactivated in the grown-up through suspension. At the moment pain, for instance, strikes, it is not related to any "cause." To claim that one feels pain because *x* happened is to take a cognitive stance in relation to an affect that, in the intensity of its happening, suspends this articulation of cause and effect. I may "know" that a knife has caused the pain that I feel in my finger, but at the point where pain pierces, its very intensity resists letting itself be related to anything outside its absolute now.

The infantile affect has no meaning: it does not communicate a signification about a referent. And still the affect has or rather makes some "sense." The affect "signals some sense"; it "makes sense." This sense is always the same: pleasure and/or pain. This minimal sense does not, however, constitute a signification. The affect signals that there is pain and/or pleasure but does not say what this sense of pain and/or pleasure means, nor to what it can be referred. The affect only and always says: there is pain/pleasure. It does not signify pain and/or pleasure; it only gives a sense of pain and/or pleasure in their absolute singularity. A pain/pleasure signals itself, it gives a sense of itself in its absolute singularity without saying what it means or to what it refers. As Geoffrey Bennington points out, it is this minimal sense that allows Lyotard to claim that the affect is still a phrase although it negates all the poles of the articulated phrase, including the pole of signification:

> The affect-phrase is *inarticulate*, meaning that, unlike all the other sorts of sentences analysed in *Le Différend*, it does not present a "universe" organized according to the four familiar poles in their two familiar axes of addressor-addressee and referent-meaning (so that in presenting a universe a sentence typically positions someone as saying something about something to someone). . . . If the affect-phrase is inarticulate and fails to present a universe, it nonetheless has a minimal point of connection with the way in which other phrases and universes are described in the book [*The Différend*], and that is around the (already rather obscure) pole of meaning or sense. . . . Rather than *presenting* a universe, it *signals* a sense which is monotonous in that it is always only a sense of pleasure and/or pain. . . . This minimal complicity of the affect-phrase with the analytic of sentences does allow other sentences to link onto it, but only in an attempt to domesticate it or to make it the object of a cognitive discourse.[7]

No more than the sense of the affect should be confused with a signification, can the signal of the affect be confused with a sign. The affect is both a state (of pain and/or pleasure) and a signal of that state. This signal does not follow the state of pain and/or pleasure, it coincides with it "immediately": "The affect is immediately its manifestation."[8] The affect is a tautogorical sign: pain/pleasure immediately signals itself, its presence. This signal must be distinguished from a sign. Lyotard elaborates this distinction via the Aristotelian distinction between logos (that is, language articulated in signifying units) and *phone*, the non-signifying voice that we share with animals and which only signals what Aristotle calls *pathemata*, that is, affects. Logos is articulated; it is cut in segments, in *articuli*, which are used to form words that can refer to the objects that they designate because they function as their *représentants arbitraires*, their "arbitrary representatives" (*LdE*, 131). The sign is a representative: it stands for the object that it signifies. The sign also presupposes a dimension of interlocution, since its status as arbitrary representative is a matter of consensus between interlocutors. Logos transmits the signification of an object to an addressee on behalf of an addressor. Since the Aristotelian logos presupposes this dimension of interlocution, Lyotard renames it "lexis." The lexis "goes from an addressor to an addressee to whom it transmits a signification concerning that to which it refers. It therefore articulates itself on two axes: destination or adressedness, and referentiality of meaning" (*LdE*, 132). The very notion of a "referentiality of meaning" suggests that the sign does not just refer to the object that it represents: it transmits a signification about its referent. It signifies that to which it refers and can only refer to it through this signification.

In contradistinction to the voice of logos, the *phone* is a confused, continuous, and inarticulate voice that does not let itself be articulated or cut up in phonemes, the building blocks for the signifying units of the words. It is akin to a "timbre" or a "tone," an "intonation" or "inflection." The timbre of the *phone* is not cut up into arbitrary signs that stand for the thing. It is not therefore of the order of representation that constitutes, as Lyotard claims, the very substance of the sign. Nor is it of the order of signification: the *phone* does not communicate a signification about a referent. What, then, asks Lyotard, distinguishes this *phone* from a mere sound? *Phone* "is a voice because it makes sense. It is a *semeion*, a signal. It is not the arbitrary sign put in place of a thing, an *onoma*. It is the sense itself in so far as it signals itself. What sense? A *pathema*, claims Aristotle, of pleasure, of pain, according to their singular nuance. Their timbre, precisely" (*LdE*, 134). The *phone* is a signal to be distinguished from the arbitrary and conventional sign of logos. While a sign is a matter of consensus between interlocutors, a signal is not. While a sign stands for the thing that it arbitrarily signifies, a signal is neither arbitrary nor does it stand for the affect that it claims to signal. The affect does not represent and signify itself as it signals itself; rather, it presents or manifests itself in a signal, a tone or an inflection, which preserves the absolutely singular nuances of the pain/pleasure that it is. It says only one thing: that it is there in its absolute singularity.

Because it does not belong to the order of representation, the affect constitutes an irrefutable witness: "the affect is indeed a witness since it manifests itself as *phone.* It is even a witness beyond suspicion in its own order: being wholly what it is, and signal that it is, it cannot lie" (*LdE*, 137). The affect testifies to itself: pain/pleasure bear witness to themselves in the signal that manifests them as they happen. Although the affect is a truthful witness within its own order, it nevertheless becomes a false witness within the order of logos:

> In order to understand the status of the affect, a difference (which I believe is "ontological"), such as that between *Darstellung* (presentation) and *Vorstellung* (representation), must be admitted. The affect as "effect" of excitation is there, but not for anything other than itself. This constitutes, at the same time, both its irrefutability and its insufficiency as witness. The affect only "says" one thing: that it is there, but it does not say for what or of what it bears witness. Neither does it say from when or from where. (*E*, 32; translation modified)

The affect is truthful and irrefutable insofar as it simply and only says that "it is there," that there is now a singular pain/pleasure. And this it can "say" in a gesture, an inflection. But that is all the affect "says." It does not say who signals this pain/pleasure to whom. It does not "say" what this pain/pleasure is about, nor what it signifies, nor when and where it happens. The testimony of the affect is therefore both beyond suspicion and eminently suspect as far as articulated logos is concerned. Logos indeed requires another kind of testimony: an identifiable "I" speaks to a no less identifiable "you" about something, a referent, the meaning of which can be established. Within logos, the testimony of the affect is therefore doomed to be judged both irrefutable (it is indubitable that there is an affect) and equivocal: since the testimony of the affect ignores and thus leaves indeterminate the four poles that articulated logos requires in order to speak (addressor, addressee, referent, meaning), the affect is a witness which can neither be heard nor speak according to the rules of logos. Even worse, it is a potentially false—because indeterminate—witness. The affect can lie and be turned into a false witness in the very gesture that would seek to impose upon it a determination that it ignores. Although it is indubitable and true that there is an affect, the determination of the addressor, addressee, referent, and meaning of the affect is open to falsification. One may even say that any attempt to link the affect to a determinable addressor, addressee, referent, meaning falsifies the truth of the affect, although such falsification is—paradoxically enough—required for the affect to become a true witness according to the rule of articulated language.

What is the relation between the toned voice, the "affectual voice" as Lyotard calls it, and the communicative voice? The inarticulate *phone* of the affect and articulated logos are "heterogeneous" to each other. They do not even constitute two heterogeneous languages since one of them, the affect, is not a language. This affect is, according to Lyotard, irreducible to articulation. This irreducibility does not mean that the affect simply stands "outside" articulated language. The *phone* is neither the absolute other nor the absolute outside of articulated language. It can inhabit articulated language, but as a squatter, a clandestine guest, an "outside within," the presence of which articulated language does not even suspect or hear. It is, within articulation, that which cannot be articulated and therefore heard. The affect is mute, claims Lyotard. Muteness does not mean that the affect is simply voiceless. It is not the absence of voice, but the condition of a voice condemned to remain unheard. Lyotard repeatedly reminds us that "mute" comes from the root *mu*, from which are derived "to murmur," "to moan," and "mystery," as well as the Latin *muttum*, which gave the French *mot*, "word."[9] There is a "murmur," and even a moaning, in all the articulated words that we pronounce. It is the murmur and moaning of affect, which the articulated language of communication "mutes" by being deaf to it, however loud, and even deafeningly strident, it might be. Logos is simply not equipped to hear it.

The affectual *phone* that passes through articulated logos (without being able to speak in it or to be heard by it) can "damage" logos by suspending or interrupting its linkages. The damage caused by the affect to logos does not, however, have to be spectacular. The affect does not need to disorganize and mistreat logos in a "massive" fashion. The *phone* can merely "infiltrate" a place of the articulated structure or one of its linkages without ever being heard by it. Here Lyotard picks up, I believe, on the two metaphors to which Freud has recourse, notably in his *Studies on Hysteria*, to approximate the unconscious affect: a foreign body but also an infiltration. An instance of this barely noticeable affectual flection would be, for instance, the literary use of the *style indirect libre*. A phrase, to be articulated, must clearly distinguish the personal pronouns "I," "you," and "s/he/it" and distinctly place these personal pronouns on the axis of destination ("I" and "you") and on the axis of referentiality ("s/he"). The affect is a "confused" voice to the extent that it may blur the clear distinction of these personal pronouns and positions. The *style indirect libre* transgresses the distinctions between referent and addressor by condensing in one place "the mark of that which is talked about and the mark of the one speaking, that is, the mark of the referent and of the addressor" (*E*, 41; translation modified).

Lyotard concludes his reading of "Emma" with the following remark: "The presence, the pure autonomy of the affect cannot be translated in a presentation or a representation. The differend is unavoidable between this affectivity and articulation. It cannot be reabsorbed in a litigation" (*E*, 44; translation modified). Now, "differend" is a loaded term. The book that Lyotard calls his "book of philosophy" was devoted to it. In *The Differend*, Lyotard distinguishes "litigations," conflicts in which a commonly accepted language may be found to resolve the dispute between parties, from "differends," conflicts for which no common rule can be found since the parties are speaking incommensurate languages. To treat a differend as if it were a litigation, Lyotard argues, is to "wrong" at least one of the parties, or both, by imposing a common order upon their incommensurability.

What, then, about analysis? Is it of the order of a litigation that attempts to reabsorb the differend, that is, the incommensurability between affectivity and articulation? Can the talking cure "treat" and, at the same time, do justice to the incommensurability of the affect, to its muteness? And what would such a justice entail?

Let me summarize Lyotard's version of analysis. The talking cure is a "treatment by phrases" in the extended sense that Lyotard gives to the term "phrase." In analysis, anything, and not just linguistic sentences, can function as a "phrase." Analysis also presupposes that all phrases (sentences, but also gestures, etc.) are *addressed* to the analyst who both occupies and vacates the position of addressee, since s/he is there only as a vacant pronoun offering itself to a multiplicity of addresses. Here arises the first philosophical difficulty: if the affect, in its pure philosophical definition, is that which negates and ignores articulation, how can it manifest itself on an analytical stage that is dominated by the presupposition of address?

The patient comes to analysis driven by an unconscious affect, the presence of which has become too intense, too recurrent, and too disruptive of the linkages of articulated life: the convulsions of the hysterics, the phobias and absences of Emma. The task of analysis consists in enabling the unconscious affect to manifest itself, to present or actualize itself. How does analysis facilitate this manifestation? Although analysis takes place within the articulated logos of phrases, it loosens up, as it were, the constraints of articulation. And this in different ways: the floating attention of the analyst, the free association of the analysand, and the weakening of the addressee pole. The analysand is asked to "free associate," that is, to put herself in a disposition where the connections and linkages from one word to the other, or from one sentence to the other, are no longer firmly settled, fixed by proper rules of linkage. This freedom loosens up the connections and, in so doing, allows for a proliferation of possible linkages. Lyotard, in his text on Valéry entitled "Disorder,"[10] likens the freedom of association required by analysis to the kind of "disorder" that requires the "poetic spirit" in action (*en acte*): spirit acts by opening itself to "the indefiniteness and unfinishedness of linkages, indetermination" (*LdE*, 119). This disorder, this opening to and of indefinite linkages, is the very condition of "fecundity."

The analyst listens in a peculiar way. S/he practices a floating attention, which suspends any judgment as to what may be important or anecdotal. By paying equal attention to the seemingly important and the non-important, s/he can begin to feel the delicate and barely noticeable affective "coloring" that permeates articulated speech. S/he pays attention and, in so doing, calls attention to these neglected affective shades: "With a delicacy both specific and severe, the analyst calls attention to the chromatics, an attention that floats on the water without prejudging the important from the anecdotal" (*E*, 33). The analyst calls attention to the chromatics of the affect in the very gesture of paying attention to it.

Another way of putting it would be to say that the analyst cannot or should not be tone deaf. The diffuse presence of the affect can be confusedly perceived in chromatic shades as well as in inflections and tones. This affectual tone can be considered as an imprint, which enigmatically stamps the articulated voice of logos. This imprint is absolutely singular, idiomatic, separate from any community and any common language. The affectual tone of a voice does not "communicate" anything to anybody. It does not "mean" anything. And it is not addressed: I do not address my tone to you. The tone, with its shifting nuances, strikes my logos and may strike you too, if you pay attention to it. But it does not address. Below and before the address, it is an enigmatic testimony to the strike of affectivity, to the traumatic blows that constitute, in an absolutely singular manner, my affective being "before" any "ego" presumably endowed with "intention" and the capacity to address enters the scene. The tone of a voice is, in that sense, a mark of its infantile affectivity, of its very birth to sensibility: a form of signature. Here an absolutely idiomatic mode of "feeling" signals itself: a signal or signature, but not a meaningful sign.

The work of analysis requires that the analyst listen not only to the network of signifiers that comes through free association but also to the tone, the *phone*, of the patient which remains the only guide of analysis. And this listening is, as Lyotard suggests, "an art" (*E*, 28) and not a science. While science presupposes the application of established rules applicable in principle to all cases, "art" deals with the absolutely singular and cannot therefore rely on preestablished rules. Listening for tone is therefore a commitment to the singularity of the case. Listening for the affectual tone also entails exposing oneself to a strange "affective communication." The analytic work seems to presuppose, at least for some analysts such as André Green, some form of "affective communication" between analyst and patient:

> Affective communication is part of the most general analytical experience. But here we are moving into uncertain territory. "Empathy," so necessary to the analyst, may soon become easy prey to the affects projected by the analyst on to his patient, beyond what is expressible, intelligible and representable, and may take a mystical turn in which scientific truth may well be lost.[11]

But should one even speak here of communication? Communication supposes the four poles of articulated language that the affect, in its strict sense, negates. Rather than talking of "communication," one might then substitute "communicability," which would mark this crucial difference. There is an affective communicability, a strange transmissibility of affect, outside the model of articulated communication. To be "affective," a transmission might then have to take place, like the affect, at a level where patient and analyst are no longer an "I" and a "you." The patient ("I") does not transmit or communicate an affect to the analyst ("you"), insofar as the affect, in its happening, negates the position of both "I" and "you." This implies that the analyst, at the point where s/he is struck by the affect, has, at least momentarily, given up the "personal" position of articulated communication and returned, as it were, to an affectability which precedes articulation, to the "before" of infantility and passibility. This affective communicability, however, does not and cannot mean "I feel your pain." In the Lyotardian terms with which I am working, such phrasing is a delusion that denies the absolutely singular quality of one's affectability. You can no more feel my pain than you can speak with my tone; my pain is, like my tone, irreducibly idiomatic. Therefore, the bond of affectivity between analyst and analysand cannot and should not mean the illusion of fusion in the "same" mute magma. It might be more of a bond in difference, a bond where the separation is inscribed and respected.

The analytic loosening of the constraints of articulation gives a chance to the affect that permeates the representative chain to manifest, or rather "precipitate" itself, in a "now," in an absolute present that punctures the diachronic time of the session. The affect is "now." It is a present that resists and ignores a diachronic time where the now is framed by a past and future now. When it precipitates itself on the analytic stage, is the affect addressed? One Lyotardian version of the analytic scenario would suggest that the affect, faithful to its intractable inarticulateness, does not address itself, but is instead *made* to address. The analytical response consists, according to Lyotard, in asking: "Why are you not saying anything to me?" This response need not be addressed only to the analysand, who remains literally silent. It is also implicitly addressed to the very muteness of the affect. The analyst, in this little scenario, which encapsulates for Lyotard the analytic move, responds with a demand. S/he demands that the affect be addressed. In other words, the question "Why are you not saying anything to me?" is not a statement of fact, a simple description of what is happening, but an analytic intervention. The analyst demands the minimal analytic requirement: that the affect be an address. Now, the affect in its strict philosophical definition, that is, in the ideal purity that Lyotard gives it, is not destined by anyone to anybody. And it is "mute," "inarticulate," precisely because it ignores the axis of destination. If this is the case, then the analyst makes muteness address. In a move, which is to be anticipated, Lyotard stresses that the analyst at this point "articulates" the silence by presupposing that it is addressed. And within his pure philosophical terminology, this articulation constitutes a violence of sorts, a forgetting of the radical heterogeneity that separates the affect from representation and articulation. The analyst willfully forces the dimension of address onto an affect that ignores it. In so doing, s/he willfully ignores the radical heterogeneity of the two orders. And it is the task of philosophy to come in to underline the potential "injustice" that such a forcing might entail, at least to someone who, like Lyotard, has tied the notion of "justice" to the respect of heterogeneity.

The therapeutic value of the move, however, is indisputable. Lyotard himself notes that this transcription seems unavoidable, and that it is called "transference." Transference, he points out, usually means that the analyst is used as the addressee for all the patient's phrases. The point is to determine to whom these phrases are addressed, to lift the silence that weighs on the "true" addressee. Nevertheless, a philosophical reservation marks itself at this juncture. The point of transference might not be a question of discovering the true, originary addressee of the affect since the affect might be originally "indifferent" to articulation. Lyotard, for his part, reduces transference to the following succinct definition: "a *phone* in the process of articulating itself" (*LdE*, 144). In other words, it is an inarticulate muteness in the process of being forced into articulation. Lyotard enumerates the various therapeutic values that proceed from this articulation. The address of transference enables the patient to hear that which she could not hear: her own affectual voice. It also allows the affect to actualize itself here and now, to present itself, to let itself be known. How indeed would we know of the very existence of an affect if it could not let itself be caught within the net of articulation?

However unavoidable and therapeutic it might be, the forced transcription of muteness into an address is still, from a philosophical perspective, a "wrong." Therapy would "wrong" the affect by making it speak, that is, by inscribing the affect in an order incommensurate to it. And this, of course, is a violence of sorts, a kind of abuse. (I would add that the violence of the analyst might only repeat the self-violence that the very decision to undertake analysis requires on the part of the patient. By the time the patient enters the room, isn't the patient already addressing the mute and crippling affects that led the patient there in the first place?) I want to make it clear that it is not here a question of proposing that this violence should or even could be avoided. If this violence is necessary, as I strongly suspect it is, does not analytic respect nevertheless require that it be acknowledged as it is performed? More importantly, isn't such an acknowledgment necessary for the therapeutic work to take place? My suspicion here is that in some cases, trauma cases for instance, such recognition is a nonnegotiable precondition to analysis.

Finally, isn't it possible to consider that the mute and inarticulate affect still resists articulation even as it is made to articulate and to address itself? In other words, in the midst of the analytical treatment, some "thing" remains, irreducible to the treatment by phrases. Is analysis about "letting go" of affects, liquidating them? Or, as it therapeutically liquidates affects by allowing them to be represented, must it not also acknowledge that the affect still remains, and that this remainder is not necessarily the obstacle of a resistance but a creative resource?

Acknowledging an intractable remainder might indeed be the minimum form of respect that the patient demands of the analyst. Traumatized patients "know," I suspect, that there is no hope of liquidating this intractable remainder. The affect will remain. To acknowledge this intractable remainder is not merely to recognize the limitations of analysis and the fact that it is condemned to stop in front of an untreatable reserve. It might also mean discovering unexpected resources in this very resistance.

"One owes the affect," claims Lyotard in one of his most enigmatic expressions.[12] And this debt can never be acquitted once and for all, he adds; it can only be recognized. One owes to the affect, first, the crippling pain that it inflicts and through which it makes its presence known. The task of analysis may not be to liquidate the debt of pain owed to the affect, but to acknowledge it while at the same time modifying it and thereby alleviating it somewhat. One still owes the affect some pain, but now it is the pain of laboring to find the words that will testify to it and let it be known. And known in its muteness. To testify to the muteness of the affect, claims Lyotard, is the task of literature, which labors to say a "secret affection" that a writer worthy of the name knows to be unsayable, irreducible to articulation.[13] This is also the task of analysis if it fixes for itself the endless task of saying, of approximating with words, the radically mute intensity of the affect. Words will, of course, fail; they will not reach the "mute affection," say it, deal with it, and be done with it once and for all. Words will also necessarily betray the muteness of the affect by articulating that which intractably resists articulation. But in this very failure a success may be found: the opening of new signifying organizations, of new possibilities. Instead of owing the affect the crippling pain that interrupts logos and threatens it with annihilation, what is now owed to the affect is the proliferation of new and as yet unheard of possible linkages that comes through the constraint of free association, or through the constraints of literary style. It is still a suffering of sorts. But it is now the pain of labor. Lots of words to say "nothing," the nothing that is the affect. For Lyotard, the unconscious affect is indeed another name for the nothing that haunts philosophical thinking and terrifies it, stretches it to its limits. The affect is indeed "no-thing" insofar as it negates—that is, annihilates—all the poles of the articulated phrase. The affect says "nothing": no meaning, no referent, no addressor, no addressee. One owes words, and lots of them, to the mute nothing of the affect. One says a lot to try to say "nothing." And one will never manage to say nothing. The testimony is doomed to fail. Writers like Beckett or Blanchot know this debt that cannot be acquitted once and for all, but which can only be endlessly acknowledged, and acknowledged in writing.

This debt to the affect—it is not just the analysand and the writer who must pay it, each in their own way. The analyst, too, must pay it, and especially when writing. In his reading of the case of the Rat Man, Lyotard pays attention to the moment when Freud confesses that he is astonished by the "singular beauties of the case."[14] Freud refers to Ernst's extraordinary resources of articulation, narration, and argumentation, to the density of his associative network. He even confesses to Jung that the density of the analytical material provided by the case threatens to "exceed" his artistic abilities in matters of presentation ("meine Darstellungskunst"), that his restitution fails to do justice to the "work of art" that the psyche has produced.[15] His work lacks "truth" because it is "incomplete."

Freud, according to Lyotard, speaks here as a literary writer who feels that he owes words to the "singular beauties of the case," words that would do justice to it, restitute it adequately and completely. He feels the laboring pain of the writer who seeks to find the "right" words. He also feels the despair of the writer: his language is inadequate to the task. Something has been missed. The restitution lacks. It is not true. Where Freud is mistaken, however, is in the identification of what is lacking. His writing does not lack, as he believes, the ability to restitute the richness of the lexical lode, or the ingenuity of the unconscious syntax. His writing has failed to testify to the "inflexible *phone*" (*LdE*, 146). Lyotard pointedly notes that only a few pages are devoted to the transferential storm that Ernst unleashed on a Freud who recognizes, in the notes of the sessions, having been quite affected by it. Analytical writing has a debt of affect: it is "en dette d'affect"

(*LdE*, 146). It owes a debt of words to the affect that it unleashed, to the *phone* that it made resonate and to which the analyst, in one precarious moment of affective communicability, resonated.

How can analytic writing begin to testify to this inflexible *phonè*? Testimony requires, claims Lyotard in the context of the work of art, that the affect be transmitted:

> We can only take up the challenge of speaking art under the regime or, if you prefer, in the tone of what I would call, by a sort of vague analogy with psychoanalytic practice, a *compte rendu d'affect*, a report or account of the affect provoked by the work. Now, one can only report on or account for an affect by transmitting it, and not by objectifying it, as Valéry has suggested.[16]

One does not report the affect simply by describing or explaining it, all gestures that would posit the affect as that which is talked about and hence missed. One may try to testify to the affect through a confused voice which blurs the so-called personal distinctions as when, for instance, Freud feels impelled to coin the expression "strangulated affect,"[17] an expression where the hysterical choking resounds and metaphorically infiltrates the theoretical apparatus designed to account for it. Or again, when he persists in using the present tense in the series of sentences that he chooses to articulate and summarize the various chronological permutations of the analysand's symptomatology, as he does, for instance, in *A Child Is Being Beaten*. More important, it seems, to report the affect entails transmitting it, that is, giving the affect the occasion to happen, to act yet again. And this, Lyotard reminds the philosophers as well as the analysts, may require taking the chance of a tone.

Jean-François's Infancy

Christopher Fynsk

Writing so immediately after his passing ("immediately" because the time has still not taken form, the "passing" has still not occurred), I cannot avoid imagining Jean-François as a reader here. I feel the presence of that precise attention to language and argument that marked every exchange with him, and then that singular devotion to the *pragma* of the discussion. I sense, too, that fine mockery that issued from so lively an engagement with the object, and I wonder how we who write now might possibly acquit ourselves.

I can just hear the withering irony that would greet any too-pious evocation of his memory—an irony all the sharper as it would be propelled by his reaction to a narcissism that he was always the first to suspect. I can sense his anger at any falsity, be it simply an evocation of his name that situated it among a set of fashionable, ultimately marketable, references. And I can feel the deep melancholic despair that would grip him as soon as he heard that note signaling the academic mode: the presentation of his work as a *topic* (however suavely it might be presented and situated in relation to other discursive sites). "Does it come down to this," I hear him say, "an oeuvre, a position in the discursive field—all of it already consigned to oblivion as discourse?" I know that he would find a comedy in it all—he would turn it in the direction of what the French language offers with the term *humour*. But it is precisely at that point of anticipating his liberating gesture that my fantasy breaks and I remember he is not there to turn the old trick—that it is up to us to achieve the peculiar transcendence he would have found. So how do we acquit ourselves? How do we constitute and assume his legacy?

When I suggest that the task cannot be one of reviewing a body of work and a set of theoretical elaborations, I do not mean to suggest that we fail to honor him by studying his texts. After all, he took his philosophical and critical efforts very seriously. What figure, working in the field of "continental" philosophy (or "poststructuralist" or "postmodern" theory, as they are called), worked more assiduously at formal articulations? And he wanted his works to be read. Just a couple years ago, for example, he took great satisfaction in the fact that *Discours, figure* was receiving renewed attention. And if his arguments were not successful (as was the case with *Heidegger and "the jews"* for some of the readers he most valued), he wanted to know why, genuinely, and even a little anxiously. His restless movement between formal *dispositifs* was not the sign of a casual attitude toward the discourses through which he moved. There was nothing cynical or nihilistic, nothing even pragmatic about his "formalisms." He worked very hard to get it right. At the same time, however, he never imagined that his theoretical labors would supply the "right" answer, "le bon enchaînement," as he put it. He sought to hold his own and to win space in a field he constructed sometimes as polemic, but he never sought critical or philosophical hegemony in the sense of the best or the "correct" representation. He was devoted not to the concept, but to thought, to winning space for thought. And more. "Sauver l'honneur de penser," he wrote. Save the honor in thinking.

The legacy is to be assumed from there, I believe: from his tireless attempt to bring that imperative to the fore and to meet it. To be sure, his efforts were coupled to a devastating demonstration of the grounds for despair; he showed in volume after volume how thoroughly the task is menaced by the forces of the market and what he called "complexification." But he also offered examples of how one might go on, how one might endure—*as though* there were a future to be prepared and to await. The lesson was not a "teaching" in the sense of a doctrine. It was more like a performance. Moreover, the performance invited repetition; it said, "here, translate this." Of course, the invitation made the best of necessity (there is no metalanguage, he insisted; do it as you will and as you can—you have no choice but to translate). But it also obliged in its generosity. As though the *as though* called upon something, perhaps even claimed something. In Jean-François's playful "translate this," there was the *Anspruch* of which Walter Benjamin spoke when he said that the past has the power to claim the present, that the present will find a freeing force in answering that claim. Jean-François, I might note, turned more than once to Benjamin's *Berlin Childhood* for traces of that claim.[1]

"Translate this." That is just about exactly the phrase by which I received that part of Jean-François's legacy that was destined or prescribed for me, that part that defines my assignment here. Decorum urges me to add, "Not for me alone, of course." But I have to grant, like one who has been before the law when its gates are closing, that it was for me alone, that the legacy I am trying to think comes singularly, even if it exceeds any single inheritance in the very generosity of its shareable address. So perhaps I will be excused for beginning with an anecdote—though I suspect that in such a context no excuse is necessary. I am sure that for most of those who write for this occasion, Jean-François's legacy is indistinguishable from his presence: that playful, seductive, mocking, brilliant, sophistic, always engaging, always loving presence. And for that reason, I am sure I am not the only one who needs to narrate his passing. Because again, like many others, I cannot believe he is gone. I cannot believe the old sophist isn't carrying on somewhere, plying his trade to meet his expenses, and saving the honor of thinking.

Anyway, this is how Jean-François's legacy was transmitted to me; or this is part of the story, for it goes back well over twenty years. I remember, first, a passing conversation during his visit to Binghamton in 1989 that turned on the topic of infancy. I don't know what prompted it, but I know that it ended with the following words to me: "I sense this infancy is very strong in you." A scene from childhood, one might say; it marked me with an affect that was at once apprehension and infantile pride. But I hardly knew what to do with it. Nor did I grasp, even belatedly, what to do with it when Jean-François commissioned me to do a translation of his essay on Kafka, the essay entitled "Prescription." I simply did not grasp what it might mean that he had prescribed for me an essay on infancy, not even after a month's habitation with that text. I didn't even get it when "Prescription" was collected in *Lectures d'enfance*.[2] Or perhaps I got it at this time after all (at least this is what I think now); perhaps I knew that I had to find my way through this question of infancy before returning to his own work on it. For I avoided *Lectures d'enfance* rather carefully. In fact, my avoidance, which ended only in the summer of 1999, lasted a full year past the time when I had completed my own work on the *infans*—work that was even dedicated to Jean-François's memory.[3]

What was I supposed to get? An assignment, I believe. Jean-François had assigned me a question that he knew concerned me intimately. His gesture was not disinterested, as I knew perfectly well from the fact that he apologized numerous times afterwards for having stuck me with a job that he needed done quickly. The assignment came in the form of a request, but we both knew that it meant "translate this," and more than once (it was the middle of the semester, after all), I found myself saying something like, "Yeah, well translate this!" But I also sensed that if he was using me, he was doing so as a teacher. By obliging me to read him in this very particular fashion, he was instituting a new form of relation between us. And I would come to understand, belatedly, that if his "translate this" was binding in its pedagogical force, it also had a freeing intent. Ultimately it meant: "Translate this infancy from your own. Bring it to writing." The assignment would fully emerge only after its goal had been realized; I would recognize it in reading *Lectures d'enfance*. But I first had to go through the writing, which occurred some eight years after I translated "Prescription."[4]

Now, I can envision working with this in various ways, even playing with it; the child being the father of the child, and so forth. And I tell the story in part because I think it touches upon some important issues concerning the teaching relation and translation itself. But here is the pertinent thing for this occasion: the assignment made visible to me in Jean-François's text something that I don't know I could have seen otherwise, at least in quite the same way. I certainly would have recognized the theme of infancy as one of his preoccupations, but I do not think I would have seen the manner in which it formed an integral part of his legacy. For me, at least, this legacy had to be handed over and taken over (in the manner I have described) before it could be visible. I had to *do* before understanding.[5] And having now accepted the assignment, I think I can begin to approach the topic of Jean-François's infancy as more than a topic, indeed as part of what made his text obliging for those of us who need to write after him and in his memory, and for those who will be claimed by his text in years to come—like those children to whom he addressed *Le postmoderne expliqué aux enfants*.[6]

I would like to begin by sketching how I link the topic of infancy to what I am calling Jean-François's legacy; because, after all, the assertion is somewhat counterintuitive. Infancy cannot normally be counted in that sum of acts and works, or even that familial burden we call a legacy. And from the perspective of the legacy's inheritance (there being no legacy apart from its inheritance), we have to recognize that a legacy is something one takes on precisely in leaving infancy. To be sure, we receive our legacies *from* a kind of infancy, starting with the very first. They come with the name and in the touches and voices that convey a history of desire. But a legacy cannot be said to be transmitted until it is spoken. A legacy is of the symbolic, and by definition, the *infans* is not, not yet. So how could infancy be part of a legacy?

Answering schematically, I would try to put it as follows: Jean-François understood himself to be writing *from* an infancy and *to* an infancy. When he pointed to the task of saving the honor of thinking, he implicitly enjoined a repetition, a translation of that address. Now, there are two senses of the term "infancy" in the phrase I just employed ("writing from an infancy to an infancy"), and I will try to develop their meaning and the possibility of linking them as I move through a set of Jean-François's texts. But to provide a hint of where I am going, I would like to cite lines from the conclusion of the ninth section of *Le postmoderne expliqué aux enfants*, a section addressed to Jean-François's own son and dated June 21, 1985.

This ninth section is devoted principally to George Orwell's *1984*. It takes up the question of resistance, a resistance that Jean-François describes as *bodily* in this text, but which he also believes must be written. Having taken his distance from "the likes of Chomsky, Negri, Sartre, Foucault" (a group of intellectuals who, in Jean-François's view, perpetuate a notion of struggle derived from the Enlightenment), and having juxtaposed to them Adorno's chagrin vis-à-vis the fate of the Enlightenment promise and his turn to art, Jean-François returns to Orwell, whom he places on the side of Adorno. He continues:

> I am not saying that the line of resistance traced by Orwell's work is without problems. On the contrary. The appeal to modern ideals was an appeal to the universality of reason [. . . and] reason is in principle universally shared. But we have seen that this is not strictly true of the body, and certainly not of the unconscious body (if I can call it that), which imprisons each one of us in an untransmittable secret.
>
> This is why I feel we must extend the line of the body in the line of writing. The labor of writing is allied to the work of love, but it inscribes the trace of the initiatory event in language and thus offers it to a sharing, if not as a sharing of knowledge, at least as a sharing of a sensibility that it can and must hold as common. (*PE*, 96–97; translation modified)

Jean-François does not take this appeal to the task of writing to be without its own problems. But he continues with these words to the young David:

The problems created by the resistance I am describing will continue to surface. It is for us to elaborate them, as it will be for you. What I want to say to you is simply this: following this line does not mean shutting ourselves away in ivory towers or turning our backs on the new forms of expression bestowed on us by contemporary science and technology. It means that we use these forms in an attempt to bear witness to what really matters: the infancy of an encounter, the welcome extended to the marvel that (something) is happening, the respect for the event. Do not forget that you were and are this yourself: the welcomed marvel, the respected event, the mingled infancy of your parents. (*PE*, 97; translation modified)

Again, what I want to remark in this extraordinary address to Jean-François's son (an address intended for every reader, even if it has an absolutely singular import as a kind of gift and a kind of obligation, a kind of legacy) is the passage from what we might call an infancy of the body to a mode of being that Jean-François thinks as an infancy of encounter. My aim is to address the nature and possibility of that passage.

I shall start with a brief evocation of the notion of encounter that is furnished by the same chapter from which I have just cited. It appears by way of a reference to what Adorno termed the "micrologies" of Walter Benjamin's *One Way Street* and *Berlin Childhood*, brief scenes of a kind that can also be found in Jean-François's own essay "Scapeland." (I think, for example, of the childhood memory from Amsterdam, or the later memory of the banister from the building in East Berlin where he participated in his own resistance against a bureaucratic totalitarianism.)[7] Of such micrologies, Jean-François writes:

They do not describe events from infancy, they capture the infancy of the event, they inscribe what is uncapturable about it. And what makes an encounter with a word, odor, place, book, or face into an event is not its newness when compared to other "events." It is its very value as initiation. You learn this only later. It opened a wound in sensibility. You know this because it has since reopened and will reopen again, marking out the rhythm of a secret and perhaps unknown temporality. That wound led into an unknown world, though without ever making it known. Such initiation initiates to nothing, it just begins. (*PE*, 90–91; translation modified)

I cite this passage for the wonderful way in which it emphasizes the sheer contingency of the event and for the way it honors the empirical, even as it underscores that the *fact* of the event for the psyche derives from the way it represents an effraction for the sensibility that undergoes it. The empirical encounter, he tells us, has a radically initiatory character. In this sense, infancy is *of* the event, not its condition (in the sense of a subsisting state). As he puts it in "Time Today": "what testifies is not at all the entity, whatever it be, that claims to be in charge of the passibility to the event, but the event 'itself.' What memorizes or retains is not a capacity of the mind, not even accessibility to what occurs, but, in the event, the ungraspable and undeniable 'presence' of a something that is other than mind and which, 'from time to time,' occurs . . ." (*I*, 75).

The radical character of these formulations answers to Jean-François's effort to refrain from substantializing the passibility to the event that he attempts to think. Infancy is not the infancy *of* a subject. Nevertheless, from time to time it is there, given in the event through an exposure of sensibility to something that exceeds its organization. But what is this sensibility if it is exposed to such an effraction? What constitutes its passibility to the event, or its capacity for what we might call an *experience*? Jean-François's answer on this point is, I think, purposefully sketchy. He appeals to a classic formulation of the unconscious, all the while acknowledging its limits. Thus while he hesitates to substantialize the unconscious (and all the more so, I think, as he embraces the lesson from Wittgenstein in his later work), and while he refuses the appeal to an imaginary of the Lacanian sort, he nevertheless evokes an infancy of the body that he calls, in his address to the young David, "psychoanalytic," or "unconscious." Borrowing a distinction from Merleau-Ponty via Lefort, he explains that there is a "phenomenological" body that links the sentient being to a world that it makes and that makes it, but also another that withdraws from the world, "into the night of what it has lost in order to be born into that world" (*PE*, 92; translation modified). A body that is *of* the world, then, and another that is hostage to the thing, *la chose*. The two must be thought together, for they form a unique sensibility: "the point of view, the point of listening, of touch, of scent" (*PE*, 92). But this absolutely singular, untranslatable manner of deciphering what arrives, this singularity of resonance, or this "idiom," as Jean-François refers to it, is divided within itself. The insistence of something "at once more familiar and more strange" (*PE*, 93) disrupts, alters, or even suspends the singular idiom of sensibility; its murmur constitutes what Jean-François terms in another essay, "a suffering in perceiving and conceiving [that] sets up fields of perception and thought as functions of waiting, of equivocations" (*I*, 21). This other voice, to which Jean-François refers in his essay on Freud in *Lectures d'enfance*,[8] this "plaint," both shapes sensibility and in-determines it, exposing sensibility to the initiating event.

But what, in turn, is the unconscious body that it offers exposure to the event? In what sense is it always already passable to alterity? In "Prescription," Jean-François attempts to develop the notion of a bodily aesthesis, a preinscription of relation (relation, once again, to the thing) that is prior to any schema, be it in the forms of sensibility or of thought, or, in general, of the law. He calls it the body of infancy:

To be, aesthetically (in the sense of Kant's First *Critique*), is to be-there, here and now, exposed in space-time and to the space-time, of something that touches before any concept or even any representation. This *before* is not known, obviously, because it is there before we are. It is something like birth and infancy (*in-fans*), there before we are. The *there* in question is called body. It is not "I" who am born, who is given birth to. "I" will be born afterwards, with language, precisely upon leaving infancy. My affairs will have been handled and decided before I can answer for them—and once and for all: this infancy, this body, this unconscious remaining there my entire life. When the law comes to me, with the ego and language, it is too late. Things will have already taken a turn. And the turn of the law will not manage to efface the first turn, this first *touch*. Aesthetics has to do with this first touch: the one that touched me when I was not there. . . . Its obligation, its constitutive prescription is to acquit itself of this insensible touch through the means of the sensible.

The touch is necessarily a fault with regard to the law. It has its place and moment in a savage or alien space and time that are foreign to the law. And to the extent that it maintains itself, persists in the mode of this immemorial space-time, this savagery or this sinful peregrination is always there as a potentiality of the body. (*TP*, 179)

Now, if the exposing touch is indeed an opening of relation, and if that relation is to be a condition of passibility to the event, not as a determining condition, but as a haunting thing which opens in the event "from time to time," then the exposing touch must have an "ontological" reach, so to speak—it must open a relation to difference. Thus, while Jean-François follows the classical schema by thinking from the ground of the discovery of sexual difference, he always understands sexual difference as indissociable from ontological difference. Here is how he puts it in his essay on Joyce from *Lectures d'enfance*:

Ulysses poses another question altogether: Is not sexual difference the same as ontological difference? Is it not from the former that the temporalizing separation of consciousness from itself is engendered? And from it that the unconscious as extramemorial past is formed?—a past that is not retained as past and that one cannot have back, that is, an inappropriable past. Is it not this immemorial that calls? And is it not writing that attempts, desperately, to formulate an answer to this remainder to which the soul is hostage? (*TP*, 205; translation modified)

The infant body, or the body of infancy, would thus be something like a persisting site of exposure, a material residue, of sorts, in the sense that it is a site of inscription, or rather preinscription, that is lost to any self-relation (including the retention of memory). At the same time, the infant body is an in-temporally persisting opening, both an exposure and the suffering of an exposure, for which such words as *désolation, défaillance, désappropriation*, and *misère* come repeatedly to Jean-François's text as always vain supplements. A bodily suffering of difference, once again—sexual difference, first of all, but as it echoes with the enigma of a nothing that is somehow there.[9] "What is the event [of sexual difference], stripped of its scientific or cognitive denomination?" Jean-François asks in his essay on Hannah Arendt:

It is the enigma of there being a relation with what has no relation: that is, in knowing that it is born and dies, the soul (aptly named) bears witness to the fact that there is not only *what* is (*what* it is), but the other of what is. Of course, this relation does not take place when it takes place, it has taken place and it *will* take place. Thus, it *will have taken place* all at once, appeared too late, disappeared too soon. And this is because my birth is always only recounted by others, and my death told to me in the stories of the death of others, my stories and others' stories. So that, inasmuch as it is essential to this relation with the nothing (whence I come and where I am going) that it be related to me, the relation with *others* is also essential to the presence of absence, for it is from there that this presence (of absence) comes *back* to me. Essential, too, is the *fabula* to which the pulsation of beginning and end lends rhythm. (*TP*, 148; translation modified)

I want to return shortly to this reference to a *fabula*, but to do so it is necessary to remark the allusion to something Jean-François terms a "soul" in the last two passages from which I have cited. The passages suggest that it is the "soul" that knows the suffering of the body. But what mediation is added here (if the term "mediation" can be used at all)? "Soul" appears to allow for the possibility of relation to what Jean-François wants to think of as an irremediable heteronomy of bodily exposure, a heteronomy that he terms in "Prescription" "premoral" or "amoral" because it escapes the hold of any reflexive reason (reason being in no way beholden to it at the level either of intelligibility or of responsibility). Clearly, some assumption of that heteronomy is required if it is to be possible to think something like an obligation for art or thought, or the possibility of "extend[ing] the line of the body in writing." Why should thought heed its call? How could it? In short, were there not something like this relation Jean-François calls the "soul," there could be no "respect" for infancy. But what is the relation between body and soul?[10]

Needless to say, these questions are not new nor are they easy. Moreover, I am not convinced that we will always find consistent answers throughout Jean-François's many meditations on infancy—though we do consistently find, I believe, an awareness of why consistent answers cannot be furnished. Once again, the schematic character of his appeal to the motif of sexual difference suggests that he does not hope to provide an "account" of the "origin." And when he does follow Freud's speculative theorizing, he makes it quite clear that theory is at its limits. I think, for example, of the uncompromising analysis provided in *Discours, figure* of the brief text by Freud entitled "A Child Is Being Beaten."[11] There, in a critical analysis which predates the appearance of the theme of infancy in Jean-François's work, but which is manifestly addressed to a certain childhood, the evidence of a "heteronomous" relation leads Jean-François to posit what he terms an "incompossibility" of subjective positions, a veritable dispersal of subjectivity in a phantasmatic utterance (a call, a "plaint") that is never articulated by the suffering patients and must be constructed by Freud to come to language. The dispersed "subject" of the phantasm, as Jean-François describes it, is never present to itself in any form of self-reflection or self-perception, and thus never constitutes a unity. For although Jean-François thinks it is possible to define a *position de signifiance* in the figural matrix that generates the phantasm, he also insists that the formal unity of the figural matrix (which is required by any description) is fundamentally disrupted. The rhythm of the phantasm of beating is marked by an arryhthmia, and thus Freud's conclusions, like his own, can be no more than suppositions. The suffering body does not lend itself to conceptual grasp, even if it is not without relation to thought.

Once again, the relation is not properly encompassed by "thought"; indeed, it is a kind of disaster for thought. It is an ongoing provocation. In "Can Thought Go On without a Body?" Jean-François terms it "an irreparable transcendence," and continues as follows:

> Not only calculation, but even analogy cannot do away with the remainder left by this difference. This difference makes thought go on endlessly and won't allow itself to be thought. Thought is inseparable from the phenomenological body: al-

though the gendered body is separated from thought, and launches thought. I'm tempted to see in this difference a primordial explosion, a challenge to thought that's comparable to the solar catastrophe. (*I*, 23; translation modified)

My point is to suggest that Jean-François never writes of infancy without awareness of that "catastrophe" or "disaster" that it represents for thought and for his own writing. It is from that awareness, I think, that he offers, in the essay "*Logos* and *Techne*, or Telegraphy" a concluding meditation on Dôgen's metaphor of a shattering mirror to define the primal event that is the "non-ground" of the mind's infancy (*I*, 55–56). Exposure to difference, Jean-François suggests, is like the timeless shattering that has occurred when a mirror is confronted with that image of the *nothing there* that Dôgen describes as a "clear mirror." "Anamnesis," Jean-François concludes, "would be [the] notification . . . to stand up towards the clear mirror, through the breaking" (*I*, 56; translation modified). I believe that the appeal to Dôgen, here, is not simply an instance of exoticism, however effective it might also be on that score. It is rather an implicit acknowledgment that what he seeks to think does not surrender to the concept or to any theoretical exposition—that if there is a passage from infancy to thought, it is not established by the concept. Figuration, of some kind, is an irreducible exigency for thought in its relation to the infant body. Indeed, the very name of "infancy," and perhaps especially that name, must bear an essentially figural status in Jean-François's text (as is perhaps already clear from my citations). Infancy, as we learn in the passage from the essay on Arendt from which I cited a few moments ago, has an irreducibly "fabulous" dimension. But this is not to say simply that infancy can only be a metaphor for something that exceeds the limits of representation, nor even that it can only be given in a narrative, a *récit*. It is to say also that infancy names the insistence, even the exigency of the fictive or the figural in conscious life (that exigency that gives the insistence of the primal scene). And it is only by a kind of engagement of that figural that the passage we are trying to think (from body to thought via "soul") can be made. Or so Jean-François supposes, and that supposition is itself offered as a willing participation in the exigency of the figural. When Jean-François writes of infancy, I want to suggest, theory is passing into a mode of supposition that is not fiction, but also not separable from it. The reference to something like a "soul" that knows, perhaps constitutes the interrupted *fabula* of its infancy, partakes of that supposition.

Jean-François describes this supposition in that same essay on Arendt, and I want to concentrate briefly on his argument there in order to begin the passage to what I called earlier the infancy of encounter. The context of his discussion of infancy is Arendt's own meditation on birth and the faith and hope that is brought to the human condition by the possibility of a creative action that represents in the natural, and always ruinous, succession of human affairs a kind of natality. "Birth," as Jean-François summarizes what speaks to him in this meditation, is "the event of a possible radical alteration in the course compelling things to repeat the same. Infancy is the name of this faculty, in that it brings to the world of being the astonishment of what, for a moment, is nothing yet—of what *is already* without yet being *something*" (*TP*, 151; translation modified).

A faculty of astonishment, he calls it this time. To understand this use of the term, we need to turn back to an earlier section of the essay where he develops what he calls "the impugnment of melancholia or the refutation of nihilism" (*TP*, 147), in other words, the possibility of survival vis-à-vis the kind of vision of history that prompted Walter Benjamin to offer his image of the backward-driven angel. Melancholia, he says, sees nothing but loss and an always withdrawing being that strips even birth of promise; but melancholia forgets, he says, the relation of the soul with being or non-being, the enigma of apparition. "Rather than nothing, being gives entities, instants, objects. Since being offers itself in 'objects,' it gets forgotten. Yet it *gives* objects, something *happens*" (*TP*, 147). Even in the extreme of a nihilistic apprehension—and perhaps, he adds, we must go to that extreme with the last man, the one who suffers and administers the banality of evil—even in that extreme, there dawns the possibility of a joy (a word Jean-François takes from Pascal), "the dark joy of a request made stronger for its being more improbable, and thus more threatened by annihilation and more openly confronted by the truth of nothingness" (*TP*, 148). A request, he says, and then falls back to what he terms a "scruple," the scruple of an "as though":

> the mind, thrust into the ordeal of nihilism, onto the road to despair and skepticism (which is permanent), knowing that there is nothing to do or say, no valid entity, no entity even which *is*, acts *even still* as though there were.
>
> In no way is the effect of this clause cynicism. Cynicism remains derivative of nihilism and perseveres, through its activism, in the melancholia of "nothing is worth it." Nor is the effect a *ludic* form, where a corpse dons the colors of life

in a grimacing and macabre irresponsibility. Nor is it an "artist's" metaphysics of will and values.

The effect is infancy, which knows something about the *as though*, which knows about the pain of impotence and the complaint of being too small, of being there late (compared to others), and (as to its strength) of having arrived early, prematurely—which knows about broken promises, bitter disappointments, failings, and abandonment, but which also knows about dreaming, memory, question, invention, obstinacy, listening to the heart, love, and real openness to stories. Infancy is the state of the soul inhabited by something to which no answer is ever given. It is led in its undertakings by an arrogant fidelity to this unknown guest to which it feels itself hostage. Antigone's infancy. I understand infancy here as obedience to a debt, which we can call a debt of life, of time, or of event; a debt of being there despite everything, and in relation to which only the persistent feeling of respect can save the adult from being no more than a survivor, a creature living on reprieve from annihilation. (*TP*, 148–49; translation modified)[12]

Infancy is the *effect* of this modality of being guided by the "as though." But it is also, as the preceding page makes clear (and I have already cited a good part of it) its non-ground. I can find no less clumsy expression, but I want to underscore that it is *from* infancy, from the relation with what has no relation, that the "as though" proceeds. The "as though," once again, does not take its freedom from the abstractions of a negative stance such as irony or cynicism (always a refuge of the self), nor does it proceed from the kind of giddy speculation that Benjamin described in his book on the German *Trauerspiel*, nor, finally, is it satisfied with the comforts of a form of aestheticism (and Jean-François is identifying a strong temptation in contemporary thinking to wed contemporary pragmatism and Foucault's late reflections on what he called the "care of the self"); it proceeds from the mind's infancy—the soul's fabulating relation to origin and end, and its "arrogant fidelity" to the unknown guest to which it feels itself hostage.

This last phrase, this "arrogant fidelity," requires, I suspect, a bit more development than Jean-François ever gives it, at least to my knowledge. Because he is identifying an inclination of the soul (as he terms it) that I take to be the original condition of any "faculty of enthusiasm" or any opening to the event. I speak of a kind of "lending" or even giving to the exposure that happens in the soul's opening to the nothing. If there is an infancy of encounter that is something other than a forced or self-deluding wishfulness, it is because the soul has opened to encounter, has said "yes" in some way to what has come upon it. Blanchot, whose meditation on infancy echoes constantly in *Lectures d'enfance*, speaks of survival not as arrogant fidelity, but as a kind of acquiescence to the refusal of what comes in the initiating event, the advent of nothing (which refuses itself because the mind cannot hold it).[13] Heidegger is thinking of such a relation when he evokes his own figure of a child in the context of his meditation on *Gelassenheit*, and Levinas is speaking of such an acquiescence, I believe, in his meditation on the "yes" in *Four Talmudic Readings*, to which Jean-François points in his chapter on "Obligation" in *The Differand*.[14] If infancy is to be something like a "faculty of enthusiasm," it is because it proceeds from a kind of yes. The child gives itself to the other, and indeed this giving takes a fabulous form, but in the fable there is a yes, a yes that echoes even among all the infantile "noes."

So a "yes" must be accented in Jean-François's account, I believe. But the fundamental point he is making in the essay on which I have been commenting holds no less. If it is possible to envision surviving the grounds for despair provided by this century (in sum, a spreading banality of evil in the face of multiple forms of devastation), it is because there survives in the mind an affirmative relation to non-being, and thus the capacity for opening to the event, for projecting upon an "*Is it happening*?" This is not a childlike optimism; the joy that is known in infancy cohabits with terror, if only the terror of the *jouissance* it has known. The "yes" is radically dispossessed; it opens, and it opens in, Jean-François says, a "desert" of desolation. Again, I would remind you of all the metaphors of destitution, of peregrination, *misère, défaillance*, etc. Nevertheless, this desert constitutes the ground, the non-ground for supposing that the event could come, for proceeding *as though* encounter could happen.

"As though." I'm going to hasten to a conclusion by suggesting that this "as though" is what invites to acts of filiation (or affiliation) in relation to his text, and thus to something like a legacy. I believe it is possible to say that it is present in every act by which Jean-François promises himself to the event—in every act of writing. Readers will remember the striking words near the end of the "Reading Dossier" that opens *The Differend*. "In writing this work, the A. had the feeling that his only addressee was the '*Is it happening*?'" (*D*, xvi). He was writing *for* thought, conceived here as an expectant, even anxious opening or receptivity to the new. He was projecting upon its possibility and passibility, committing or promising himself to it—as though it could come. Now, I shall not review the traits of infancy that already mark Jean-François's descriptions of the event in *The Differend* (I think, for example, of his remarks concerning the "weakness" of the phrase). But the words I have already quoted from "The Survivor" should suffice to allow me to say that he was committing himself to the infancy of encounter there. To no particular reader, therefore, but to every reader who would be affected by this modality of projecting upon the possibility of thought, this impossibly confident manner, almost messianic in presumption, of proceeding as though it could happen.

But why should any reader find an invitation in that address, a provocation, even? I will answer briefly, rehearsing what is perhaps already quite clear. The invitation lies, I think, in the *as though*. But we must understand this leap of thought in all its complexity, that is, with all the complexity of the passage to which I have tried to point, the passage from the infancy of the soul to the infancy of the event. I will reduce this complexity by speaking of a double movement, but let me try, nevertheless, to offer the following sketch. I would suggest that Jean-François's identification of his addressee as a kind of coming thought, a coming reception of encounter, leaves the reader in a kind of abandonment, even as it invites this reader into the promise or the commitment that is made. Following the invitation could always prove, in fact, to be no more than a "spectating," though even this aesthetic relation would engage the fictive or fabulous dimension of the "as though" and thereby engage to repetition. But this invitation would be gentle, in no way constraining or provoking (however stimulating it might be), were it not for the fact that it is doubled by a dimension of obligation, an obligation that stems from the fact that the projection upon an infancy of encounter proceeds from an infancy that it re-marks, or even summons, as it promises itself to the encounter. The commitment, the address to the infancy of encounter repeats the "yes" of infancy that is its non-ground; it brings it to speak. Even *The Differend*, I think we can say, reverberates with Jean-François's infancy, and this is all the more true of those more writerly texts that thematize this infancy. There is a saying of infancy that occurs throughout his writing. Jean-François points to it explicitly in the preface to *Lectures d'enfance* when he writes of the thing that haunts the text in its separation from it. "Let us baptize it *infantia*," he says:

> What does not speak. An infancy that is not an age of life and does not pass. It haunts discourse. The latter does not cease to put it aside, it is its separation. But it stubbornly persists thereby in constituting it, as lost. Unknowingly, therefore, it shelters it. It is its remainder. . . .

> Blanchot wrote: "*Noli me legere*," you will not read me. What does not lend itself to writing in the written calls perhaps upon a reader who no longer knows, or does not yet know, how to read. (*LdE*, 9)

That call, we may presume, has all the traits of infancy; it says abandonment, weakness, misery. But it also says "yes" to the exposure in which it has opened and to which it has willingly exposed itself in this yes. It says exposure. That exposure, Jean-François assumes, has an ex-posing force. It is for this reason that it obliges, or that it can be shared. As Jean-François said in his address to David: "The labor of writing is linked to the work of love, but it inscribes the trace of the initiating event in language, and it offers it in this way to a sharing, if not the sharing of knowledge, at least as a sharing of a sensibility that it can and must hold as common" (*PE*, 96–97, translation modified).

Writing, as Jean-François understands it, presupposes, *must* presuppose the communicability of its exposure. Its commitment to infancy presupposes the reader's infancy. I am tempted to give "pre-suppose" an active sense, and say that writing supposes and pre-supposes, or supposes and de-poses, since the communication of infancy opens a kind of dispossession. And it is in this double movement that it prompts to repetition; it dis-poses, let us say, to repetition of the as though, of the commitment to thought. Again, Jean-François's promise, or his manner of promising himself, always proceeds from the relation to what has no relation. Its "suppose" is always redoubled with the dis-posing saying of infancy.

For this reason, his saying works very much in the manner of that address that opens Blanchot's own "primal scene" in *The Writing of the Disaster*: "You who live later, close to a heart that beats no more, suppose, suppose this."[15] This is an invitation not simply to entertain the narrative that follows (the narrative of the birth and death of the *infans*), but to perform that narrative, to write it from the ground of the infancy that comes to that writing. "Suppose this," Jean-François says; "partagez le récit." There is an obligation in that address, once again, but it must be assumed, or rather reassumed, in an act of writing. An act that constitutes, from its own destitution and exposure, what Jean-François calls at one point in his essay on Arendt "true" or "real" filiation.[16] His legacy of infancy will happen, I want to say, if we write it; it will have been up to us, his abandoned, arrogantly faithful children.

On the Unrelenting Creepiness of Childhood

LYOTARD, KID-TESTED

Avital Ronell

From Socrates' predatory urges to Locke's invention of the "Ideot" or Hegel's racist assignments—for the moment I shall take this no further—philosophy has demonstrated a need to impound those who could not speak for themselves, who had not reached a certain legislated majority. Under the reign of Locke, Hume, and Condillac, empirical philosophy assembled the figure of the idiot in order to put some reality behind established hypothetical assumptions.[1] The idiot pinned down the first folds of language in the essays on human understanding. Made to stand for an epoch, lost to civilization, of originary memory, the idiot spanned the chasm between nature and culture. His entry on philosophical pages helped, moreover, to rehabilitate the "empirical" basis of empiricism. Much can be said about the induction of wild children, savages, idiots, and infants into the realm of philosophical speculation, and it would be important to investigate more fully the peculiar yet crucial status of these minorities as philosophy conducts its adult raids. No doubt Nietzsche may be seen to have turned this state of affairs on its head when he invited the animals to participate in a new tropology.

Now comes Jean-François Lyotard, who talks to children. No matter how polymorphously perverse, punctually pampered, or pacified, these are the distressed among us, the fearful and hungry. They squeak and peek and try to get their meaning across. They panic, then smile and burble, then panic. Held in abusive custody by the laws of becoming, they hang on to your finger for dear life. From the get-go, the reality principle sneaks up on them to snap them out of the domain of the pleasure principle (of course this is a complicated relay, as Lacan has shown, for the reality principle is always in defeat; but still, it goes after you). As in Goethe's ballad, the Erlking is out to get them, poised to snatch the child from the arms of momentary reassurance. In the case presented by Lyotard we are faced with the figure of the minor, often oppressed, for whom language and representation may not be entirely foreclosed, though surrender, the predominance of muteness, and a repertoire of stammers often govern the thwarted scene of childhood. Still, there are reprieves and the event of memory; language, however jumbled, mimetic, deregulated, occurs and belongs to the existence to which childhood—something that eventually goes into remission but returns in waves throughout the lives of the wounded—is fitted. Interiority does not necessarily take hold at the early stages. Yet even when these children are silenced or a hand is laid on them, they are traversed by what Lyotard understands as sheer feeling—maybe a pinch of joy, a sting of melancholic regret, a straitening that cuts both ways, a body memory that trembles. With no language of interiority to vouch for feeling, the children are more or less stranded, bared to colonializing projection.

Vaulted and shut, their subjectivity—if there is one—offers little in the way of an account; even so, in most cases they surpass or at least scramble the master codes of philosophical claims made on their behalf and elude the cognitive scanners that try to detect and classify them. The child constitutes a security risk for the house of philosophy. It crawls in, setting off a lot of noise. The figure of the child, which in the end inserts an imaginary lesion in philosophy—a condition that calls out for endless symbolic repair—may be borne by the anguish of the differend. That is to say, it enters, or is entered into, the places where speech falters and language chokes in the throat of a political body, where the question of fair representation is peremptorily dismissed or simply not addressed. But it is not as if the child had the means of representation at hand. The child is given over to extreme forms of defenselessness: dependency, Lyotard indicates, is too weak a word to describe the condition of such a minority being, the ever haunting condition of childhood.

How did they stumble into philosophical headquarters? Well, their prototype, the essential child—the idiot—appeared alongside or at the head of the train of blind, deaf, or mute subjects (whose implications for subjecthood, precisely, provoked crisis) and was most closely leagued with the prestige accorded to the construction of the wild child—the teachable idiot. They were pressed into service, assigned to uphold mythic assurances of the humanly clean slate, presenting such a possibility, in theory, at least, to the extent that they—idiots—donated their bodies to the cause of a science that staked everything on what appeared to constitute observable traits of human origins. Recruited to the cause of philosophy to make a philosophical point, the idiot belongs outside the philosophy whose integrity it promotes. The child, as I said, crawls in at unexpected moments or morphs, as in Kant's critical reflections, into the ambivalent purveyor of genius—the irresponsible, often puerile excess to which we owe the poetic word.

In *The Inhuman*, Lyotard, for his part, writes of the debt to childhood that is never paid off. A matter of the traces of an indetermination, childhood continues to hold us hostage. The obscure savageness of childhood reminds us that all education is inhuman "because it does not happen without constraint and terror."[2] At once savaging and civilizing (there is never one without the other), education straitens the little one, who is cornered by cultural demand. Childhood, in any case, will leave us with inhuman surges of deregulation, with a level of fear and distress that can come up at any point in the trajectory of so-called human development: "Shorn of speech, incapable of standing upright, hesitating over the objects of its interest, not able to calculate its advantages, not sensitive to common reason, the child is eminently the human because its distress heralds and promises things possible" (*I*, 3–4). Lagging behind itself, the child's "initial delay in humanity," moreover, "which makes it the hostage of the adult community, is also what manifests to this community the lack of humanity it is suffering from, and which calls on it to become more human" (*I*, 4). The irrevocable creepiness of childhood is the place from which an ethical call is placed—be it made by the day-care crowd or the operators Antigone, Christ, and Isaac, all loyalists to the child's camp, even though their identity as children must remain at once undecidable and settled. (For some reason—or unreason—some figures of ethical calling are tagged essentially as children, even if by other measures they are plainly in midlife crises when they are tried.) Lyotard asks: "What shall we call human in humans, the initial misery of their childhood, or their capacity to acquire a 'second' nature which, thanks to language, makes them fit to share in communal life, adult consciousness and reason?" (*I*, 3). Childhood enters a breach into the very concept of the human and makes us ask, once again, what it means to be human. Yet the decision to claim the human is split between the early episodes of initial desolation and the later cover-up schemes that language supports and the community payrolls.

More severe words are reserved for the provocation of childhood in another, later text. In "Mainmise" the child is lined up with the slave, with the one whose destiny is put in the hands of another.[3] Like the slave, the child does not belong to itself, having, Lyotard says, no claim to himself (there is no play of "/herself," so out of a sense of frustrated probity I will repeat the complete oppression of the girl-child): "He is in the hands of another. Dependency is too weak a word to describe this condition of being seized and held by the hand of the other" (*H*, 1). By childhood Lyotard means that we are born before being born to ourselves: "We are born from others but also to others, given over defenseless to them. Subject to their *mancipium*, and to an extent that even they do not recognize" (*H*, 2–3). The offense is such that even the offenders, by necessity repeat offenders, operate on the level of an unconscious siege. You may want to know when exactly the sneak attacks strike: childhood is an age that is not marked by age—or rather, it does not age but recurs episodically, even historically. Childhood can last a whole lifetime if you find yourself throttled and unable to root out some representation of what is affecting you; this can happen every day: "I am speaking of this condition of being *affected* and not having the means—language, representation—to name, identify, reproduce, and recognize what is affecting us" (*H*, 2). If I am not mistaken, Lyotard uses childhood to resist the modern Western ideal of emancipation; he manages to deflate the reverie that has you thinking you'll get out from under the grip of the *mancipium*.

The *mainmise*, which travels in many disguises (parental love "may have been a calamity—it may have engendered such a *mainmise* over the child's soul" [*H*, 3]), often remains unknown to the child as an adult. Something is taking her down, even as she meets the world with measurable instances of "success." Under the thumb of an invisible yet persistent *mainmise*, the adult child regresses to minority following an unpredictable rhythm of being that beats the drum of an impossible emancipation—the emancipation promised by humanism, whether Christian or secular, which teaches that "man is something that must be freed" (*H*, 3). As for the nature of this freeing, "there are many different possibilities, from Augustine up through Marx" (*H*, 3). These promises say in effect that the *mainmise* can be thrown off, even dealt with definitively, according to some calculable program or redemptive ground plan. If we could get over it—this would suppose that we had a reciprocal grasp of what is keeping us down.

The *mainmise*, a condition of extreme captivity, can be so powerfully effective that the adult, like the child, has no access to it by means of memory or cognition. To bring the terms of this condition to bear on us, if only by projective inversion, it is almost as in that episode of *The Twilight Zone* that ends with a shot of a miniature house where normalcy was played out under the gaze of a giantess, a playing child. The shadow thrown on you was in a sense too big to be perceived, much less fought off. One is left dumb and unknowing about the *mainmise* that nonetheless accompanies your every move and persists in calling the shots. The imprint is so profound that the child, well, "it will not even occur to him to rebel, nor will he have received the gift or grace to pray that his *mainmise* be lifted" (*H*, 3). Because of the untraceable fingerprints of the *mainmise*—I am surmising here, as Lyotard is unclear about how this works—the condition that he describes should not be subsumed merely by structures such as those underlying severe neuroses or psychoses ("I am not just talking about severe neuroses or psychoses" [*H*, 3]). There is no account or narrative that could contain or point reliably to the *mainmise*, no anamnesis, as he likes to say. At the same time, the surrender is so pervasive that it need not be pathologized in order to be heard. You do not have to be psychotic to understand that you're barely out on bail on good days and back in the hovel of wretched captivity on other days of your so-called autonomous being. The possibility of a given freedom—freedom as unquestionably given, and before all else a given, thrown in with the *da* of our Dasein—in other words, the kind of freedom that Jean-Luc Nancy, with his Kantian signet, posits, seems to be absent from the scene.[4]

The hold on the child translates into an irrevocable wounding on which childhood in fact depends. The timing may be slightly off, because in this instance Lyotard hints that pleasure may be felt prior to the wound, while elsewhere he indicated, I thought, that the wounding hold had first dibs on the child. To the extent that the rhythm of unconscious time bombing is included in the depiction of these experiences (which often bypass "experience"), it would be petty no doubt to insist on strict synchronicities. Lyotard offers this wo(u)nderful observation: "For the child, everything is a wound, the wound of a pleasure that is going to be forbidden and taken away" (*H*, 3). The *mainmise* is raised as a sign of what is about to happen, namely, of what has always happened: it is raised to slap the pleasure out of the child. In this round the *mainmise* is, we could say, the hand of time. Time beating pleasure, given over to the stranglehold of the reality principle: "The suffering that results and the search for the object, something analogous, in short, to emancipation, arise out of this wound" (*H*, 3). The emancipatory urge, prompted by the early experience of essential deprivation, starts with this figure of analogy, weak but soldering. (In Lacan's reading of Freud, the fundamental desire—the incestuous one—is prohibited in one of the starts of life: everything else flows from the initial withholding pattern, including the battering search for the object neither entirely lost nor altogether found.)[5] Alive with the memory trace of early forfeiture, the subject tries to free itself, at least enough to cover the losses. Thus originates the call, a call to emancipation or of exodus—a call, in any case, that initiates the movement of flight. The call positions the constrained child in relation to elsewhere. The children of Israel (why are they children?) are said to have taken the call as they headed for trouble or, rather, more trouble, and elsewhere.

Lyotard links the temporal wounding to the flight from Egypt. In the essay he observes, in reference to the exodus of the Hebrews, that they "escaped the Pharaoh's *mancipium* only by placing themselves under the *mancipium* of Yahweh" (*H*, 2). The fantasy of a promising elsewhere is broken. It is not as though there would be a locatable exteriority to the primal hold. Permit me to introduce an analogy, another hand to play in the negotiations with the *mainmise*, for it is still necessary to elucidate the difficulty of ever obtaining a truly valid exit visa when it comes to the anticipation of an exodus. As with the plight of addiction elaborated by Thomas de Quincey, one can move only from one addiction to the other, even if the second term is that of a cure; the oppression of dependency, the demand of adherence to the addiction or to that which opposes it, is structurally the same.[6] What joins the disparate events consisting in the *mainmise* of the child, the flight from Egypt, and the call from elsewhere (Lyotard persistently figures the flight from Egypt as a response to a call, a "vocation") is the unknowing in which they originate and continue effectively to hold sway. One is dumbstruck, somnambulizing, rising to a call that cannot be identified or in any meaningful way secured. Perhaps it comes from the past or resounds in a future dimly awaited. "It comes from beyond me and within me"—this is how Heidegger locates the call, the aphonic call of conscience in *Sein und Zeit*.[7] At any rate, one cannot account for the call that has a hold on me or, disrupting any conscious itinerary, that puts me on hold without my consent, surpassing my initiative or the knowledge I think I have about the way things go as I crawl through the playing fields of Being-in-the-world.

Attentive to that which, defying cognition and eluding memory, stultifies, Lyotard tries time and again to trace the call. There is something that grinds Being, knowledge, memory, even health, to a level of indifference, something that defies all conceptuality or generalizable principle. He stays close to the ground and keeps his receptors open. There is a grand coherency in the fact that when his narrated *Lebenslauf*, his *curriculum vitae*, established in *Peregrinations*, evokes the call on an almost ontological frequency ("there is something like a call"),[8] Lyotard claims a lifelong interest in the notion and doctrines of indifference. Something in Being menaces thought, undermines writing, with a quiet, sort of pernicious consistency. In the distant past, Lyotard offers, he was committed to the encounter with that to which we remain deaf and sluggish—to the "groundlessness of Being which constantly exerts a fascinating threat over thinking and writing" (*P*, 9). He writes his M.A. dissertation on "Indifference as an Ethical Notion." A paper investigating a kind of originary stupor that involved the Epicurean *ataraxia*, the Stoic *apatheia*, the extreme Stoic *adiaphora*, the Zen not-thinking, the Taoist nothingness, and so forth, it later on leads to considerations of other stultifying modalities of Being. I would not hesitate to go as far as grouping his concern with reflective judgment in this category or to mobilize for this thought-numbing area of the work his discussion of Freud's call to let the mind float: "'You have to impoverish your mind, clean it out as much as possible, so that you make it capable of anticipating the meaning, the 'What' of the 'It happens'" (*P*, 18). The poverty-leveling of mind does not oppose itself to thought but allows something to arrive, something that we associate with the possibility of meaning.

The advent of the event, moreover, is, as Lyotard contends, itself dependent upon the ability of mind to scale back its holdings, that is to say: "No event is at all accessible if the self does not renounce the glamour of its culture, its wealth, health, knowledge, and memory. . . . Let us make ourselves weak and sick the way Proust did, or let us fall truly in love" (*P*, 18). The only possible existential glitch here resides in the suggestion that one would be positioned to *make* oneself fall ill or in love; this, no doubt, is said with that smile of irony for which Jean-François Lyotard was known by his friends. Still, it must be admitted that, in the strict sense, renunciation implies a supplement of will—the *ability*, precisely, to disable, when mind exercises its ability to disable the self. That is the only hurdle I see here, and perhaps I am placing it too firmly in this deserted landscape where debility rules. There is a splitting that seems to be at issue, an almost Fichtean split of self according to which one of the selves, the transcendental self, watches the other, more empirical one crash into the wall of necessary failure. It is hardly probable that Lyotard, smile or no smile, would permit such an idealist formulation to prevail at this time. I will have to suppose that there is not a rescued self that survives the crash or that is shown determined to play the weak-and-sick card.

In order to attune one's being to the event, in order to prime for the advent of meaning, a thoroughgoing impoverishment, an extreme ascesis, needs to be welcomed and assumed. Yet, because it involves a supplement of will, this degree of ontological deflation still does not sink to the level of being that in "Mainmise" he later on associates with the *mancipium*. Acts of self-depletion are somehow engaged by the subject as it renews the encounter with the limit-experience of deficiency. The depleted condition,[9] which Lyotard eventually reads in terms of the stakes of knowledge, opens the channels in his work to art and politics—inscriptions that run on empty, forfeiting the support of cognition and its corresponding power players. Another way of putting this is that art and politics are not simply rule based or governed solely by preexisting contracts or criteria. In a Kantian turn, Lyotard thus argues that both art and politics are exempted from the hegemony of the genre of discourse called cognitive (*P*, 21). In Kant's terms, such an exemption means that we have no use for the sort of judgment he called determinant judgment. Among other things, this explains why we are essentially bereft—left clueless, off base, and in a cloud of obscurity.[10]

Reflective judgment implies the ability of the mind to synthesize data, be it sensuous or sociohistorical, without recourse to a predetermined rule. Lyotard writes: "Accordingly, thinking advances through clouds by touching them as enigmatic cases, the reason for which—their 'what they are'—is not given with them, with their 'that they are occurring'" (*P*, 20). Determinant judgment operates differently. "The problem at the heart of the latter is the following: a concept being defined, one must find the available cases to be subsumed under it and so doing begin to validate the concept. In other words, understanding possesses a rule of explanation and is trying to select references to which it can be applied. This is a formidable way for wandering through thoughts; it is the way called science" (*P*, 21). Determinant judgment gives way to the technoscientific universe, announcing the place of the Heideggerian *Gestell* as the modern way for thinking to be related to Being. It would appear that determinant judgment has won out by securing a type of cognitive base—a calculable grid—that compensates for the backsliding returns and depletions that were earlier at issue.

Lyotard shows that in spite of the triumph of determinant judgment in the contemporary world (in the values of programming, forecasting, efficiency, security, computing, and the like), "other games or genres of discourse are available in which formulating a rule or pretending to give an explanation is irrelevant, even forbidden" (*P*, 21). This is particularly the case with aesthetic judgment, with taste, which introduces a kind of cognitive humbling, an essential passivity: "No concept, no external finality, no empirical or ethical interest is involved in the reception by the imagination of sensations coming from so-called data. There are only the most humble syntheses. . . . The conceptual rule under which the data could be subsumed must remain inactive" (*P*, 22). Lyotard in fact ends the first lecture of *Peregrinations*, "Touches," by putting out a kind of ethical call—one might say, in keeping with the logic he unfolds, an ethical call without ethical interest or prescriptive pathos. He says, concluding the lecture, that to "respond to a case without criteria, which is reflective judgment, is itself a case in its turn, an event to which an answer, a mode of linking, will eventually have to be found. This condition may be negative, but it is the principle for all probity in politics as it is in art. I am also obliged to say: as it is in thinking" (*P*, 27). No predetermination, Lyotard maintains, exempts any thinking from the responsibility of responding to each case. Thinking is responsible to the singularity of each case, being answerable to the unsubstitutable demand placed upon it. It is delusory to give a meaning to an event or imagine a meaning for an event by anticipating what that event will be in reference to a prior text. "But it is indeed impossible to avoid this way of thinking completely, because it offers security against the calls or touches of the big X" (*P*, 27). Traveling through a space between the active and unconscious breaches of mind, the big X marks the spot where sheer receptivity can be located, on the other side of any claim of knowability.

The big X has to do with the "something" that may occur—in the case of Cézanne, under or on his eyes "if they make themselves receptive enough to it. This 'something' is a quality of chromatism, a color timbre. To achieve this is a matter of a 'passivity' without pathos, which is the opposite of either the controlled or unconscious activity of the mind" (*P*, 19). X addresses the uncanny "fact" that "there is" something here and now, regardless of what it is. "It is as if something hidden inside the Montagne Sainte Victoire, say Being, or that entity Kant calls 'the X in general,' was playing in a game against the painter by making 'moves' with chromatic material" (*P*, 19). One cannot psyche out the "X in general" or know what it's up to. On good days, one can simply acknowledge, follow, or, if your name is Cézanne, somehow paint its disposition. Placing us in the grips of a major double bind, it lords over us like the immovable power play of the *mainmise*. On the one hand, we strive to let go in order to avoid being hard of hearing when the big X puts out a call: in order to be attuned to the call, we are not supposed to know, grasp, or force subsumption on the uncanny fact that it occurs. It hits us as an appeal without precedent, a circumstance without cognitive netting. There is no other hand (which by no means lessens the grip of the double bind). Yet things go on as if there had always been another, perhaps a first hand—this turns us over to the shriveled authority of the *manchot* of which Lyotard writes, the missing hand ("By freeing himself from the tutelage of the other, the *manchot* takes back his hand, takes things back into his own hands. He thinks he is getting over his castration, that the wound is healing. This dream of being able to get over lack, over what is missing, is the very dream that gives rise to emancipation today" [*P*, 5]). This missing other hand is the hand played by the supplement of will that we detected earlier, that is, by the action of self-mutilation that permits one to exercise control over a stretch of destiny. Like the crab that loses its claw or the animal tearing off a limb or paw in panic, the *manchot* takes things in hand, albeit in the clutch of a missing hand. The rhetoricity of this moment is impossible, for the *manchot* is shown taking back a hand that no longer is. The inexistent trophy dominates the promissory note of political rhetoric. According to Lyotard, the violence that suppresses castration dominates and blinds the politics of emancipatory struggle today.

Although his thought edges toward the chasms of absolute impoverishment, inscribing the mind and taking the body down with him, Lyotard often pulls back from his insight, in the end entrusting his elaboration to a surplus of linguicity. He shares this tendency with Lacan. Lyotard, for example, has named a hole in Being but then recoups by saying there are other games, other discursive genres. Yet he has himself traced a movement where no game plan or map of discursiveness would hold. This indemnifying gesture signals a tension in his articulation, which we have noted in his prescription for making oneself weak or rendering the mind inactive—as if the passivity without pathos that he equally promotes were not possibly coextensive with all the efforts of Being. For what is *mainmise* but an originary condition of oppression, a lower gear in the death drive that in fact tramples the subject-elect prior even to the irreversible alienation of language?

Now all this comes down to the ordeal or trial of the call, to the call of the big X, or Being, or the mountain, or God. On top of Being or God, even the mountain calls. The call is not necessarily of language or entirely without language. It is hard to situate with any certainty. In *Sein und Zeit* Heidegger had said of the call—the aphonic call of conscience—that it comes from within me and from beyond me. In order to heed the call one has to have emptied oneself, have undergone a personal kenosis (which, to the extent that it empties, drops off the "personal"). In any case, there is nothing on the order of knowledge to guarantee the call or ensure its referential authority (we shall see how the call without knowledge or ascertainable origin becomes the call of the father). Lyotard himself began the essay with such a stamp, miming its necessity by splitting himself off from his own intention. He began in the twilight of unknowing. About the observations he was prepared to unfold, he said of their origin that they "do not come from the place of some presumed knowledge. For I know nothing of what I have to say here. Nothing of this love of knowledge and wisdom that the Greeks instilled in us under the name of philosophy" (*H*, 1). In this sense, according to the logic of the argument he subsequently develops, Lyotard has worked through the seduction of woman. According to the biblical fable, she exists in order to make man forget that he does not know (you know, the fable of the apple: "woman's desire is that man forget that he cannot have knowledge" [*H*, 8]). Correspondingly, there is something like a false call that is posited in the fable—a false and therefore also a true call, and primal man has been shown falling prey to the false call, the call to knowledge or to forgetting his castration (already in paradise there was castration!).

These calls test man, constitute his trial, ordeal ("the letters of the Torah that designate God's asking find their best approximation in the German verb *versuchen*. This word means trial, attempt, tentative, even temptation. Yahweh tries Abraham by asking him for his son" [*H*, 9–10]). The essential test of childhood, "a great uncertainty concerning childhood," writes Lyotard, involves the binding (*liaison*) and the unbinding or disconnection (*déliaison*): "That is to say, concerning the very core of what governs emancipation. This uncertainty concerns the status of the call and of that which calls, which is to say, the status of the father" (*H*, 7). This goes very fast, but we have already seen that the feminine can pull a fast one and place a false call ("the evil that speaks in woman"). At the same time the *mainmise* is that of the father, even if he has employed a wayward operator:

> Jesus' response to the question "Who is the greatest in the kingdom of heaven?" quivers like an arrow that has hit its target; it is the little one, the child (Matthew 18:1–5), *parvulus* in the Vulgate. That is why the child must not be "scandalized" [Gr. *skandalisei*: offended, made to stumble] (Matthew 18:6). Using the term *wound*, I said that this scandal or stumbling block (what Freud called seduction) is inherent to childhood insofar as it is subject to the *mancipium* of adults. And *mancipium* must be taken in both senses here: the one that the adult exercises over the child, and the one that their own childhood exercises over them, even while they are exercising it over the child. (*H*, 7)

Reflecting the double track of *mancipium*, Lyotard understands the term "childhood" in two ways: the childhood that is not bound to this time but is "the celestial model of what has no need to be emancipated, having never been subjected to any other *mainmise* than that of the father; and the subject that is inevitably subjected to scandal, to stumbling blocks, and thus to the abjection of what does not belong to the truth of this call" (*H*, 7). The scandal or stumbling block "is everything that sidetracks this call—violence, exclusion, humiliation, and the seduction (in the original sense) of the innocent child" (*H*, 7). The one by means of whom the scandal or stumbling block occurs exercises a *mancipium* over the child, thereby misguiding and keeping the child away from his only *manceps*, the father. Splitting man from the father, Lyotard affirms the disturbing plight that pulls the child from the paternal domain: "This stumbling block and misguidance are necessary. It is necessary to be *bound*, expropriated, appropriated by man rather than the father" (*H*, 7). Man in this case stands for woman, who intercepts the call and runs it through a scrambling device that endangers the man-child: "The woman's desire is that man stand up and rival the Almighty—thus no longer obeying the Almighty's call, no longer being bound to his *mancipium*. Such is the wicked emancipation that the hysteric whispers to her man: you are not castrated. This emancipation is paid for by suffering, labor and death" (*H*, 8). Woman calls on man to block the call, to disconnect from the divine call-forwarding system in order to come into his own. She disrupts the Edenic paternal flow and throws her man to the winds of time, repetition, and death. Introducing pain into the destinal equation, she levels at the "beyond" of "beyond the pleasure principle."

Somehow or other, the only two boys who will not have been led astray by the feminine, which Lyotard collapses into the maternal *mancipium*, are Isaac and Jesus, whose moms were not entirely women ("Their mothers will have barely been women" [*H*, 8]). This is so because of the effects of maternal time warp: one was with child too late, having been barren, and the other too soon, having been virgin. Sarah welcomes impregnation with a laugh that is to become the name of her child (Isaac: "he laughed"). Lyotard compares the incredulous, vengeful laughter of Sarah to the Virgin's simple faith, framed by a smile. Because of these traits that unwoman them, the Jewess who is on the mat too late and the Christian whose womb conceives too soon are granted a certificate of exemption from the sphere of endangering maternity. These two women, Sarah and Mary, are exempted "from the fate of the mother as seductress. Hence the two sons, Isaac and Jesus, will have been only slightly led astray, or perhaps not at all, by the maternal *mancipium*" (*H*, 8). The barring of the women—barren or humanly inconceivable—allows for the unintercepted call to come through to these boys: "It is from the father himself that the trial of the binding and unbinding comes to the son" (*H*, 8). Mother takes her place at the sidelines, steadily transforming herself into the figure of mourning. Always in the grips of a lose-lose situation, mother appears to have the choice between damning herself as invasive seductress or effacing herself under the insistent beat of a death knell.

Lyotard continues his reading of the fable, though he no longer signals its fabulous contextual hold. Instead he focalizes what he now regards as good emancipation—what amounts to an extreme form of paternal binding: "For the child, good emancipation has to do in both cases with rising to the call of the father, with being able to listen to it. It is not at all a matter of freeing oneself from this voice. For freedom comes, on the contrary, in listening to it" (*H*, 8). Freedom is signaled, one could say, within the Heideggerian conjunction of *Hören* and *Gehorsam*, of hearing and adhering. Listening is an extreme form of obedience, of opening and giving oneself over to the voice of the other. Paul sketches the switch-over from one master transmitter to another when he writes of an abiding enslavement within different registers of address: "For just as you once presented your members as slaves to impurity and to greater and greater iniquity, so now present your members as slaves to righteousness for sanctification" (Romans 6:19). Lyotard comments: "One is emancipated from death only by accepting to be 'enslaved to God,' for 'the advantage you get,' [Paul] continues, 'is sanctification. The end is eternal life' (Romans 6:22)" (*H*, 8). The enslaved may respond to a different master, but the condition of enslavement does not in itself undergo significant modification. Lyotard does not spend much time tracing the slippage from freedom to sanctification but concentrates on the emancipatory drive that may with more or less success satisfy its aims.

Jews and Christians have observed a tacit agreement in one area—the area that covers the reception of the other. They are similarly disposed at the reception desk of the transcendental intrusion, watchful and ready to take note or direct a command. For Lyotard, the Jewish side of things is unambiguous in terms of receiving the call. "On the Jewish side," he writes, "there is no need to comment further upon the listening, which I would wish to call absolute or perfect (in the way one speaks of a musician having perfect pitch), that is, upon the ear that Abraham or Moses lends to the calling of his name" (*H*, 9). I would like to ask that you lend your ears to this flattering mystification of the Jewish pitch. It grieves me to add a sour note to the assertion, yet how can one's ears, trained on the inaudible, not prick up when provoked by the friendly foreclosiveness of the utterance "there is no need to comment further"? Affirming Lyotard's own ethics of responsiveness, one must *enchaîner*, one must produce phrases around this silence, even if it should rest on the silence of presumed perfection. The statement calls for something of a midrashic intervention, for it may be wrong to stabilize the calling of the name or what Abraham thought he heard that day (we leave Moses to another treatment, perhaps a psychoanalytical one, as when Lacan, discussing *das Ding*, offers that the burning bush was Moses's Thing). Let us put this call momentarily on hold and proceed. Lyotard continues: "On this point Jews and Christians are in agreement—emancipation is listening to the true *manceps*" (*H*, 9). Both sides of the divide agree upon the essential structure of subjection to a higher force, located in the commanding voice. This is the agreement that modernity disrupts when it tries to imagine and bring about an emancipation without an other. "Such an emancipation can only appear, in terms of the Scriptures, as weakness and impurity, a recurrence of the Edenic scene. . . . Jews and Christians agree on the impossibility, futility and abjection of an emancipation without *manceps*, without voice" (*H*, 9).[11] Nonetheless a profound disagreement divides them. It stems, Lyotard offers, from the value that each ascribes to sacrifice. Paul makes virtually no reference to the trial of Abraham, contesting instead the Jews' ritualistic faith, which is commemorated in the annual sacrifice, marking the division of the Temple into two tabernacles, the second being reserved for the sovereign sacrificer. Paul omits mention, Lyotard points out, of the call that Abraham received—namely, the one by means of which Yahweh asks Abraham to offer up his son, or rather submits him to the test of sacrifice but then calls off the test: "There will be no sacrifice of the child. Only a perpetual threat. The threat that Yahweh may forget to send the ram" (*H*, 10). (Lyotard invites another to speak: "As George Steiner puts it so well in his little book entitled *Comment taire?*,[12] every Jewish son knows that his father might be called to lead him up the hill that is now named *Adonai-Yerae*, that is 'God will provide' [rabbinic translation], so that he may be sacrificed to Yahweh. Not being sure that God will provide" [*H*, 10]. For what it's worth, I do not see the earth-shattering insight here; could one not say that every Christian son knows he might be nailed by his father? Is not every father, at least every imaginary father, the foster parent of the child Oedipus, out to get him at some level of unconscious deliberation?) The point here is that the bond fastened round the body of Isaac, its "binding," its *liance*, can be undone, "thus marking the precariousness of the binding, almost inviting the people of Israel to forget it, inviting renewed sin and trial, endless rereading and rewriting" (*H*, 11). God backed off, the supreme hand desisted. Which is to say: He can always make a comeback. The Christians, on the other hand, went all the way on the issue of sacrifice. Even Jesus was surprised that he was not Isaac and that the game was not called off at the last moment. But just because the game was not called off and the sacrifice played itself out, this does not mean that it amounted to what Lyotard has called a "good emancipation." The transfiguration of suffering, humiliation, and death into passion "is *already* emancipation" (*H*, 11). The flesh was "redeemed or pardoned [*graciée*]" (*H*, 11). In this regard, the sacrifice cut both ways.

"Certainly, this confidence in pardoning or remission can give rise to bad emancipation, to appropriation, privilege, and worldly powers. Protestants knew this and so protested" (*H*, 11). Lyotard ends the elaboration by pointing to a differend between the Torah and the Christian New Testament, which pivots on the question of forgiveness. Hannah Arendt writes in *The Human Condition* that forgiveness is the remission granted for what has been done. "Not a forgetting but a new giving out, the dealing of a new hand. One would have to examine the relationship between this and emancipation" (*H*, 11–12); the problem is, can *mainmise* play with a new deck, or would such optimism merely set the stage for new *Deckerinnerungen* (screen memories) concerning the unrelenting terrorism of childhood?

There were two test sites for us Westerners, then, two figures of children who more or less transcended their putdowns. In a sense, however, testing in terms of the Christian reinscription was called off, or, more precisely, rigged. Indeed, a differend has emerged in the church's reappropriation of Christ precisely where it refuses the test. A genuine test has been consistently denied by the church, called off or deemed out of line with the exigencies of erecting an untestable deity. The testing structure is repelled to such an extent that when the issue arises of Christ being put to the test, it becomes a marked scandal. There is the matter of the unavowable temptation. Unsublatable, the temptation fades under the worldly scepter of bad emancipation. Even when popular modes of expression try to put the trial back in the Passion—as in the filmic articulation *The Last Temptation of Christ*—the church sends out its delegation to make street noises and block entry into the body of a tempted, troubled, tested son of God. Christ untested guarantees a certain narrative stability, no doubt—the stability of repression—but it interrupts the disturbing fable of the becoming-god.

I want to stay on this side of the fence and leave the Christians to the transfiguring humiliations, the passions of which so much has been said and what Lyotard sees bolstered, I think, by dialectics as so many counterfeit test sites. Let us, though, return to the trial of Abraham, if only to read, in response to Lyotard, the ambiguity of the call that came through on that fateful day. If rising to the call of the father offers a fighting chance for good emancipation, then let us check in on the way that call was placed—or, as the case may be, misplaced. Someone's father took the call, and some kid paid for it. . . . Listen:

"Abraham!
Abraham!"

The call befalls you and you cannot prevent the "falling" which you are: it throws you. You are thrown [*geworfen*]—thrown off before any "I" can constitute itself or any subject can be thrown together. You are called to come to the world and answer for yourself. In fact, "called" is your most proper name, prior to any nomination, any baptism. This is why the call concerns only you. Your being is being-called. But why, why did God call twice? This is a matter that Lyotard does not take up, but it has a bearing, I think, on the way we encounter—or fail to acknowledge—the *mancipium*. For if the oppressive hand weighs so heavily upon us and has left a lasting thumbprint on our being, then it is necessary to recall that there is trouble on the line, and difficulty in assigning the call with any certitude. Given the static, moreover, that harassed the line and lineage, it remains difficult to determine whether the position of father can be stabilized and does not itself jump, fall, leap back into childhood's regressive posturings. Even God had to double-deal, or deal at least with two pressing moments, when placing the call. These two moments have divided God against himself, effecting once again the weak point of the "big A," *Autre*. While Lyotard allows for a false call inadvertently to come through in his reading and has something to say about that which sidetracks the call, he retains a sense of the truth in calling. As if it were ultimately possible to clear the static. God, for his part and party line, stutters: a hapax. Even though he is constantly repeating himself and renewing his threats, I do not believe that in order to make himself clear he has had to stutter the way he does over the name of our Ur-patriarch.

"Abraham! Abraham!" Why did God have to call out the name twice? Why does God have to say Abraham two times? Or are there two of him? Had God surrendered from the start to the temporal predicament of the addressee, or was he himself split by the destination of his call? In this double call or the call of the double, Kafka, as if fielding Lyotard's call, situates a parable.

"Abraham! Abraham!" The call came through as a gift that surpassed his initiative, indebting and obliging him before he could undertake any decision. I am not saying that the voice is a phenomenon or a *phone semantike*: perhaps you hear it without hearing. Yet as inaudible and incomprehensible as it may be, it never lets up on calling you.

I want to consider in light of Lyotard's focus on the calling structure that held Abraham in thrall, this virtually unknown text of Kafka. Titled "Abraham," it begins by splitting the addressee: "There must have been other Abrahams." My perspective, if that is what we can call it, would have been that of the child Isaac, switching, at times, also to that of Sarah. "And Sarah laughed," writes Kafka.[13] But mostly I fell for the child Isaac, the one who was benched in the last minute of an ancient homegrown world series, where the trace of sacrifice, the sacrificial punt, still exists. Isaac, in any case, was benched, pulled off the playing field of a transcendental rumble: Isaac sacked. The story depicts him, if we need to find a cultural diagnosis, as a mostly masochistic lame loser. "Loser" may still imply too much agency, though. Kafka rereads the call that was taken on that fateful day in terms of a terror that was nowhere articulated in the sedimented responses that have accrued to it: the terror of becoming ridiculous. What could it mean to have to sacrifice your sacrifice, which is to say, the father's sacrifice to which you have been assigned—or rather, to find yourself stripped even of the sliver of will that implicates you in his sacrifice, in the sacrificial act that is not even your own? The grammar of Isaac's failure to sacrifice, that is, to be sacrificed, is even more abject: what could it mean for us today that Isaac's sacrifice was sacrificed, called off? In *The Gift of Death*, Derrida writes that death is the place of one's irreplaceability, unsubstitutability, for "sacrifice supposes the putting to death of the unique in terms of its being unique, irreplaceable, and most precious. It also therefore refers to the impossibility of substitution, the unsubstitutable."[14]

Now we come to Lyotard's assertion of Jewish perfect pitch as exemplified by Abraham. Let us recall the resolute way in which Lyotard pitches—or rather, ditches—the problem. On the Jewish side, he writes, "there is no need to comment further upon the listening, which I would wish to call absolute or perfect (in the way one speaks of a musician having perfect pitch), that is, upon the ear that Abraham or Moses lends to the calling of his name" (*H*, 9). At this point I want to convoke a counsel of elders, one from the field of literature, the other from the philosophical domain. Both are ironists who have reached deeply into abysses. They were fearless when it came to reporting what they had found. Kafka and Kierkegaard, on the trail of the great patriarch, shared an insight into the ridiculousness of Abraham. Kierkegaard's example of foolish faithfulness, which he takes up at length in *Fear and Trembling*, is Abraham: "Abraham believed and did not doubt, he believed in the preposterous."[15] Kafka's parable "Abraham," which ponders the deconstitution of the primal patriarch, evokes Kierkegaard (and Don Quixote). Multiplied and serialized, his several Abrahams are ridiculous creatures—the world would laugh itself to death at the sight of them, one a harried waiter taking an order. Their performance of insurmountable foolishness inscribes them in an unforgettable saga, dividing while sealing a first letter to the Father.

The great patriarch, the *Erzvater*, from whom, as Kafka reminds us, we are said to descend, shares decisive motifs with those figures of error and misconception that tend to be thematized in his stories and novels. Inevitably set to provoke the world's laughter, the retakes of Abraham begin by naming the spiritual poverty of the patriarch ("Abrahams geistige Armut"; *A*, 36) and the inertia it spreads, the indifference that clouds his ability to see the diversity of world. And then, outrageously, as if capable of sustaining a competition with the Almighty, the text itself conjures and calls up the man, the primal one, creating for itself another possibility of Abraham ["Ich könnte mir einen anderen Abraham denken—"; *A*, 36]. The "I" thinks up an Abraham who, though prepared to satisfy the demand for a sacrifice immediately, first freezes upon receiving his marching orders. This one stumbles, namely, over the constative utterance in the Bible, which unleashes a performative necessity: "He set his house in order" (*A*, 37).

The narrative can't get past the fact of this house, whose ordering it posits (the Bible does not set great store in having Abraham clean house, Kafka read it off some wall).[16] The parable insists: Abraham had some property. He had a house; moreover, it had to be set in order. The house of being or a small estate, the house already contained Abraham, bestowed upon him specific, worldly properties, and established somewhat of a prescriptive routine. He was bound by this house. It had to be put in order before any other, higher orders could be followed, much less heard. Housebound, this Abraham, who "certainly would have never gotten to be a patriarch or even an old-clothes dealer," was prepared to answer the call with the promptness of a waiter, but was unable to bring it off "because he was unable to get away, being indispensable; the household needed him, there was perpetually something or other to put in order, the house was never ready" (*A*, 37). The issue of sacrifice implicates readiness, a giving up of property. The concern evinced by Kafka is presacrificial. How can a house be ready when the call comes through? A house needs to be ready so that a call can be received. The reception of the call would deliver the host to an outside that is more intimate than the hearth. What is the link between the call and the order of the house? There is the insinuation of a state of house arrest: he'll never leave the house, not even by leaping out the window. There is the other issue of the leap, Abraham's leap, which does not appear to take place.

The problem with this Abraham, says the narrator, is that he already had the house, something to fall back on, something to leave: "If he had not had a house, where would he have raised his son, and in which rafter would he have stuck the sacrificial knife?" This Abraham, who displays greater evidence of style than the more popular, the impoverished one, becomes his substitute, becomes the more "real Abraham," who is, however, "an old story not worth discussing any longer" (*A*, 39). So why are we discussing it?

There is something about the old story that cannot be put to rest; it calls us, repeating itself ever as an old story whose recurrence marks it as a founding story, the story of Abraham, the one who received the call. This one "had everything to start with, was brought up to it from childhood—I can't see the leap." The narrator supplies logic where the leap is missing. If this Abraham already had everything, then something had to be taken away from him, "at least in appearance: this would be logical and no leap." Where is the famous leap of faith promoted by Kierkegaard, of a sudden, unaccountable narrative breakaway? The logic of sacrifice seems too close to calculative simplicity here, resembling in a prefigurative way that of Job, from whose vitality so much was taken. "It was different for the other Abrahams, who stood in the houses they were building and suddenly had to go up on Mount Moriah; it is possible that they did not even have a son, yet already had to sacrifice him. These are impossibilities, and Sarah was right to laugh" (*A*, 39). But Sarah's laughter is not addressed to the most ridiculous of possibilities, only to impossibilities that make sense and fail to produce a leap. What makes sense? There were Abrahams who were called before they were ready, that is, before their houses were readied, much less built. These were pure sacrificial beings who were prepared to surrender that which they did not have. This sacrifice, following the logic of the parable, is greater even than that of the Abraham who had someone to give up to a higher power. These Abrahams gave what they could not offer. Hence Sarah laughs at the gift that, never having been given, is already, "suddenly" (*A*, 39), given away and somehow redeemed. She laughs at the peculiar nothingness of the gift, the danger and disruption of the gift that bears no present. Her laughter, as Lyotard sees it, contrasts with the sublime smile of the Virgin. But he does not present the immaternal mother in a particularly theoheretical light. Laughing, Sarah doubles the gift's unfathomable givens, for according to Freud and Nancy laughter "itself" would be gift as well—the *Geschenk* or *Gabe* inhering in the surrender of giving up (*Aufgabe*).[17] Laughing, she surrenders an unnamable gift. According to the program notes provided by Baudelaire, her laughter would be that of a she-devil, breaking and entering into the house of limits, bursting and busting (she bursts into laughter) the steeliness of man's calculative grid.

The narrator continues: "But take another Abraham" ("Aber ein anderer Abraham"), in which the "aber" and "abra" and "aba" converge, an other father, one who in principle inhabits the leap and passes through a loop of warping disjuncture, if only to be stopped at the moment itself of reception. This other one got everything straight, he "wanted to perform the sacrifice altogether in the right way and had a correct sense in general of the whole affair." There was a problem of address, however, scorched by an impossible presentation, the sheer negativity of exposition. He had the right sense of things, "but could not believe that he was the one meant, he, an ugly old man, and the dirty youngster that was his child. . . . He would make the sacrifice in the right spirit if only he could believe he was the one meant." It is not the case that this one does not believe in God; no, what he does not believe is that the call was meant for him to take. He does not believe in himself as destination; he cannot believe that the call will have arrived if he were to respond to its demand. This might be an intercept, a matter of mistaken identity in the divine call-forwarding system. In fact this Abraham, old and capable of presenting only his ugliness, fears mainly the metamorphosis. "He is afraid that after starting out as Abraham with his son he would change on the way into Don Quixote" (*A*, 39). He would turn into the ridiculed figure of the seeker, the improbable hero of thought, a fabulously bumbling tourist of the imaginary. Worse still, he would have turned into literature; that is, he would have turned himself into the authority of a literature which strip searches the sacred, consistently enraging world: "The world would have been enraged at Abraham could it have beheld him at the time, but this one is afraid that the world would laugh itself to death at the sight of him" ["die Welt werde sich bei dem Anblick totlachen"] (*A*, 39–40). The other side of the world's rage at Abraham consists in this laughter, a laughter-to-death that threatens extinction. Kafka's text thus presents another version of *Totem and Taboo* where, instead of producing a blood-and-guts murder of the primal father, the world-horde emerges as capable of laughing itself to death, to his death, in a broad sweep of castrative derision. The trope of ridiculousness subverts the gravity of biblical patriarchy or shows what was always there, left untouched. It prepares the ground for a world-class masochistic introject, for another internalization of the first father, humiliated and steadily miniaturized. Freud's horde got theirs, too. Conscience-bitten, they were felled by remorse in the end, or, rather, they were henceforth to stand by remorse and a father for whom love arrived in the ambivalent aftermath of an immemorial murder. Their father, however, stood tall, with haunting authority.

Reversing the flow, the new caller ID system puts the presumptive addressee on the line. The one who thinks the call is meant for him alone and is heading straight for him, with his name on it, is subjected to particularly brutal forms of ridicule ("And Sarah laughed"). We learn from Kafka's narrator that ridiculousness has the power of agency and aging. It is not merely that his ugliness makes him ridiculous, but, more to the point, that ridiculousness increases his age and ugliness, further sullying his son. Ridiculousness is imbued with divine powers of negation, and so a subtle tautology enters in a contest that resounds with laughter: "However, it is not ridiculousness as such that he is afraid of—though he is, of course, afraid of that too and, above all, of his joining in the laughter—but in the main he is afraid that this ridiculousness will make him even older and uglier, his son even dirtier, even more unworthy of being really called" (*A*, 41). The ridiculous is exposition: it will expose him, nearly eating into his skin, *making* him older and uglier, transforming him as it presents him, rendering unsightly as it inspects. It is, moreover, hereditary, for it exposes the son to even more dirt on his father, "his son even dirtier" (*A*, 41), tainted, destitute. An improper sacrifice acts in fact as the destruction of sacrifice (something that Kafka accomplishes but that, as we come to understand, God could not: the end of sacrifice). The son, Isaac, if he is to be offered, must be given up as a clean sacrifice, as that which is clean in itself, a clean cut, a proper offering. The parable takes up the other side of the biblical obsession with cleanliness, zooming in on a stain that cannot be removed: the possibility that Abraham was dirty, his child even dirtier. The proper mode of responsiveness depends upon erasing the stain, which, however, proves to be ineffaceable. Under the circumstances, how can Abraham make the cut or take the call? Ridicule stalks him like a ghost.

Abraham finds himself in a bind: he must of course answer the call, because it addresses him; when rising to answer the call, he becomes ridiculous for responding to it as if it had been meant for him, Abraham. Ridiculousness, which comes after the call, reverses the charges, turning temporality around on itself, for it bestows upon Abraham the predicament of having not been called—not really called ("wirklich gerufen zu werden"; *A*, 40). It has the ability to return the call on itself and reoriginates it as mistaken, off pitch. The ridiculous diverts and cancels the call. So that God "really" could have made the call to this Abraham, the call "nur für Dich bestimmt," intended only for you, as the doorkeeper in another parable says to the man from the country. This Abraham could have been God's intended, the intended destination of His call, which was to be canceled when the ridiculous supervened as a kind of devil on the line of divine transmission. But ridiculousness has effected a mutation in the addressee, who was no longer the same as the one called. Abraham did not become ridiculous until, believing in his own perfect pitch, he answered the call. Answering the call, he annuls it: "An Abraham who should come unsummoned!" (*A*, 41).

The narrator of the parable fades the sequence into a pedagogical analogy of contemporary consequence, deriving a scene wherein the class *Dummkopf* hears his name called on commencement day. An institutional ritual has been disrupted: the student body writhes in laughter. In order to understand the folly of Abraham's pitch, we are regressed into another childhood drama, another scene of humiliation: "It is as if, at the end of the year, when the best student was solemnly about to receive a prize, the worst student rose in the expectant stillness and came forward from his dirty desk in the last row because he had made a mistake of hearing, and the whole class burst out laughing" (*A*, 41). The dumbest of the dumb rises to the occasion of solemn bestowal, having heard his name and felt himself to be addressed. A notably Christian moment can be seen to occur when the meek comes up from educational death row, the last row and lowest rank, to inherit, unaccountably, the prize. He is crucified by class difference; betrayed within a different hierarchical standard by which he is downgraded, his insufficiency provokes a unanimous peal of laughter. The class *Dummkopf* is too dumb to know that he cannot be the smart one beckoned forth on this day, he leaps up—here, finally, comes the leap—to claim the prize meant for the best student according to a scorecard that he proves unable to decipher. All he knows is that he heard his name called. Again, this morphed Abraham, the childish patriarch, is associated with the improper: his desk, dirty, has not been put in order, yet he hears himself called. There is a film of disgust trailing Abraham, a minor dust storm kicking up in the wake of father. The solemnity of the event is broken. The unclean father, a constant Kafkan obsession, returns to its once auratic source exposing the father as reflected in a dirty child or lame student. There is one thing, *the Thing*, that occupies a shared imago and shatters its integrity. It arrests the stain, inevitably disfiguring the face of authority without lessening the severity of that authority—lending it, rather, the power to induce even more anxiety. Crumbs on a newspaper, dirty sheets, a tear in a picture: these lesions in being whose precise punctuation already marked Abraham. The presentation has been absolutely sacrificed, appearances materialized and degraded, beginning with the dirty desk in the back row, the loser's place. How could an Abraham, stained and disheveled, originate in the back row except by hearing impairment or random draw—the deformity of an improper address?

One possibility remains constant: that his name has been called out, if only, the text says, in punishment. The contest of the faculties enfolds the question of contesting faculties, for if he can believe his ears maybe the teacher's understanding is at stake: "And perhaps he had made no mistake at all, his name really was called, it having been the teacher's intention to make the rewarding of the best student at the same time a punishment for the worst one" (*A*, 41). Kafka does a retake of the great Book, displacing and condensing the value of reward, the necessity of punishment. How was the truth of Abraham tested? There are two parts to this test. Although in the Bible Abraham's obedience was tested—he passed the test, won back the boy, got God on his side—in Kafka the test, though schooled and standardized, is scrambled, the test results rendered inconclusive. Did he pass? Did he fail? Did he not need always already to have failed in order to pass? Or did he think he passed but was failed by the multiplication of Sarah's laughter booming through the chorus of his classmates? Did he accidentally skip a grade when he was supposed to be held back?[18]

His faculties contested, little, dumb, dirty Abraham answers to the call of the faculty, a call meant as punishment but where no one can be entirely sure anymore who is being rewarded as best student or punished as the worst one. All we know is that the punished and rewarded are collapsed into the same figure that accounts for the fiction of the father. The most exalted and secretly ridiculed of beings owes his existence to the undecidable nature of the call, its meaning or address, its intention and value. By answering to his name, he has already offered his sacrifice, whether or not the teacher will call it off—whether or not it is even in the power of the faculty to recognize the difference. The final irony is that, having been called, Abraham comes unsummoned. As unforgettable source, seared by the trauma of universal laughter, he is measured in Kafka by the consistent shedding of self-worth, bowed by the incursion of unrelenting indignities.

Consistently lapsing into the stupefying commands of childhood, he remains hostage to those subliminal acts—they are a matter largely of passivity, of following a sacrificial order—that risk exposing him primordially to the most naked core of sheer ridiculous being.

The teacher, the master, or God plays his part in the sullen destitution of the boy, Abraham, our father. What we learn from Kafka's parable, if the teacher means us to learn anything, concerns the failure of presentation. Ineffaceable, the lesion surfaces, as in "A Country Doctor," in the struggle over presentation. There is always a smudge of dirt where anointment occurs. As much a sign of the missed appointment as of a missed anointment—the appointment is made dependent in Kafka on having missed the point—the calling of Abraham disarranges hierarchy, subverts class expectation (why should the poorest student inherit the prize?), so that the good student is always tainted by the worst student who can come around, according to the order of a new curve, and be commended as the most prizeworthy. Yet the text at no point effects a dialectics or a genealogical switch as it swings over the breakage of singularity. The bad student does not turn into the good one according to a logic of secret negotiations with a higher power. He wins the divine lottery, but as a loser.

A lot depends in the parable on Kafka's use of *gleichzeitig*, on the simultaneous wish of the teacher to present reward and punishment. How can simultaneity be instituted and observed? Even God cannot practice simultaneity; he must call out Abraham's name twice, if it is indeed Abraham's name that is being called—the question mark around which the parable rotates. We have a hard time imagining the voice that summons as a stammering one, resembling the syncopated speech of Moses. The voice of God has been reported to be clear, though not always, and there is some probability that somewhere voice can be cracked, split, even in His case. Kafka does not say whether the voice summoning Abraham was disarticulating or hoarse, whether on the contrary it rang out with unparalleled acuity. In a sense, it doesn't matter. God was not heard on the first try. God Almighty for the most part must submit His calls to the laws of temporization, which in order to be heard have to be repeated to begin with. Not to speak of what could have been *meant* when the call was made. Intention, when the name is called, remains rigorously unreadable. The best student may be Abraham—yes, maybe, but this story, the old one, we are told, has lost all interest. Neither God nor the teacher can have access to the intention that motivates the calling of the name since both are limited by the one name, by the oneness of a name that strictly defies spontaneous serialization. However well the intention has been mastered, it does not in the end allow one to know which or who was called, for even in the utterance of the one name He can always conceive of another Abraham ("Ich könnte mir einen anderen Abraham denken—"; *A*, 36). As for the name, it cannot be reduced to the same or difference. To the extent that it remains impossible to call out two names at once, the intention must be split, as with the cut that binds Judeo-slash-Christianity.

Assuming that Abraham did not sacrifice the child Isaac (though according to one midrash the son was executed),[19] the question remains of how and whether Isaac survived the near-death experience—how he survived a psychotic father, that is, everybody's primal father, Kafka's, yours and mine, even, or *especially*, when they are in sync with the Law, practicing the ineluctable *mainmise.*

Isaac, for his part, became a figure of traumatic repetition; he dug holes in the earth where his father had done the digging before him, puncturing Mother Earth, producing holes already marked by Abraham. The son reproduces holes, digging and emptying, as if responsible for a dumb show whose interpretation Hamlet subsequently imposed on Western consciousness. What Isaac was "getting at" we still do not know or cannot tolerate knowing. In any case, he turned out to be a bit of a loser, if he was anything at all in the end, the almost sacrificed son. It cannot be said with certitude that he survived, or that anyone survives that which we are calling childhood. One supposes that the child Isaac would have been better served had his destiny not been summed up in the Dostoyevskian freeze-flash of the nearly executed. Deprived of a martyr's grandeur, relieved of his stake in establishing an unprecedented contract between God and man—he had been a wager, he was dealt out—Isaac was condemned to live in the trauma zone of childhood's empty repetition, digging for a truth trove that was never to be found. The serial digger displaces the dagger, punctuating earth with the unreadable hieroglyphs of another story, that of another, untold Abraham. There could have been, there must be, yet another Abraham.[20]

As for the child, Isaac: the biggest bluff, for all that, may have occurred when the delusion was implanted, the hope nurtured of a chosen people. Isaac, he was, and was not, called. More radically uncertain than persecution (when you know they're after you, you're already dead meat, you *are* the ram caught in the bushes), is that of being cheated by the call. Too stupid to know if your name was called, you are ridiculous. You are ready to go up for the sacrifice, but in the last moment you are benched. They don't need you. An animal will serve the purpose, your purpose. This call told you that you were the one, the chosen. You set yourself up to receive it; you were set up. It was no longer recognizable whether the call meant to serve as punishment or reward. Your father took the call. You inherited it, with all the expected static; you inherited his burden, which you thought you could lighten. You followed your father in mute complicity, split between the father and God. As you were walking, as he was preparing to give you up. You could not tell, you simply could not decide whether this call that expelled you from your house was a blessing or a curse.

Passages of the Maya

Philippe Bonnefis

What I do is simple, expressed in Buddhistic terms: I use my life to attempt to express a passage of the Maya, as Maya.
—André Malraux

Facing life, the life-work of André Malraux, Jean-François Lyotard through his book (*Signé, Malraux*) puts us in the position of that Brahmin or fakir whom Malraux glimpsed under monsoon clouds at Benares and "who dansed," let us remember, "and who was doubled up with laughter squealing 'bravo' at the illusion of the world."[1]

Why then couldn't I also indulge in the only demonstrations this book so obviously summons? Thus rendering it justice. . . . I would be sorry indeed if my title were ambiguous. At no point was my intention to reopen the interminable trial on which Malraux put biography. Suffice it to underline its precisely vain and interminable character. So perfectly vain that it would quickly appear, should we refer to his texts and grant their contradictions, that neither the provocative expressions ("Let's scrape the fresco to shame; we'll find the plaster in the end")[2] nor the feigned surprise of the ironist congratulating himself (in *Les voix du silence*) that no one had yet dreamed of subjecting "the Italian campaign tactics to Josephine's adultery" or "the modification of Maxwell's equation to an Einstein adventure,"[3] none of this could definitively overcome Malraux's incredible determination to win fame through a genre that he vehemently condemned.

After all, how many times hasn't the work of Malraux shown him, biographer at study, tapping impromptu a few scales, practicing? And what, for example, are the life stories of Alexander or Mayrena (Marie I, king of the Sedangs) but freehand sketches, attempts to put in form. And this is not the least important, forms that all go in the same sense. The story of Mayrena's exploits is credited to the Baron Clappique, and thus to a fictional character that Malraux in his *Antimémoires* deliberately, it seems, dragged out of the limbo where he had rested since *La condition humaine*. Alexander's epic, moreover, finds its Homer in the incredible female prophet whom the director of national museums, wondering about the authenticity of a piece of fabric submitted for his appraisal, very seriously consults.

Here we need to explain in detail, to unfold in the extent of its "far-fetched" complications, the scenario of rites of passage to which Malraux's biographical writing feels obliged to sacrifice, in words that every time are authorized only by the improbable itself. A scenario that, in this respect, recalls the one that at the same time is implemented by Blaise Cendrars, another unrepentant and irresolute biographer, who no more than Malraux "knows how to go to the very end," who lingers in beginnings, in foreplay. Rather as if both had the intuition that in fact biography can only be written in the mode of the unreal.

Is it out of forgetfulness that the author of *Le démon de l'absolu* abandons his hero right in the middle of the ford and leaves him for dead? In any case dead to the story, which is interrupted then and there, stopped on the image of Colonel Lawrence absorbed in *The Boy's Book of Colonel Lawrence*.[4] Reading, you understood of course, the narration of his own story. . . . A romanticized story to be sure, an edifying story, addressing children—but his, well and truly *his* story, which not only ironically comes back to him thus, but also ricochets, reaching Malraux himself. The irony of the situation is double. It invites us of course to put on the magic spectacles of childhood to reread the biography of a legendary hero. What's more, it requires that Malraux have gathered only at the end the conditions that might allow his book to be written. A book, it's clear, done backward, thus neither done nor to be done.

The text is contrary to Jean-François Lyotard's admirable book, which is admirable even if the reasons for which it is admired—all excellent, I don't doubt it—seem to me to overlook its principal quality. When Malraux himself becomes biographer, he attributes to that act fragility, he lends it illusiveness, he makes it irremediably chimerical. Lyotard, if I am not mistaken, in his biographical gesture conforms to this kind of chimera, for which Céline had the beautiful word *féerie*.

First sentence of the book:

> The slender young woman, deep purple eyes veiled by a wide-brimmed hat, had enveloped him in her mourning that March day in 1903, and from the coach coming down through the Place Clichy, the tot with his big eyes watched the passage of a cab, a bearded bowler hat, an omnibus, long-haired errand girls basket in hand, a horse carting tins of milk, work trousers with legionnaires' belts, smoking dung piles, a convertible automobile and considerable stone façades adorned with nymphs, hatters' signs, and live-music cafés—all that waddled along behind the car, and he felt that nothing of this agitation was real, that it was all decor, farfetched cinema.[5]

Spells, chromos: "bewitchment," Céline whispers again. Spells that spare nothing and no one. Not even you listening to Lyotard's phrase, embracing the staccato rhythm, jumpy and a bit dry, not knowing, as you heard the first sentence, that you became film on the way. Bit by bit, "transformed film"; soon "film yourself."[6] No longer existing, it's your turn to exist only a little, as we exist in cinema, that art of phantoms. Phantoms "filling the screen,"[7] phantoms filling the room. Phantom itself. Limbo's object, par excellence. Hamlet-like and ghostly. . . .

Cinema, because it appears to some as "the supreme Maya [*sic*]," as "the supreme degree of the ephemeral,"[8] because it knows how to persuade us that the real is but appearance, that there is nothing behind appearances (in which the invention of cinema, we don't think of it often enough, supposed nothing less than the death of God)—from every angle of consideration, cinema is not very different from the mirror, lure that the biographer examines in Malraux's works. He walks with it a moment on the great paths of the human adventure, then abandons it. A mirror that fixes on nothing, no fragment of history, or rather only on fragments. Made for un-fixing: this is Malraux's verb, and it says it all. What has become of the lives of Mareyna, Alexander, and Napoleon? Film projects. Unpursued projects. Projects, moreover, abandoned as soon as they were formed.

And let us note that Malraux suffers not the least feeling of dissatisfaction. As if refraining from production were faithfulness to cinema, faithfulness at least to its spirit. This fidelity for him that meant approaching as much as possible the secret essence of an art that has lived a long time, and we can no longer ignore that fact, because of the awareness of its volatility, and because of the assurance, reconfirmed daily by the imperfection of its chemical means, that it was promised only a very short life. To the point that it impressed writers as different as Cendrars, Giono, and

Céline as the only art suitable to the twentieth century, "the most pathetic of all centuries but also the most conscious," the century that will have taught us that "the peculiarity of man is to disappear."[9]

Not long ago, Jean-François Lyotard dreamed of the possibility that his book might pursue a career on the screen. What sense should we give this call for the benediction of cinematographic adaptation? What Lyotard asked of cinema was surely not a consecration, but something like what Malraux asked Buddhism to help him express: "the passage of the Maya." He said also "the sentiment of appearance." This is in him a sentiment animated, outside any reference to a thought of Being, by an obsessive and constant fear of precariousness, and reposing upon a certitude, shared by Lyotard in whom this ecclesiastic will finally have found his biographer, that reality is irrevocably nil.

If Jean-François Lyotard's book is beautiful, it is because it gives its reader a novelistic inference. It is beautiful, Lyotard's book, above all for having, à la Céline, successfully transformed its rather cumbersome hero into a "detached I." But *detached*, let us hear Céline well, and right to the end: "*You must be more than a little dead* . . . you have to have been *detached*."[10] The feat was to lead its reader—from the opening lines—to adopt a distant point of view on the flashy life of spectacle, if there ever was one like it, of the public figure. Such is the dilettante point of view of butterflies, and of Méry, Malraux's character, added as an afterthought to the *Antimémoires*.[11] Méry, who began to collect butterflies when he knew he was facing death. In *Les chênes que l'on abat*, Malraux lends him these words, which he hastens to peddle to the General:

> Often, now, I put myself in the place of butterflies. . . They are 260 million years old, and the average life of a butterfly lasts two months. They know their regions in Malaysia, their islands. In Java, in Bali, they were well before men. . . So they no doubt exchange butterfly stories: flowers left trees to become offerings, to adorn hair. . . Humans came one after the other, and massacred each other, naturally. They succeeded one another. Madmen. . . Be sure that, for butterflies, the only vaguely serious part of humanity is women, who do not massacre each other. . . After all, they no doubt say, we have been the same butterflies for so long, and those poor stories of men.[12]

Same old song, new lyrics. With the idea, unknown to the refrain, that facing death, we become butterflies. It is exactly death that Jean-François Lyotard's biography puts in the beginning, disrespecting the rule according to which a biography at the very least begins with a birth. It's the least one could do. . . . Don't count on it, though. Modest as our requirements might be, they won't be granted. No, death is given first. Given death, happen what may. That is, if something, whatever, can still happen.

Such is the nature of the enigma this book explores. At all risks, as its author liked to say (in the plural), gone on a quest, in the footsteps of Malraux, for the hypothetical happening. Courting the "apparition" whose arrival he awaits under "the big mudslide of appearances"—his White Whale (*SMX*, 332). Harpooning the Whale—he calls that signing. No event, *stricto sensu*, without signature, and thus, few events. For if everything is good for signing—disaster, resistance, horror, or distress—every signature is not good, and, case in point, it is the impossible that must be wanted. Surprising, then, that a life as eventful as this one seems, when the balance sheets are drawn, could be so desperately poor? The wealth we suppose it is but façade covering over misery.

Reason for Malraux's memoirs being *Antimémoires*: for, if memoirs are the written relation of important events in a person's existence, the *Antimémoires*, which more prudently wish to be a book of encounters, come up against the double difficulty of having to rule each time on the validity of the encounter (was it one, really?) and on the legitimacy of valuating it (if there are more than one, can there be a sum total?). . . . Reason for Lyotard's biography of Malraux not being a biography, but a "hypobiography": the word, slipped in as an aside, in false modesty, at the very end of the work.[13] By its very place immediately redoubling the effects of the modulation in minor. Or the effects of small proportion, no doubt, as if inverting the plus and minus signs, signs of elevation and decline.

The morphology of the name shows clearly enough, if we only think of hypogeum (hypocenter, hypocaust), that, in preference to lofty values, hypobiography concerns itself with all that comes from below and rises from the deep. From the oceanic night, full of sleep's swarming octopus, which frightened Tchen so. Trenches, graves, and coffins, their music boxes. Melodious carrion (listen to them sing, and how well they know their song, and how together they resume at the refrain the great tune of repetition). Those lands remote in space and time—we call them deserts, jungles, or sierra, it doesn't matter. They have no defined name. Now kingdom or reign of the fly prince, in Malraux; now engulfed by the shadows of the deepest wilderness, they're the alcove where the dancer reposes, in her vermin finery.

No doubt, our fables, our beautiful fables, pretty tales of our childhood, need rewriting. Need being subjected, one after the other, to the hypocritique of infamy, from which alone it appears at the end of the day that they, as numerous as they are, draw the authority they continue to exercise over grown-ups, even before they grew up. What would Robin Hood be, the same Robin to whose adventures Malraux, his whole life, in Annamite rice paddies or under Catalan olive groves, will have unceasingly added new chapters, what would he be if, by a sort of asceticism, he hadn't made it a rule to affront terror so regularly, what would he be without "Robin Larva," always on the verge of being barred from humanity, scandalously countersigning, so as to authenticate it, his each exploit?

For the two go together, for larva equals butterfly. To resolve this equation, such is at least the task that its author assigns to hypobiography. A prefix, need one emphasize this? And, as if on purpose, the same, Lyotard recently observed, as in "hypothesis."[14] Considered from this angle, a hypobiography is a hypothetical biography. It is what remains of narration in a life story when the event is uncertain. When, for the least fact reported, the questions are asked of how the miracle of a fact can still be produced, and whether life that we stubbornly call upon in a confused witness is something other, as we'd prefer to think, than a pure and simple phantasmagoria.

In short, these are the nuances to which the hypobiography will have done justice fast. Hardly is the book open, and there is dancing, pirouettes, agitation in every sense. Malraux, and Jean-François Lyotard with him, enjoys the joke, that this agitation—political fights, wars, commitments in good and bad faith, power intrigues, comedies of love, on which History slips arrogantly and childishly—will be taken for "Malraux's life." Playful, lying, temperamental more than his share, acrobat when he plunges into things, there is a d'Artagnan in this man: Malraux rewrites even Dumas. According to a letter from Charles de Batz, held in the Archives, he rewrites Dumas,[15] while, for the general's edification, he redoes the battle of Agincourt, won, he explains learnedly, by cats,[16] 120 cats in a row: that can't be made up. Or it makes itself up. The cat, in Malraux's work, personifies the fable. Whimsical, fantasy maker. To attest to it, an anecdote (the anecdote, in the *Antimémoires*, is always a witticism, revenge of the witty man on the imbecility of History), an anecdote that stages, in New Delhi, the minister of culture and the pandit Nehru:

> He read General de Gaulle's letter giving my credentials, put it on the table and asked me, smiling wider:
>
> "So, you're a minister . . . "
>
> The sentence did not mean: you are part of the French government. A bit Balzac, and especially Hindu, it meant: this is your last incarnation. . . .

"Mallarmé," I responded, "told this story: one night, he's listening to cats conversing in the gutter. An inquisitive black cat asks his cat, a good old tomcat: 'And you, what do you do?' 'Right now, I'm pretending to be a cat in Mallarmé's place. . . .'"[17]

Can we reasonably envision transposing the principle of reincarnation to the scale of an individual existence? Imagine conceiving of a biography as the history of migrations of one soul in one and the same body. Such a fancy is mad, from the point of view of Buddhism itself. Yet it's the one that comes to the most Buddhist spirit of Malraux's characters. I mean the butterfly chaser, the painter of *Vanitas* who spoke a moment ago of his whims, who seems to come straight out of a Nabokov novel: "I would like to write," he says, "a book of memoirs that Buddhists should have written, that they never wrote: ten chapters during which I would always be unknown to my character in the preceding chapter, you understand?"[18]

As for me, what I understand, or think I understand, and as far as I know, is that if Malraux in the end resists the temptation of writing a book like this, which would have been the most farfetched of all had he written it, his biographer on the other hand cannot refrain from thinking seriously of it. Buddhist, Jean-François Lyotard's biography? It depends. But Buddhist at least virtually. If we only took as proof the advertisement, the program if you prefer, as it is explained on the book jacket: "Here is the Malraux of Indochina and of Spain, pillager of temples and minister of culture; orator and writer; rebel and notable; comrade and Gaullist; son and lover; solitary child of Bondy and thinker of the imaginary museum."

What kind of mechanics is this anyway? And-and, and-and, and-and, and-and. . . . What does *and* mean, if the conjunction here has to express at the same time a disjunction? Unless we suppose that the Buddhistic wheel, insofar as it is the wheel of impermanence and discontinuity, is really the motor that drives the story's development. Drives it, leap after leap, we would say, if the situation, if the game that opposes our players didn't require that we borrow from Mallarmé the feline term *bound.* Bound after bound.

Nehru, we remember, had just laid down the reincarnation card, when Malraux, straightaway, responded with a cat, his master trump. Nine lives, think of it! Superstition credits them with nine. But to none of those nine in particular do they grant their faith. In the end, they don't believe in them. Never in what they do, in what they are. Always pretending.

To be cats (if you're with me). The cat is a pretender. He pretends only to be a cat. But in this case, no more and no less than Malraux, when he jungles, when he brings down the house on all the stages of the great theater of the world, Malraux who pretends to be Malraux in Jean-François Lyotard's biography. Did he not sign, and that would be in order, with a cat's silhouette?

For they sign, those devilish animals. The French language still carries the traces:

> Cats sign by scratching. The people used to name them *greffes, greffiers*, or clerks, but they sign also the indefinite of space and time by whimsical comings and goings sometimes gay, sometimes spiteful, stopping on thresholds unseen by us, where they smell some "present beyond." The beyond of a below, that which hums, rumbles, or purrs in their throats. They're just animals, no heavier than a bird, destined soon to die, and who have a savoir faire. Familiar creatures, they do not hesitate to share warmth, plate, and bed with us, and with their fellows in beauty, in misery. Yet never quite here, unruly, haunted. They make of their spontaneous distraction a kind of style. They marvel. They slip away and spring up. Ellipsis, they know all about it. And the name of this life on the threshold, the name of the door ajar, of the questioning, is limbo. (*SMX*, 349–50)

What to add to the wonders of this sumptuous coda? One thing, perhaps, which, better than I could, gives the book's tone: a cat story, very brief—they all are in Malraux's works.

The action takes place in La Boisserie. In the immense shadow of Saint Bernard: Clairvaux is a step away. "A Chartreux cat jumps on the desk. Where could it come from? The door is closed." The tiger's pounce, dear to Michaux. A grey and golden flash. Spirit of the air, a cat is caught in flight. . . . If you can catch it! Like the bird, master of the art of slipping away. A strong presence, this "convulsive fur,"[19] we can't deny it, but a presence, or at least we should be prepared for it, which will not re-present itself. A cat. Fancy that! "Where does it come from?" Well, it comes: what more can be asked? Pure value of appearance. Value, to paraphrase Lyotard (himself paraphrasing Merleau-Ponty), which each time forces sight to "arise along with it" (*SMX*, 342). Not a second to lose!

Thus is this uncomfortable manner of dwelling in time, sometimes called an event. No more than the cat does it announce itself, does it forewarn. There is no time for the event. The events. Even less for signing them. Signing, you understood, those that deserve it. Those that approach legend, that defer destiny, and of which Malraux prophesies that they will always offer the same characteristic of appearing like a "springing up of the unforeseeable."[20] Leaving no other trace of their passing than a point on the long duration of dead times where we float, helpless. Just a point. A final point, perhaps. It depends on who signs them.

In Latin, *punctum. Punctum*: a needle point [*piqûre*]. From *pungere*: to puncture. To sign or to riddle with needle points. Not so much to mark as, by action, speech or writing, to spur on, to stimulate. An acupuncture of the world: Malraux is an acupuncturist. In "Asia of the *laisser-être*" (*SMX*, 64)—yes, in that "region of Mothers" (*SMX*, 111) where we are told that will seems madness—it is in Asia that he will have drawn this power to snatch from the shadows where they rested, sleeping beauties, and, whatever name the museums might give them—great works or masterworks—to restore for us the value of *intensity*. In a word, which by the way is Buddhistic, to make of them what Jean-François Lyotard, about to throw in the pen and leave Malraux, calls his "fetishes of awakening" (*SMX*, 332).

I said that this biography begins by the end. Truthfulness requires me now to say that it ends by the beginning. Let the sun rise on its last chapter. For this last chapter, extra, yet giving the directions for the whole book, Lyotard reserves the passionate examination of Malraux's writings on art, of this "interminable self-analysis" (*SMX*, 334), where we see Malraux, always ready to marvel as does "the child on the beach, before the empty shell which starts to move,"[21] leaning right over the source of presences, and by his own authority, provoking, sometimes, the miracle.

The miracle of this ecstatic instant, spasm, or blackout, which Malraux calls metamorphosis or myth. In the sense that a myth "is not the imitation of a chrysalis." It is "the butterfly. Metempsychosis of nations, India would say."[22] And miracle in which I discern something of the resurrecting gesture that Baudelaire lends the artist. I hear something of the "Lazare veni foras!" whose echo rumbles in the walls of his Salons [*Salons de peinture*]. I perceive something of the sepulchral light he shines on Delacroix's paintings, and that, for me, will illuminate hereafter with its dubious twilight the cycle of rebirths to which the disenchanted charmer Jean-François Lyotard, under the voluntarily frivolous title of biography, will have devoted this moving narrative poem, which would become his *Vie de Rancé*. I would like to make it last a little longer, beyond its own limits, by pronouncing, after him, with that voice he had, barely audible and as if exhausted (*mutique musique*, whose presence only the artist or the writer, from the bottom of the lump in his throat, knows how to flush out), the words he addressed to Albert Ayme: "The painter is, in anyone, he who cries out to the light of the world: why have you forsaken me? Chant of Shadows, Friday of anguish. Even the greatest colorists who celebrated the Earth's glistening did so despite the bewitchment their eyes suffered, and against it. The celebration of color is won over its abomination. So the tomb opens, and the shades appear in glory. . . . This is not Christmas, it's Easter. I said ceremonial because the pictorial gesture demands the desire that color appear *anyway*. This desire, or this will, is a grace. The grace given to Lazarus."[23]

Translated by Monica Kelley
Translation edited by Zrinka Stahuljak

Lyotard Archipelago

Michael Naas

Already more than a year after the event, a singular event, that is, the arrival of a phrase, a single phrase—"nouvelles si tristes"—addressed to me in Athens by a loved one in Paris, the temptation is now so great to link on with something other than silence, which is all I knew how to do at the time, and to speak as I would have never dared do before of the life and work of Jean-François Lyotard. The temptation is now great to speak of Lyotard in a more complete or comprehensive way, and to try, if not to encapsulate or summarize his work, at least to identify its principal land masses and mark out its limits and horizons. With the initial surprise and sadness now past, with an anniversary and its inevitable colloquia and tributes come and gone, the temptation is great to survey the entire corpus from above, to represent the whole in a few phrases of remembrance, and to try to give an account of a body of work that is large and heterogeneous but that, we now know, is not without end. More than a year after the event, after that single, singular phrase attached to an article from *Libération* of April 22, 1998, the temptation is now so great to fly over Lyotard's archipelago and make a map or, even worse, map in hand, take a cruise.

For there will be, we are tempted to believe, no new phrases to surprise us, no shifts in genre to interrupt our panoramic vision or make us revise our panoptic pronouncements. Having visited and explored the last of the islands in the scattered corpus of what I now risk calling, to borrow a word from him, his archipelago, having read the last books on Augustine and Malraux,[1] on the life and work of Malraux, and on the very possibility of writing a biographical text—which shows that Lyotard too must have felt this urge and this danger—it is now so tempting to draw the lines of influence and confluence, to mark out the trade routes, and then to sail or cruise leisurely from one island to the next.

One could visit, for example, the island of Marx, since Lyotard was one of the truly great thinkers and analysts of capital, of political economy and its relation to libidinal economy. Close by, to be sure, would be the island of Freud, all of Freud, but especially, and from very early on, a persistent, repeated, almost compulsive return to *Beyond the Pleasure Principle*. And while on the island of Freud, one would want to read everything Lyotard wrote on psychoanalysis, on Lacan, Winnicot, and Klein, for example. And then again close by the island of transgression or eroticism, the island of Sade, Bataille, and Klossowski—and you can imagine the sort of reception that awaits you there.

And then there are islands that are rarely visited nowadays, where it is easy to get lost, and so difficult to learn the language, to know the history. For example, the land, the period, called *Socialisme ou barbarie*, when Lyotard wrote political articles on, among other things, the war in Algeria. Lyotard as colleague and comrade of Lefort and Castoriadis. It is perhaps not so hard to follow his thought there, but when you read, for example, his own scathing assessment of this period in *Libidinal Economy* it is difficult to feel the intensity or appreciate the stakes. Less foreign might be Lyotard's more recent writings on political and social issues, on the role of the university, on May 1968, on the fall of the Berlin Wall, the Gulf War, and so on, and so forth.

On the other side of the archipelago or the campus—for the archipelago is also a university, with its various faculties—would be Lyotard's thought on aesthetics. Not only on other thinkers of aesthetics—Adorno, for example, who remains a constant reference in Lyotard's work, along with Claudel, Dufrenne, Merleau-Ponty, and Malraux—but on the arts themselves, cinema, music (Kagel, Cage, Berio, Xenakis, Schoenberg, Boulez, even Zappa and Hendrix), theater (Artaud and Brecht), literature (Sterne, Diderot, Mann, Mallarmé, Max Jacob, Kafka, Joyce, Beckett, Stein, Orwell, and his longtime friend Michel Butor) and art, perhaps especially art (Giotto, Fra Angelico, Cézanne, Lhote, Warhol, Morley, Guiffrey, Rothko, Escher, Malévitch, Klee, Kandinsky, Duchamp, Delaunay, Newman, Wesselmann, Francken, and, of course, Adami, Arakawa, and Buren).[2]

Were one ever to leave this island of literary and artistic intensities, there would still be the island of linguistics (Lyotard as a reader of Saussure, Jakobson, Beneveniste, and Frege) and then the island of theology (Lyotard as interpreter of those moderns named Paul and Augustine, or Pascal and Buber) and then, of course, the island or the many islands of philosophy, where entire colloquia and collections could be devoted to Lyotard on Plato, and on Aristotle, Descartes, Burke, Hegel, Nietzsche, Bergson, Husserl, Benjamin, Wittgenstein, Bachelard, Arendt, and, of course, Kant, for whom an island of his own should be reserved, or rather an archipelago within the archipelago. Indeed it is in his reading of Kant, particularly in *Enthusiasm*, that Lyotard speaks most directly and at length of the archipelago, of the heterogeneity of faculties in Kant and of the passages between them. And then add a very large island for Heidegger—a heavily visited and much conflicted island, where even this word archipelago, with its roots in the Aegean Sea, suggests a problematic tendency toward the Greco-German axis.

A series of islands would also have to be set aside for Lyotard and his contemporaries. A generous but demanding and uncompromising reader of his contemporaries, Lyotard was committed, it seems, to a discursive agonistics with those with whom he fundamentally disagreed as well as those to whom he felt close. Lyotard, then, as one of the first and best readers of Deleuze and Guattari, of Derrida and Baudrillard, of Lévi-Strauss, Lefort, Ricoeur, Lacan, Barthes, Marin, Irigaray, Rorty, Habermas, and, for me, Levinas, since, in texts such as "Levinas' Logic" and *The Differend*, Lyotard's analysis of the ethical phrase regimen has been fundamental to my reading and understanding of Levinas. And while on the subject or island of philosophy, it would be a temptation of the Occident not to mention Lyotard's interest in Eastern philosophy, his master's thesis on the theme of indifference in Buddhism, in Zen, and particularly in Dogen, work that, it seems to me, never left him and probably influenced not only his ideas but his style, a writing at once incisive, committed, and yet sublimely detached.

And then there are islands defined less in terms of proper names than themes: Lyotard on technology, on time, on the inhuman, childhood, or narrative. Lyotard on phenomenology, one of the very first islands, and, why not, Lyotard not on but in narrative, an island in the archipelago defined in *Pacific Wall*. And then there is, of course, Lyotard and the postmodern—Lyotard and *The Postmodern Condition*, a slender book with an already long and remarkable history. Lyotard as the inventor of the postmodern, the postmodern sophist—a word that does not have a negative valence in his work—who traveled around the world, from Paris to Los Angeles, Bogotá to Tokyo, peddling his postmodern wares, which included, it should be said, a scathing critique of philosophy in the service of profit and economy.

Again, these are just a few of the islands Lyotard did not simply visit but actually inhabited, places where he has left us not just passing and random thoughts but a veritable corpus within his corpus. Few thinkers in our century could claim a corpus this diverse, with such heterogeneous interests and competencies, though in a couple of moments I will suggest one, André Malraux, one of the most recent islands in the archipelago, one of the very last and, I will argue, one of the best for understanding—or not understanding—the whole.

Because of the force, lucidity, and rhetorical power of Lyotard's thought on any of these islands, spending time on any one of them inevitably changes the way you look at and conceive the entire voyage. For each island can tell you how to understand or interpret the voyage itself, each risks, with various levels of success, framing and relativizing the rest. Multiple *mises en abyme* of the archipelago are thus possible, like a Borges novel where each island in the archipelago contains the archipelago in which it is found: one's voyage on the archipelago might thus resemble a multi-formed aesthetic experience, a movement from one libidinal intensity to the next, an exploration of different language formations or genres, or else, having spent too much time on the island of Capital, where one is taught to package and capitalize upon difference and desire, a voyage in the service of some intellectual tourism. Each island would thus tell you how to think not only other islands but the cruise ship itself, which is never a neutral place, but a vehicle that always frames and programs the whole in advance, bringing along its own food, entertainment, and narratives about what is to be seen, done, bought, and felt on each island.

I too will have thus ceded to this temptation, not to say it all—I had no pretensions to that—but at least to give some idea of the extraordinary scope of what I'm calling Lyotard's archipelago, or rather, more than a year after the event, the time for a possessive genitive to be subsumed, the "Lyotard archipelago." I know, of course, that so much escapes me, not only islands, as I said, where I feel my incompetence, where I do not speak the language, but phrases I could never hear: phrases of desire, of hesitation, anxiety, irritation, and pain. Unpublished, unpublic phrases. And I know that what escapes me in reading the published works of

Jean-François Lyotard is, precisely, his human condition, which is to say, I think, his inhuman condition, his animality, all the places where his understanding failed him, where he was not himself but was scared or foolish, horrified or silly, in a word, *bête*—yes, in the end, it is his *bêtise*, all of his *bêtise*, that escapes me.

Cruising from one island to the next, knowing what we are, where we come from, and where we are going, what we would risk forgetting in this intellectual tourism would be precisely the passages between islands, as we end up understanding not just the other islands but the passages between them on the basis of one of the islands visited. What we would end up understanding, and thus forgetting, would be forgetting itself, the *lethe* or oblivion between one regimen or phrase and the next, so easily forgotten in the interest of some genre, with its stakes and claims over the *"Arrive-t-il?"* of language, over its event. In the end, Lyotard was interested less in the islands themselves than in the passages between them, the heterogeneity between and within them. Indeed, were we to look at the whole corpus from above, to try to summarize and encapsulate a corpus this diverse and heterogeneous, one would surely have to begin with a thought of diversity or heterogeneity itself. Heterogeneity is what would have remained the same from the very beginning of Lyotard's work right up to the very end. And that is precisely what we risk forgetting when we try to represent and see it all, and so protect ourselves from what is heterogeneous, unseen and threatening, in the frame, what affects us or wounds us or perhaps even interrogates us before we even are what we assume ourselves to be, there where, as we will see, we are an "I" without a self, an "I" without "me."

In every subject he took on, in all these heterogeneous projects, Lyotard was interested in what resists within them and in the dangers of resisting and thus concealing this heterogeneity and this resistance. Whether it was in an analysis of capital where the rule of money reduces everything to a single value and threatens to overtake imagination itself, or the grand narrative (for example, the modern narrative of emancipation) that attempts to co-opt and engulf micrologies and small narratives (all that resists in the name of the pagan), or the reduction of all work to the single criterion of efficiency or optimal performance (a reduction that risks silencing philosophy itself), or the contemporary development of development that threatens the arrival of the event itself, or the sovereignty of representation that threatens to stifle the voice or eclipse the space of the unrepresentable, or the meaning of a discourse or painting that threatens to overcome the opacity of its matter, tissue, or figure (its material support), or a form of memory that risks forgetting, or the control and channeling of desires in their pulsional state through certain apparatuses, libidinal genres, if you will, that put these pulsions in the service of more comprehensible, representative ends or ideologies, or the critique of Marxist ideology that risks co-opting or subsuming more local politics or strategies, or the comprehension and reduction of all that resists the subject or the community in the name of, say, the "jew," the sublime, the remainder, the intractable, the thing, or sexual difference, or else in the differend between genres where a rule of judgment coming from one party does some wrong to the other, Lyotard is interested, always and everywhere, in what is heterogeneous to the subject, to representation, to the state, to meaning and to narrative, to what tends to get factored out, factored out precisely because it is factored in, that is, into some economy, whether political, libidinal, or some other economy. In each case, Lyotard not only spoke—indeed, still speaks—for the other side, for the oppressed, but for a way of speaking that is heterogeneous to the master discourse and not simply opposed to its position. To various forms of mastery, whether of capital, technology, power, or representation, Lyotard speaks for what resists and for ways of speaking that resist within the system, that resist but make it work, give it energy, intensity. Lyotard thus bears witness to what does not and cannot have an ear within the system, or to what can only have an ear but cannot be represented by the eye. Force, affirmation, repetition, intensity irreducible to profit and efficiency—these are what resist, and Lyotard tries everywhere and at all times to identify and then maximize the possibilities of such resistance. This is Lyotard's politics, his definition of the political: to maximize and multiply intensities, to release possibilities, to lend an ear to voices outside the genre, or, as he once put it in an essay on the different styles of European and American philosophy, to "keep watch over our archipelago."[3]

Attentive always not only to the themes of genre and style *in* texts but to the genre and style, voice and time, *of* texts, Lyotard's work forces us always and everywhere to pay attention to the style and genre of his texts, that is, to the generic differences between islands.[4] It forces us to pay attention to different modes of address, to the inclusion or exclusion of the reader as explicit addressee, to *vouvoiement* and *tutoiement*, to voices masculine and feminine, and to differing genres, dissertative, philosophical, polemical, pedagogical, and so on, so that even at the level of style Lyotard's writing is heterogeneous, a corpus held together, unlike Orpheus's rent body, not by an organic relation between parts, but, as I have suggested, precisely by a shared heterogeneity, by the differences—irresolvable differences, differends—between the styles and stakes, the genres.

And yet across genres, we could say, there was always a signature, an "I" countersigned in various ways. An economic, condensed, sometimes elliptical style, where one is never quite sure where the accent lies, whether to discern amusement or irony. A style charged with affects without affection, intense without ever being earnest or self-important, sharp and incisive but always playful. Wise and knowing and wise in knowing that neither he nor we really know; serious because the issues are serious but never self-serious. A style that conveys a sort of wisdom, even if, even when, he would later think he was simply recounting *des bêtises*. Wise in the moment, wise about the moment, wise in knowing that it was necessary to respond and yet experienced enough to know that there is no last word, that there will always be other phrases to follow.

Because of the extraordinary heterogeneity of both his corpus and his style, the fear—my fear—is that islands in this archipelago, that the entire archipelago, comes over time to be forgotten, that the Lyotard archipelago comes to be less and less frequented, the works of Jean-François Lyotard less and less read. And so we must, I believe, in spite of the dangers, make some links, draw some connections, compare heterogeneities, group resistances, remember and recollect various forgettings. To save this thought, we must remember its forgetting, remember all that Lyotard has taught us about forgetting, about heterogeneity, and resistance—in other words, about the human-inhuman condition. I would thus like to visit here that island of forgetting, heterogeneity, and resistance, that is *Signed, Malraux*,[5] that *Chambre sourde*,[6] if you will, that soundproof chamber or room, where we hear nothing but the cries or stridence of our own voices, a cry in our throats, an island isolated from the rest and yet containing them all, an "archipelago of death," to use Malraux's phrase from *Lazarus*.[7] I turn to Lyotard's last texts on Malraux not simply because they have been less well explored than others, because they came near the end, so close to his death, but because they speak so powerfully, perhaps like no others, of our human-inhuman condition, and of the heterogeneity, forgetting, and resistance in the entire archipelago. These two books, particularly *Chambre sourde*, into which I will enter momentarily and from which I will be unable to escape (and if you hear me screaming to get out it will not be with your ears but only with your throats, which will mean that you are in there with me), these two remarkable books, among the *eschata* of the archipelago, are, in their very emphasis on forgetting, heterogeneity, and resistance, works of an unexpected fellowship and communion.

So as not to forget the passage I would thus suggest not flying or cruising there but swimming, together, like friends, in the direction of Malraux and *The Human Condition*, and so in the direction of China, doing the crawl like Mao, whom Lyotard describes swimming across the Yangtze River in his essay "Several Silences."[8] Swimming, then, doing the crawl, like Mao alone or with a friend, so that there is "not domination" of the body, "but metamorphosis," "not mastery of the body, but dissolution into workings." An "I-without-me," body parts on the beach, as bodies part on the beach, at least for a time, allowing for contrast and comparison. . . .

For example, Lyotard and Malraux. The philosopher, professor, and itinerant sophist on the one hand, the adventurer, aviator, government minister, and novelist on the other. Apart from a common lineage in Nietzsche, nothing would immediately suggest their conjunction, nothing would seem to overcome their heterogeneity—nothing but, as we will see, a common resistance and heterogeneity. Both were thinkers, both were men, of resistance, of resistances, and both were thinkers of heterogeneity, and of heterogeneous subjects—philosophy, politics, art, literature, and the differences between East and West. In *Tomb of the Intellectual*, Lyotard himself speaks of Malraux precisely in terms of heterogeneity, citing him in fact as his lone example: "Although the same person can indeed fill two or three functions—indeed, cases of this have been observed (Malraux, for example)—these functions are not any less heterogeneous to each other in all their aspects."[9]

Not unexpectedly, Lyotard enters *Chambre sourde*, this book of 1998 that bears the subtitle *Malraux's Anti-Aesthetics* to echo Malraux's own *Antimémoires*, with the questions of time, narrative, and voice, questions that have been at the center of his thought for decades: "It's been a century now, as history counts it, that Nietzsche's anti-voice pronounced the funeral oration of modernity" (*CS*, 19). In the wake of this oration, writing has gone on, not as usual, certainly, but as testimony to the end of modernity, and the names Céline, Bataille, Artaud, and Camus are cited as exemplary figures of this writing. To this list, Lyotard announces, he would like to add the name of Malraux, who, despite his penchant for adventure, his flamboyant public persona, is just as much plunged in "ontological nausea," in the "experience of a body and soul exposed to abjection," as these others (*CS*, 20). Opposed to the linear narratives of modernity, Malraux would be a witness to the cyclical degeneration and regeneration or what I would call the "eternal replay" [*la redite*] of all things—plants, insects, animals, and humans—a witness to what Malraux calls the "unknown power" (*CS*, 23) beneath all things, insect larvae as well as human beings, stars as well as civilizations.

From the very beginning, Lyotard claims, Malraux tracks, or lets himself be tracked by, this unknown power. In both his work and his life, which are, in the end, impossible to distinguish, Malraux gives himself over to this inhuman condition seething beneath the human. Beneath the political critique of fascism, Nazism, and eventually Stalinism, beneath all ideologies, all human intelligence, there are animals, from scorpions to mad cows, termites to panthers, innumerable beasts, in other words, "que des bêtes, que des bêtises." Though humans may communicate and transmit their concepts and techniques for a few centuries, "man is a chance occurrence," for Malraux, and "the world is essentially made up of forgetting" (*CS*, 29). What is required, then, is a "penetrating lucidity" with regard to this forgetting, which, in the modernization of the Orient, risks being forgotten in the Orient as well as the Occident. In Malraux, Lyotard finds this lucidity, this non-forgetting—which is not the same as a memory—of this forgetting, a listening to the inaudible, a witnessing on behalf of the forgotten voice, all forgotten voices, including the ones that the final solution would have wished to silence (*CS*, 36–37).

After summarizing in a few pages many of his speculations concerning narrative and voice in modernity and postmodernity, Lyotard turns to the question of narrating a life—writing a biography, his own *Signed, Malraux*, for example, being implicitly put into question, or an autobiography, Lyotard thinking here no doubt of Malraux's comments on this very impossibility in the *Antimémoires*.[10] Both biography and autobiography usually have to assume some form of unchanging identity, some identifiable subject; but what exactly is this subject, this identity, when the "*bios*, lacking any finality, is but the deceptive moment of a death more complete than death: cosmic death" (*CS*, 44)?

Beneath life and death there would be only immortal, cosmic death—of which we can gain only a glimpse. And yet, without hope or glory, without the modern narrative to subsume death into some greater story or meaning, something, for Malraux, still resists the nothing, without aim or project something resists, a mere "feeling of existing," as he calls it, a feeling that is not to be confused with "self-consciousness," "an instantaneous existence and not a life that lends itself to biography" (*CS*, 46–47). As Malraux writes in *Lazarus* and as Lyotard recalls—Lyotard, who undertook to write a biography of Malraux—"It is the narrative illusion, the biographical work, that creates the life story. . . . One has no biography except for others" (*L*, 74).[11] As Lyotard spins it, "The spider has its nest within the me" (*CS*, 44), and "the autobiography of the spider is unthinkable. It says I but has no identity" (*CS*, 51).

Having quickly situated Malraux in his time, having raised the question of writing, of writing for Malraux and of Malraux, dispensing for the most part with the facts and figures, the life and times, the works and days of André Malraux, a task fulfilled, though in Lyotard's inimitable way, in the hypobiography *Signed, Malraux*, Lyotard in *Chambre sourde* wastes little time in heading straight for the inner chamber, a chamber within a chamber, a soundproof, secret room, isolated from all others, a larva cell with neither doors nor directions but, as we will see, in communication or communion with others through writing, through an exemplary text of 1973 called *Lazarus*. Lyotard recalls that Malraux wrote this little book from within the chamber, cell, or tomb that was his hospital room at the Salpêtrière. Stricken with a nearly fatal disease of the nervous system, oscillating between life and death, in and out of a coma and stricken with vertigo, Malraux finds himself out of bed one night wandering around in the dark on all fours in his room, crawling back and forth, up and down, walls indistinguishable from the floor, "cut off," as he says—amputated—"from the earth," "a life without an identity" (*L*, 84). Prize-winning novelist, war hero, government minister, all that is undone in this silent, darkened chamber where Malraux encounters an "'I' without a self," not dissolution into nothingness but, he speculates, "an animal consciousness?" (*L*, 84). Wandering through what he calls the "archipelago of death," which "disregards any sequence of events, lays bare only the most inchoate and most intense consciousness, the convulsive 'I am'" (*L*, 79), Malraux experiences a consciousness "passionately determined to exist, simply to exist" (*L*, 85), a resistance to nothingness. And Lyotard notes, "The point of this resistance, infinitesimal, intense, is called the *je-sans-moi*, the I-without-self or the I-without-me" (*CS*, 48).

At the center of *Chambre sourde*, then, there is the "I-without-me" of—let's call it for the moment—Malraux, though it resists all identification and appropriation. At the center of one of his very last books in the archipelago, there is Malraux wandering in the archipelago of death, crawling on all fours, struggling, resisting like an animal, seized by a horror without object, by "a sacred horror [that] inhabits us" (*CS*, 49; *L*, 92). With God dead and the self, the "me," moribund, what remains, Lyotard writes, "is the animality that 'I' am, that the me knew nothing about and would be horrified by," the "vermin [that] resists in the me," and says "'I' with a voice that no one is any longer around to hear" (*CS*, 50–51).

This I, this vermin, is a "monster without interlocutors" (*CS*, 51), a monster of the absolute, or, as Kyo calls it in *La condition humaine*, which I would prefer to translate here not as *Man's Fate* but as *The Human Condition*, an "incomparable monster."[12] This monster is the "I-without-me," a phrase from *Lazarus* that Lyotard will not cease to meditate upon in *Chambre sourde*. The "I-without-me": resistance and that which is resisted. While "the me bears a proper name, is located in a dated time, in particular places, participates in activities, in the commerce of phrases, in the community of humans" (*CS*, 53), the "I" resists all identity, discourse, and community; it cries out but encounters nothing to recognize, reflect, or respond to it.

Between the "I" and the "me" there is, in a sense, a differend, a differend between the senses. An emblem, a key to this differend—yet another chamber recalled by Malraux in his hospital room at the Salpêtrière and explored by Lyotard in *Chambre sourde*—is the scene near the beginning of *The Human Condition* where Kyo hears and scarcely recognizes his own disembodied voice on a phonograph. Though every scene of Malraux's novels, Lyotard says, bears witness to "a single convulsion: the agonizing subject, the monster that resists in it" (*CS*, 65), this scene is clearly exemplary for both Malraux and Lyotard, for it later gets replayed in both, after having obsessed *The Human Condition* from one end to the other.[13]

Man's Fate, The Human Condition, is haunted from beginning to end by the inhuman. The inhuman seethes beneath the novel, from its famous opening scene where Ch'en murders a weapons dealer lying in bed beneath mosquito netting—a man inside his larva, so to speak, with the world of insects, animals, and humans that is Shanghai teeming below—all the way to the darkened prison cell where Kyo, Katov, and the other revolutionaries await their execution at the hands of Chiang Kai-shek.[14] But the scene with Kyo is, as Lyotard tells us, the shibboleth of the story, and, I would say, of the differend between "I" and "me." Kyo and his comrades are gathered near the beginning of the novel in a store that sells phonograph records for language instruction, records that are now being used by Kyo and friends to pass secret messages to different parts of China. When Kyo hears his own voice played back on the record, he experiences a surprise and incredulity that is today rather commonplace but surely was not in the 1920s. Kyo's father Gisors later explains the principle of this alienation of the voice:[15] "It's undoubtedly a question of means," says Gisors, "we hear the voices of others with our ears" and "our own . . . with our throats" (*MF*, 43). This is the key to Kyo's anxiety, the shibboleth: a question of voice, of a secret that must pass by way of the body, one particular body, one particular throat. A question of means, says Gisors—a differend of the senses, between hearing oneself (in the throat) and hearing others (through the ears), between a "me" for others and an absolute "I." Between the "I" without voice, perhaps even without question, and the question "Is that really me?" no synthesis, no biography is possible without forgetting the "I" without voice. "Once inscribed in the common register of the audible," Lyotard explains in *Chambre sourde*, "the singular stridence is stifled, its exception neutralized, and the first and true alienation that places the voice out of the range of the audible is itself abolished" (*CS*, 92). Unable to be both addressor and addressee in the same phrase, one cannot hear oneself as oneself but only as another. The I-without-me is thus perhaps a way of speaking of a "me" who has been interrupted in my capacity to take up the position of addressor, to speak and have a voice that would penetrate the soundproof box of my thorax, to participate in a conversation or dialogue with myself and others. A differend between the senses or, indeed, between what can be sensed and what can only be felt. For there is an abyss between the voice heard by the ear and the stridence of the throat, between the "me" and the "I-without-me" (*CS*, 96–97). Although we might want to convert this pair into an internal dialogue between the self and itself, what passes by the throat is not an object of perception and so cannot be recorded. Stridence, vibration, and resonance are incommensurable with speech, perhaps even with voice. Lyotard thus speaks of a "stridence that awakens the latent horror slumbering within hearing" (*CS*, 86), a "strident cry that calls for the sacrifice of the ego" (*CS*, 88), a voice from elsewhere that resides as close as possible to us, in the depths of the body, deep within the throat. "After the great modern voices," writes Lyotard, "the voiceless monster: to exist. . . . With the me in agony, an anonymous I touches for an instant the changeless night" (*CS*, 99).

Kyo is haunted, tormented, by this memory of the phonograph and by his father's explanation of it. He wonders what he in fact is when he hears his own voice, when he hears his own life, with his throat. He concludes, "A kind of absolute, the affirmation of an idiot: an intensity greater than that of all the rest. To others, I am what I have done" (*MF*, 53–54). Here is the difference between the "I" and the self, the "I" and the "me." To and for others, the "I" is always reduced to the "me," to what it has done, to a voice that could be recorded and made public on a phonograph. The only exception to this rule can be found in love, where the other has a glimpse of the "I," apart from the self, a sense of the "I"'s solitude apart from its public, phenomenal life. Only with his wife, May, then, does Kyo share this solitude, this engorged isolation. "To May alone, he was not what he had done; to him alone, she was something altogether different from her biography. The embrace by which love holds beings together against solitude did not bring its relief to man; it brought relief only to the madman, to the incomparable monster . . . that every being is to himself" (*MF*, 54). So that this thought does not dissolve into some ideal of romantic bliss, Malraux is quick to specify that this feeling between Kyo and May was not happiness but "something primitive which was at one with the darkness," "the only thing in him that was as strong as death" (*MF*, 54). The only thing as strong as death for Kyo is thus not some vision of immortal glory, some ideal for which to die, but a shared inhumanity, a shared experience of the incomparable beast—our human condition. There are thus two kinds of inhumanity: one that seeks to escape the human condition through ideology, sacrifices to a cause, narcissism, and so on, and one that seeks to share in the primitive night this human-all-too-inhuman condition. Lyotard writes in *The Inhuman*:

> There would be then two kinds of inhuman, and it is necessary to keep them apart. The inhumanity of the system in the process of consolidation, which goes by the name (among others) of development, must not be confused with the other, infinitely secret inhumanity to which the soul is hostage.[16]

An archipelago within an archipelago, or rather, a *mise en abyme* of the archipelago, *The Human Condition* explores the various possibilities of escaping or confronting the inhuman within us, the inhuman that is our human condition; it distributes all the roles for Malraux, and perhaps for

Lyotard, already in 1933: Ch'en, the revolutionary who seeks to transform terrorism into a mystical union with the self through the attempted assassination of Chiang Kai-shek (see *MF*, 155); Ferral, capable not of love, but only of an eroticism that brings him together with himself (see *MF*, 242); Gisors, the father of Kyo, a wise old opium smoker, aesthete, and teacher of Marxism; and Kyo, whose fight for the workers, for "Pouvoir Ouvrier," we might be tempted to say, will eventually lead to his death, and whose love for May provokes a veritable "catastrophe"—Lyotard's word—in the novel. It comes when May tells Kyo—or Kyo-Malraux, as Lyotard calls him, because the figure of Kyo is in a sense that of Malraux—that she has slept with a colleague at the hospital. At this point something changes in their relation, and May becomes an other for Kyo (see *MF*, 207); she becomes alienated from him not simply because of her marital infidelity, but because "her throat comes suddenly undone from his. Breaking their absolute and up until that moment shared separation" (*CS*, 94). The only thing that will move Kyo back toward May will be the "death mask" she puts on before him, and then a look as "poignant as pain in animals," an "inhuman" mask (*MF*, 210) that leads to a "fellowship of death" and a "communion" (*MF*, 213). As Gisors later explains, such communion is not a knowledge, which is always a "negative feeling," but "the positive feeling, the reality . . . the torment of being always a stranger to what one loves" (*MF*, 235; see also *MF*, 82, 235–36).

A novel about politics and aesthetics, love and philosophy, and resistance: one is not surprised to find Lyotard attracted like a moth to *The Human Condition*—and to the "I-without-me," the hidden voice box within the self, within Malraux within the Salpêtrière, within that chamber called *Lazarus*, which opens out, in its very isolation and separation, to others in fraternity, in communion. For in addition to love, there is, in the works of Malraux, an escape from absolute solitude through *fraternité* as brotherhood or fellowship. As *The Human Condition* draws to a close, little seems to escape the desperate, terrifying, seemingly meaningless vision of man alone before the inhuman, either ruined by inhuman ideology or else abandoned to the inhuman cry. In the darkness of prison, Kyo hears as he awaits his execution only the voices of his fellow prisoners, "voices so close to death" (*MF*, 295), "obscure beings . . . like colossal insects" (*MF*, 296; see also *MF*, 319). The workers' insurrection led by Kyo and Katov has been crushed by the troops of Chiang Kai-shek, its leaders condemned to the gruesome fate of being burned alive in the engine of a locomotive—itself an enormous, inhuman insect that burns without remainder, leaving no trace, no glory, no resurrection, no triumph of the will. Awaiting their execution, Kyo and Katov experience a "dread," "not fear, but terror, that of beasts, of men who are alone before the inhuman" (*MF*, 312). With no hope of being saved (see *MF*, 318), and little hope of their deaths being redeemed by some larger cause, Katov and Kyo are joined "by that absolute friendship, without reticence, which death alone gives" (*MF*, 315).

As the executioners come to burn the prisoners one by one, Kyo takes possession of himself by committing suicide, swallowing the cyanide capsule he, like the other leaders of the insurrection, carried on his person. He commits suicide as a final act of self-affirmation, or rather, of affirmation of the "I" without self, without "me," without hope, glory, or resurrection. Alone in the dark, faced with only the inhuman dread of torture and flame, Katov thinks of doing likewise when two comrades are brought in to await their execution beside him. Both younger than he, they sob uncontrollably as they think of what will happen to their flesh when they are burned in the furnace of the train. Katov thinks to himself, "A man could be stronger than this solitude," and so he makes a "gift of something that was more precious than his life not even to bodies, not even to voices, but to the warm hand resting upon him." Reaching out not to comrades of the insurrection, not even to voices in the dark beside him, but to the warm hand that touches his own, he makes the gift of his own cyanide, which he breaks in two, like a host, in communion (*MF*, 322). Eschewing the recompense of glory and even of recognition or gratitude, all he asks for in return is a chance to press that warm hand for an instant in fellowship, in "that pitiful fraternity, without a face," of the inhuman (*MF*, 323).

This is the fellowship of the human condition—the inhuman-human condition that we seek to flee, says Kyo's father, through different forms of intoxication, through opium or hashish in the East, in the West through love, and through trying "to be more than a man, in a world of men," through dreaming to become a god (*MF*, 239). Gisors reflects, "It is very rare for a man to be able to endure—how shall I say it?—his condition as a man" (*MF*, 238).

Could it have been this condition, this fraternity or fellowship, that Lyotard found or at least sought in these final books on Malraux, an "absolute friendship . . . which death alone gives"? All we can say is, perhaps. Any comparison between Lyotard and Malraux is fraught with peril, for we risk concealing the absolute singularity of one or the other. And any speculation about what Lyotard thought or felt, apart from what he has left us in the written record, is even more perilous. All we can say is that Lyotard during the last years of his life wrote two books on André Malraux, and one of them not only heads straight for the scene of the phonograph in *The Human Condition*, but follows, it would seem, the trajectory of this novel. With such early chapter titles as "Lost Voice" and "Me Moribund," *Chambre sourde* follows the fate of this incomparable monster called the human right up to a final chapter entitled "Communion." Moreover, Lyotard follows this trajectory not simply through Malraux's novel of 1933, but through Malraux's ruminations about it some forty years later, as he slips in and out of consciousness in the Salpêtrière hospital. In his extraordinary work entitled *Lazarus*, which seeks, according to its author, "the crucial region of the soul where absolute Evil is pitted against fraternity" (*L*, 4), Malraux recalls the scene of the phonograph, though he can no longer recall to whom it occurs, unable, as it were, to recognize his own voice (*L*, 140–41), and he evokes the sharing of the cyanide, what he calls "the most striking instance of fraternity I know," though he wrongly recalls Katov giving it to Kyo and not to the two other, lesser-known comrades (*L*, 119)—as if death and oblivion were coming to sever Malraux from his own work, to swallow him up in forgetting, to fuse and confuse memory and fiction.[17] Indeed, when Malraux was arrested by the Nazis in 1940 and put into a prisoner of war camp, he himself, as a member of the Resistance, was carrying a cyanide capsule, so the scene of the Shanghai prison from *The Human Condition* would seem to him a sort of premonition of his own fate (*L*, 119). In 1973, close to death, Malraux recalls this premonition of 1940 about the novel he had written some years earlier. And Lyotard begins with these recollections and premonitions, which start to expand by a powerful metonymy to embrace the evil of the entire century, an apocalyptic vision of all the horrific deaths of the twentieth century and of all the possibilities for fellowship within it.

For what does Malraux do in his hospital bed in 1973 apart from noting his own experience of being an "I-without-me," an incomparable monster close to death? He begins to rework a manuscript begun in 1940 in the prison camp, most of which was destroyed by the Nazis and never published. This novel, *The Walnut Trees of Altenburg*, recounts the gruesome details of the first poison gas attack by German troops on the Russians in 1916 near the town of Bolgako on the Vistula River, and the fellowship, the genuine fellowship, that grew out of that attack. It begins in

1940 with a conversation among French prisoners but then flashes back to the beginning of World War I so as to follow the German Major Berger up until the time of the gas attack of 1916. Again, rooms within rooms, an archipelago of memory, chambers connected to chambers through torture and suffering.

With this first poison gas attack "Satan reappears in the world" (*L*, 5), says Malraux, "the slavering demibeast [*demi-bête*]" that "emulated the defiant gesture of Prometheus" (*L*, 6). And yet along with the beastly inhuman comes fellowship, as Major Berger (Berger being Malraux's name during the Resistance, a name that, Malraux says, sounds good in both German and French) and the other Germans discover—and then themselves begin to feel—the incomprehensibly abominable effects of the poison gas they have just released, an inhuman weapon that brings out the inhuman best within the human beast. With the battlefield reduced to a field of struggling, burning larvae, to an inhuman horror, the boundaries between friend and enemy are dissolved, and a fraternity without equality and without liberty is born, a fraternity more profound, more inaudible, than that founded on any ideology. Malraux writes in *The Walnut Trees of Altenburg*, to which he returns in *Lazarus*: "The Spirit of Evil was even stronger here than death, so powerful that Berger felt compelled to find a Russian, any Russian who had not been killed, hoist him onto his shoulders, and save him" (*L*, 41). It was "this fraternal corpse which protected him against all that he was running away from" (*L*, 42), moved not so much by pity as by "a more obscure impulse, in which anguish and fraternity were coupled in the same frenzy" (*L*, 48). This is not fraternity as we normally conceive it; it suggests not a community, as Lyotard sees, but, anterior to all individuation, a "heteroplastic grafting of throat onto throat" (*CS*, 102).

What interests Malraux is not, he says, simply the struggle of Berger, but "the ageless voice of humankind, the primeval voice of the German soldiers in the trench, of the French prisoner in the camp" (*L*, 6), the voice "of the only species that knows—however dimly—that it can die" (*L*, 22).[18] *Mise en abyme* of the archipelago: Lyotard, ailing, or at least having been diagnosed with leukemia, writing in the mid to late 1990s about Malraux in the Salpêtrière hospital in Paris, taking up as one of his very last works one of his very first, an account of the Germans' first use of poison gas in 1916 and the possibility of bearing witness to this event. Malraux writes: "The Germans of Bolgako . . . were *witnesses*. . . . witnesses—of what?—before the vast indifference of the trees" (*L*, 137–38). "Phrases in dispute," we might be tempted to say.

Malraux's *Lazarus* goes back and forth between his reflections on death in the 1970s, his experiences and thoughts of World War II, the concentration camps, and the narrative of Altenburg, where German soldiers near the beginning of this horrific century discovered that the only thing that allowed them to survive after the gassing of the Russian troops was a feeling of "fraternity." From the death rattle he hears in the room next to his in the Salpêtrière, to the sounds of the Russian and German poison gas victims of 1916, to the voices of French prisoners in 1940, to the victims of the Nazi concentration camps, to the "blurred, twitching figures in the photographs of Hiroshima" (*L*, 93), Malraux in 1973 replays a short history of death in the twentieth century.[19] "Haunted by the struggle against the poison gas" (*L*, 93), "by the Russians and the Germans in the Vistula forest, by the word *convulsive*" (*L*, 136), obsessed, he says, by torture (*L*, 128), Malraux attempts to discover a fundamental human voice. "Ever since *Altenburg*—more than thirty years ago—I have been preoccupied with the thought of fundamental man. Man identical with himself from the earliest civilizations" (*L*, 137). What he finds is not some new foundation for man, not some new humanism, but a multiple voice: "Man," he writes, "is the voices of the French prisoners in the camp, the voices of the German soldiers in the trench" (*L*, 75).

Rooms within rooms, Chinese boxes, voice boxes buried within voice boxes, hospital chambers and gas chambers, stifled cries, *la chambre sourde* within *la chambre claire*.[20] If *Lazarus* countersigns *The Human Condition*, as Lyotard contends, then *Chambre sourde* countersigns both. But the "me" only countersigns what the "I" signs; for while the "me," the self, takes sides, goes to war, says yes or no, fixes friends and enemies, the "I" writes, allowing fellowship and a fraternity of the throat that opposes not a common enemy but the very taking sides between enemies, of saying yes or no. Which is why Malraux's writing must be recovered—and this is precisely what Lyotard has done—from those who would see it only as a sort of wartime journalism or an attempt at the historical novel. Malraux writes in *Lazarus*:

> I had written that each of us hears the sound of his *life* through his throat, and that of others through his ears, except in fraternity or love. The book was called *The Human Condition*. Since then I have had much experience with death. (*L*, 141)

Again, a question of means, and in fraternity there would be a sort of reversal of the means. We hear the voices of others—of the other, perhaps—with our throat, and our own, our own as another, our "I" as a "me," with the ears. In ethics, in the ethical phrase regimen, we are addressees of the Other and never addressors; gripped, penetrated by the Other, held hostage and terrified by the Other, who cries out with and within our throat, before we are able either to hear or to speak in other phrase regimens, before the return of a cognitive self. "Like the sacred," Malraux writes, fellowship "escapes us if we strip it of its primitive, irrational element. As mysterious as love, and as divorced from right-mindedness or duty; like love—and unlike liberty—it is a provisional sentiment, a state of grace" (*L*, 117). Enigmatically related to death, says Malraux, this fellowship, this "communion is often as powerful as death itself" (*L*, 136). In this communion lovers or comrades do not, says Lyotard, form one voice from two, for "the only companion of separated, wretched, injured beings is the inhuman" (*CS*, 67). With the promise of neither survival nor redemption (*L*, 96), the only thing to resist in the face of this inhuman is sacrifice, the sacrifice of Katov (*L*, 95, 144), and, for Malraux, the work, the work of art that vibrates, that punctuates its medium with the "I-without-me," the "I" that resists and writes like a stylus, that tries to invent a style to capture an unheard stridence, a "work of art [that] puts into communion absolute solitudes, with one another and with the stridulation of the cosmos" (*CS*, 111). Only in a work of art are we able to make heard the "silent experience of the I-without-me without violating its silence" (*CS*, 54). The work of art, which ultimately means nothing, represents or expresses nothing, least of all the subjectivity of its "author," in the end undoes the me, undoes the human, "coming from nothing and going to nothing" (*CS*, 63).

Why there are works at all is, we could say, a mystery, as mysterious as why there are phrases—and yet it is a fact (*CS*, 69), a poetics of ellipsis, for Malraux, that is supported by an "ontology of the nothing" (*CS*, 72), an " 'agnostic' mystery, desperately nihilistic, with neither Dionysus nor the Crucified," wherein "the eventual perpetuity of works can be understood" (*CS*, 95). Lyotard writes in "Communion," the final chapter of *Chambre sourde*, "the gods can die, and humanism as well; anxiety is immortal. No matter what figure it takes on in the course of the ages, it will no doubt, one day, somewhere, be shared. 'Heard,' by the throat" (*CS*, 104). Yes, somewhere in the archipelago, between islands, within every island, as we crawl rather than fly or sail between them, on all fours, an archipelago no longer of identifiable islands with names and themes but a labyrinth of soundproof boxes, linked to others only by the throat, a passage through which we crawl toward one another, hearing only a larval existence, the echo of others in our cells, no man an island but an I-without-me in the Gulag archipelago.

To have spent so much time on the island of Malraux in the Lyotard archipelago may appear, I realize, to be the worst betrayal of both thinkers' singularity. But what is their singularity, according to one and the other, but an "I-without-me," a singular resistance that writes without a proper name, indistinguishable, then, or repeated and distinguished only by an inarticulate sound, by larval phrases, larva phases that follow one another like the generations to pass through the Salpêtrière. "Here," writes Malraux, "the sick succeed one another like generations upon the earth. But generations do not recover" (*L*, 60; see also 83).

Whatever Lyotard's reasons for turning to Malraux, accidental, professional or, as I suspect, more personal, the fact is that he spent much of his last few years of life thinking about the life of Malraux, and years that he surely knew to be limited in thinking about Malraux on life, on the possibility of narrating that life in a biography, and about Malraux on death and death's relation to fellowship. Not just one book on Malraux but two, one, we could say, on the "me" of Malraux, on the self insofar as it lends itself to biography, and one on the "I-without-me," a book that does not totally neglect the biographical facts of Malraux's life but looks with a penetrating and sober lucidity at what we could call Malraux's "posthuman condition," his "inhuman condition." Although the autobiography of the spider is impossible, its "I-without-me" can perhaps be spun through the biographical web of another.

Chambre sourde attests like no other book of Lyotard to this fellowship—a human fellowship of the inhuman. Like Malraux's *The Human Condition*, like *Lazarus*, linked to them, it seems, in an archipelago of death and resistance, it speaks of heterogeneity or, better, it speaks heterogeneity itself. It lets the inaudible voice be heard, lets it resonate not in the ears but in the throat, that is, not on one island or another of the archipelago, not in some particular phrase universe, regimen, or genre, but in the place of the phrase's event, the place of its arrival, where its stridence has yet to be situated, stabilized, or explained by some phrase of explanation, justification, or even mourning, where its cry bears witness to nothing other than the absolute singularity—even before proper names—of a passage.[21]

Childish Things

Geoffrey Bennington

("Childish Things": not only that I will talk *about* childish things in Lyotard, taking that as a theme for my supposedly mature or adult gaze; but also that *what I say* will not escape being childish, shot through with all the uncomfortable naiveté and violence of a child coming to what Lyotard calls "a great uncertainty" about childhood,[1] and therefore about adulthood, paternity, the place of the father, the dead father, the father as always already dead, before the surviving child. These childish things are also, then, an autobiography, a confession.)

Whatever became of Jean-François Lyotard?

Lyotard goes on—before.

Before: i.e., what precedes in time, with respect to a given reference point, some "now" point, be it current or not. "Before" is said, in a current sentence, of a time prior to that current sentence; or is said, in a current sentence, of a time positioned as prior to a given reference time, itself positioned by the current sentence as prior or subsequent to it. In the phenomenological analysis of time, around which Lyotard turns a good deal in the latter years of his life, and which seems to call from long ago the posthumously published work on Augustine, *before* makes sense only in correlation with *after*, the turnstile of *before* and *after* pivoting on the peg of the *now*, and the possible displacement of that *now* from the time of the current sentence, allowing narrative representations of all sorts.

Already in this current, all too current conception of time, *before* divides and takes its distances, because what precedes us in time is just as well behind us in the spatializing representation of time we could never manage without (and which is part of that conception of time, a last resort that is also no doubt its best, its first resource). Behind us, already past, so that we are in front of it, before it; we are before *before*, which has gone before us, got ahead of us, inciting us to run after it, catch it up, make up our delay, our belatedness, according to the most insistent motif in *La confession d'Augustin*. (And, I confess, how belated I had become in the last ten years with respect to Lyotard! Books I had scarcely read: *Lectures d'enfance* and *Moralités postmodernes* for a start; then the two books on Malraux, *Signé, Malraux* and *Chambre sourde*, whose existence I found so hard to motivate in terms of my previous understanding of his work; finally the posthumous *La confession d'Augustin*. I confess it here: indeed this essay is nothing but that confession, a necessarily belated attempt to catch up on that delay, and to understand something of this work since the late 1980s—and this confession involves, as I hope will become clear, measuring up to a complex thought of *childhood* that entails an irreducible *biographical* question which cannot avoid a certain troubling *sexual* element. I offer those three "themes" as a way of finding some orientation in a zone of thought where orientation itself may be the least available, and least appropriate gesture, and where a certain disorder is not to be avoided.) *Before* is a word for my belatedness or prematurity; *before*, gone before us, is still before us, yet to come. *Before* precedes me, I run on before, after before. And the one who went on before, forever before us now here today, by the cruel definition of death, Jean-François Lyotard, is still before us, here and now, still to come.

This paradox of *before* goes on to affect any temporal expression that refers more or less directly to it: for example, the concepts "younger" and "older," which are clearly dependent on before and after, are struck by the paradox of *before*. My age has with the age of the other a relationship that never stops flipping over: the elder is the one who was already there before me, when he was younger; as the younger, I arrive later than my elder, he and the world have aged, I bear the weight of this time past, I am already old, while he, the elder, and even the elder's elder, is as young as can be, from the world's infancy. It is always the elder who bears the youngest infancy. The first man would thus be *both* the youngest and the eldest. The elder—the father, if you wish, and that's always what one wishes—will always give lessons in childhood, readings in childhood, *Lectures d'enfance*, to the child, will explain childhood to the child, and that's why we do not really know what a child is—nor, for that very reason, what a father is. If, as Lyotard's biography of Malraux remarks, "the son makes himself the father's father,"[2] and therefore his own grandfather, according to a schema that is quite classical, do we not also have to read this formula in reverse?[3] If we think we can understand reasonably easily what a son does in trying to become the father, and even the father's father (even if the son becomes a father always too early, as Lyotard says of himself on the opening page of *Pérégrinations*, or too late, as he intimates later in that text, as we shall see), what about the father who becomes the son, or the son's son, his own grandson? Or who, perhaps more radically, claims to be younger than the son, without even being the son's son? What would a father be who was no longer his son's son?

> [The words] have retreated, helping each other out, already wounded in a war already over, in many wars. As many wars as texts. Wounded because they rarely die. They are in tatters, but the tatters of words are good. Like their childhood given back to them after they pretended to obey, to be grown up and go off to war. That's how you find them, already read and ordered by the warlords (writers, scribblers, translators), made illegible by defeat (for every text is a defeat), left to their own devices, hobbling along on crutches, gathering into groups of idle survivors, saving their skin. That's your famous baggage. Your past, the one that isn't yours, but, as it should be, older and other than you. The past that is neither your son nor your father. Who has nothing in particular to do with you.[4]

A past that can, then, still be read, today and in the future, after his death, older (and other) than he—and therefore always younger (and other) than he. The tatters of Lyotard's words, childhood and old age, birth and death of Lyotard, still before us, still here, us, gathered into an us as indebted survivors in mourning, readers who "read because we do not know how to read."[5] I would have liked to call this text "Lyotard's Childhood" in homage to his admirable youthfulness, which always seemed exemplary for me and, I imagine, all his more or less youthful friends and colleagues. The elder is, then, in a sense always younger than the younger—the younger, surviving witness, nonplussed to find himself growing older, finding himself later before the enigma of this turnaround or about-face, the younger one, trying here to hold back his tears and to behave like a grown-up, properly, and finding himself obliged in spite of himself to subtitle his text "My Childhood." This paradox of the older/younger is what allows Lyotard to write, at the beginning of what he calls his "hypobiography" of Malraux, that Malraux "was growing in childhood," at the end that he "grew old in childhood," and, a little later, "The child is old? So much the better," or, around a remark of Malraux's about Goya: " 'What genius does not save his childhood?' Well, the one who has not aged enough."[6]

What can be the relationship between childhood in the apparently transcendental sense of a radical *before*, and empirical or biological childhood? That "transcendental" childhood is the survival of biological childhood: in the sense both that it survives biological childhood, and that it is nothing other than biological childhood surviving or outliving itself. There are very many invocations and descriptions of childhood in Lyotard's writings from the mid-1980s onward (I was tempted to use the text on Kafka collected in *Lectures d'enfance* as simply "Prescription," but first delivered in 1989 under the title "Avant la loi," opening a complex space for debate with Derrida's 1982 text on Lyotard and Kafka, called "Devant la loi"[7]—the relationship between Lyotard and Derrida, which would, beyond the crossing points enumerated by Derrida at the beginning of that paper, more recently also go via Augustine and Paul, being to say the least a complex question which I shall not open here), but the clearest derivation of this sense of childhood is probably the one given in a text on Hannah Arendt, "Survivor," from which I will need to cite a long and dense passage:

> Now what is this event, stripped of its scientific or cognitive denomination? [Let me leave in suspense for now the referent of "this event" in the immediately preceding paragraph of the essay.] It is the enigma that there be a relation with what has no relation: that knowing that it is born and dies, the soul . . . testifies that there is not only *what is, what it is*, but also the other of what is. And this relation obviously does not happen when it happens, *it happens* and it *will* happen, then, all at once, it *will have happened*, appeared too late, disappeared too soon, because it is only and always recounted. My birth recounted by others, and my death that is told me by narratives of others' death, my narrative and those of others. So that, it being essential to this relation with nothingness (whence I come and where I am going) that it be itself recounted to me, the relation with *others* is also essential to the presence of absence, from whom it *returns* to me. And essential too the *fabula* that gives its rhythm to the pulsation of beginning and end.
>
> [There follows a development in which he argues that the ability to "form complexities," to "begin" would just as much be the sense of "survival" as the melancholy sense of the truth of nothingness alone—we are all dead children, as Christopher Fynsk might say, but what survives in this death *is* childhood.]
>
> Perhaps we must go to the bottom of nihilism with the last man, who knows the "banality of evil," who suffers or administers it, or both, in order to

discover a *joy*—I'm deliberately picking up this word from Pascal, the word of the spiritual—the somber joy of a demand that is all the stronger for being improbable, and therefore the more threatened by annihilation and the more openly affronting the truth of nothingness. [. . .] The spirit plunged in the trial of nihilism, in the passage to despair and skepticism (which is permanent), the spirit which knows that there is nothing to be done or said, no entity worth its name, or that even *is*, behaves as though it was *anyway*.

The effect of this clause is in no way cynicism. . . . Neither is its effect *ludism*. . . .

The effect is childhood, which knows all about *as if*, all about the pain due to impotence and the complaint of being too little, about being there late (compared to the others) and having arrived too early, prematurely (for its strength), who knows all about broken promises, bitter disappointments, failings, abandonment—but also daydreaming, memory, question, invention, obstinacy, listening with the heart, love, truly listening to stories. Childhood is the state of the soul inhabited by something to which no response is ever made, it is led in its enterprises by an arrogant fidelity to this unknown guest whose hostage it feels itself to be. Childhood of Antigone. I understand childhood here to be obedience to a debt, that one can call a debt of life, of time or event, a debt of being-there in spite of everything—only the persistent feeling of this, i.e. respect, can save the adult from being only a survivor, a living being on stay of annihilation.

It is true that one learns quickly that death will prevent one from acquitting oneself of one's debt, that it will come always too soon. . . . But childhood consists in the fact of being and behaving *as if* the point was to acquit oneself of the enigma of being there, to make fructify the inheritance of birth, of the complex, of the event, not in order to enjoy it, but to transmit it and that it be passed on. (*LdE*, 64–67)[8]

Is it by chance that Lyotard talks so much about childhood in these "late" texts? The child is old? So much the better. "What underlies everything is that *there are no grown-ups*," he likes quoting from Malraux,[9] himself quoting—is it a coincidence?—a father confessor.

God, before whom the confession is made, would be the one who confirms the childhood of man while marking its limit. So, in *La confession d'Augustin*:

The event comes about before writing bears witness, and its deposition is then that it is past. The confession reiterates this condition of childhood measured by the standard of full presence: I will always have been little compared to Thy grandeur. You had no childhood, you are not carried off in the criss-cross of the too early and the too late. And thus is formed the infantile imago of the perfectly erect, pure act, Verb absolved from antecedents and consequents. The little one honors the very great with tiny little names; *hoc, id, id ipsum*, this that, that very thing: that the deictic without an object which in ontology stands in as a name for what has no name, anonymous eponym. (*CdA*, 47)

Is childhood, before God, as it were, anything other than what he sometimes calls, with terrible ambiguity, accepted as such, against everybody, "the 'jews'": "A people unprepared for the revelation of the alliance, always too young for it. *And by that very fact* too old."[10] Always too old *because* too young. And this would be a principle of complication in the "history" of his analysis of the Jews and the "jews," which of course traverses the whole of his oeuvre: how could we reconcile the "overevaluation" of the father, according to the analysis in "Figure forclose" with the complication brought to this concept of father by the theme of radical childhood developed in the texts from the 1990s, a theme that clearly bears a relation to that of the "jews," even if the nature of the relationship remains obscure, for good reason.

When I was a child, I spake as a child, I understood as a child, I thought as a child: but when I became a man, I put away childish things. (1 Corinthians 13:11)

In his later writings, Lyotard's evident animus against St. Paul never leads him to quote this famous verse. And yet could it not reasonably be said to sum up everything Lyotard comes to loathe about Christianity and what we might call its extensions through the tradition? Put brutally, "childish" here easily assimilates to "Jewish"; putting away childish things means putting away Jewish things (the law, works, in Paul's understanding) in the gesture of Christian repression denounced in the *Hyphen* text and elsewhere; and the "childhood" or "infancy" that is the major focus of much of Lyotard's thinking in the last ten years of his life has an essential, though only allusively thematized, relation with Jewishness. In "La mainmise," for example, the proximity of these two motifs is patent:

By childhood, I am referring not simply to an age that is, as the rationalists would have it, lacking in reason. I am speaking of this condition of being *affected* and not having the means—language, representation—to name, identify, reproduce, and recognize what is affecting us. By childhood I mean that we are born before being born to ourselves. We are born from others, but also to others, given over defenseless to them. Subject to their *mancipium*, and to an extent that they do not even recognize. For they themselves are also children, be they fathers or mothers. They are not emancipated from their own childhood, from their wound of childhood, nor from the call that arises out of it. They thus do not know, and indeed will never know—however hard they might try—just how much they affect us. Even their love for a son or daughter may have been a calamity. I mean that it may have engendered such a *mainmise* over the child's soul that the *mainmise* itself remains unknown to the child as an adult. The child will thus be affected to such a degree that it will not even occur to him to rebel, nor will he have even received the gift or grace to pray that his *mainmise* be lifted. I am not just talking about severe neuroses or psychoses. For the child, everything is a wound, the wound of a pleasure that is going to be forbidden and taken away. The suffering that results and the search for the object, something analogous, in short, to emancipation, arises out of this wound. The flight from Egypt is also called a vocation. We have been called by our name *to be* this name; we did not know who or what called us, and we do not know to what we are called. We know only that it is impossible not to heed this call and that fidelity to this demand cannot be avoided, no matter what we do and even if we try not to heed it.[11]

Could we say that the concept of childhood in these late writings provides the *mediation* for the passage from Jew to "jew" that seemed so brutal and even shocking around the time of *Heidegger et "les juifs"*? Not if we take that concept seriously, because "childhood" or "jew" here is just what, according to Lyotard, resists all mediation, dialectization, and sublation. And, as I shall try to show, what I have previously called the "terrible ambiguity" of the concept of "the 'jews'" is in many ways exacerbated and obscured by the concept of childhood, so that the specificity of the Jew, already opened up by the descriptions of "the 'jew,'" is increasingly lost in the apparent generality or generalizability of childhood. That generality, which contains, as I shall show in a moment, an insistent metaphorics of violent anal penetration, allows what are, formally speaking, predicates of "jewishness" to be exemplarily attached, in the posthumous book, to Saint Augustine. What are we to make of this final turn? Is it to show that even the Christian tradition would be profoundly infiltrated by "jewish" structures, and that its attempt to forget them would be doomed to failure? Or else is there here a softening, or an inflection of what often pushes Lyotard into reserving a singularity for the Jew? This possibility is such that the type of separation postulated between Jew and Christian in the *Hyphen* text should not really be possible at all. For does this gesture not introduce a principle of confusion into the distinction he still appears to want to exacerbate, the "blank" he wants to maintain against its hyphenated crossing in the *Hyphen*?[12] To put this more polemically, we might want to say that maintaining the type of marked difference Lyotard often seems to want to make between Jew and Christian is itself essentially a "Christian" gesture, or cannot fail to invite accusations of complicity with a Christian view of the Jew,[13] whereas recognizing the infiltration of "Christian" structures by "Jewish" features would be more "Jewish." To refer this rapidly to the thematic of childhood, this would be like saying that childhood in Lyotard's sense is eminently a quality of the adult. Such a gesture would not eradicate what I have been rather mildly calling "ambiguity," but would tend to exacerbate it beyond the grasp of the concept of ambiguity itself. Which of course would not necessarily make Lyotard's gestures any the more acceptable to Jew (or even "jew") *or* Christian. And perhaps what is a more powerful operator than ambiguity here is a logic of witness as treachery: a priori false witness, betraying that for which it bears witness: "Witness to the extent that he is not a witness and that there can be no witness" (*CdA*, 24); "The witness is a traitor" (*LI*, 215; the last sentence of the book).

If childhood is such a privileged figure, though, might we not expect to find it already there, or its anticipatory childhood, childhood's childhood, from the beginning of Lyotard's oeuvre, a key to writing his philosophical or intellectual biography? Following the paradox of the younger/older that will not stop tormenting us here, we could, for example, take up the little book *Phenomenology*, both his youngest and his oldest book,[14] and be more or less naively surprised to find many themes and motifs that return in later work (especially, perhaps, a remark on the constitutive "contradiction" of phenomenology: "the originary, once described, is no longer originary insofar as it has been described").[15] Would we then be falling into the retrospectivist trap of intellectual biography, finding everything already there in embryo at the beginning, and which would then see only developments and results—at best dialectical ones—in everything that follows, which can in this case look so discontinuous, an intellectual trajectory made up especially of breaks? If we find *before* already there in the first texts, already there before, in a sort of childhood, are we not just doing banal and classical biographical work that he would certainly have repudiated? Does bringing everything down to *before*, finding the truth always before, not amount to a promotion of biography (and therefore, as he said to journalists come to interview him about the Malraux project, stupidity, or, in the words of *Chambre sourde*, "repetition [*la redite*], like biography itself: you will have been what you were to be, could not fail to be" [*CS*, 45])[16] into a transcendental position, happily rolling out classical plots and narratives, in which the end is always already in the beginning—the whole narrative web that *before* was, we assumed, supposed to precede and undo?

Can we avoid constituting as an oeuvre, the oeuvre of a life, these more or less *dispersed* writings, binding their events by making them into a story to be told here and now, gathered around an inaugural secret? Is this not precisely the sort of archaeo-teleological set-up he would have denounced? Before, he mildly reproached me for claiming in my book *Writing the Event* that what underlay this intellectual life was always the thought of the event (his work therefore in my account culminating triumphantly in *Le différend*):[17] here, I am apparently claiming that before the event or the differend as truth of the event there would have been *before*—but the gesture would be the same, that of perversely saving a beautiful totality faced with a *de facto* dispersion which *also affirms* dispersion (for example, under the name *dissentiment* in *The Postmodern Condition*, or in the interesting and problematic figure of the archipelago of discursive genres in *Le différend*).[18]

But, no more than, for example, "figure," "desire," "postmodern," "sublime," "event," "presentation," "differend" (and many others), *before* will not be presented here as the proper name of some "thing" (and indeed at one moment which is not just any moment, at the end of the 1980s, he nicknamed it "Thing," after Lacan, this thing that is no thing), the proper name of one same thing that he would supposedly have striven to name, and failed to name, from one end of his work to the other, according to the logic stated in the book on *Phenomenology*, where he says that "the defeat of the philosopher is certain,"[19] repeated in the language of defeat we saw in the foreword to *The Lyotard Reader*. *Before* is not the name, could never enter into the play of nomination and ostension that is the subject of those wonderful analyses in *Le différend*, for example. I am not telling a story here, nor sketching a biography: rather, I am picking out bits of text, tatters, as he said earlier, cuttings or coupons, as he might have said, as I once heard him say, in which the question among other things is that of what makes such a biographical project untellable. Given what we have said about *before*, and what we could have seen differently with respect to event or presentation, these cuttings or coupons do not allow themselves to be bound by narrative form. *Before* is neither the beginning nor the end of a story, nor even the sort of *in medias res* that always still needs beginnings and ends, and that he discusses at the beginning of *Chambre sourde*. We are not reading *before* in the early texts as a seed or embryo of what was to come next: rather the contrary. The *before* that comes after allows us to read in the "early" texts what was *not* simply in them, before—the event of *before* in his texts, its childhood, is itself always after the event, too early or too late.

This is what will allow *Signé, Malraux* to propose a whole discontinuous meditation on the genre of biography, all the time reinscribing the question of life and its writing in the life to be written, that of Malraux. What Lyotard calls "the roots of the 'Malraux' equation" would already have to do with biography as relation between *bios* and *graphe*. The *bios* whose *graphè* Lyotard is doing is already split between *bios* and *graphe*. This equation would, apparently, make this relation essentially one of the relation between the sexes: life would be essentially the return of death, the rotting engendered by engendering itself, against which *graphe* would provide the possibility of a saving virile filiation: "a father, whatever he be in the biological order, is he who attempts the gesture of resigning (from) this order and who transmits the trace of this gesture" (*SMX*, 105). *Résigner cet ordre*: not only to withdraw from it, but to measure up to it—resign is also, following one of the book's most insistent motifs, indeed the one that gives it its title, to re-sign, to countersign, to sign against dead life and the female matrix. Which means that life must already make itself writing *in* "life" (a word he therefore puts in quotation marks), so that "mythopoiesis . . . fictions so-called life" (*SMX*, 19), and will lead not only to the secret of Malraux's life, not only solve the "Malraux equation," but lead also to "the secret of biography according to Malraux: it is in no way the faithful narrative of a life, it is, right on this life [*à même cette vie*], the legend that fictions itself there *in actu* . . . one is still *writing*, one is only writing, when one signs a gesture right on banality, when one metamorphizes a fact into an event by this gesture" (*SMX*, 118–19). So what should we do about biography in the current sense? How can one write the life of one whose life was already a passion of writing right in that life? Is it not impossible? Malraux, as Lyotard recounts, gives up on his project of writing a biography of Lawrence of Arabia: "'The most subtle parts of Lawrence's adventure would be rendered much more intelligible by fiction than by the analysis I'm doing,'" says Malraux quoted by Lyotard, who continues, "Now fabulating was not the law of the biographical genre. Why did he venture into it? To see if one could write without imagination?" (*SMX*, 274). How can we avoid asking the same question of Lyotard: why did he venture into it, at a given moment in his more or less legendary and mythopoietic life? As often in *Signé, Malraux*, it is difficult to work out here what belongs to Malraux, what to Lyotard. The systematic use of free indirect discourse often renders undecidable the signature we were trying to identify: *Signé, Malraux* is signed Lyotard, according to a logic of countersignature that does not stop there—the use I too have been making, from the start, of free indirect discourse, follows this troubling of the play of signatures: signed Malraux, signed Lyotard, signed Bennington, and so on. But is it by chance that the only reflection on free indirect discourse in the book should turn around sexual difference: "Thanks to free indirect discourse, Malraux mixes the woman's voice into the man's soliloquy" (*SMX*, 243), which will not stop both feeding and troubling the fantasy of virile filiation you will not fail to suspect here.

So *before* is not *the* name. Unnamable, then. But not necessarily unnamable in the sense of disgust or horror, which would only be a determined figure of it, like those of putrefaction and decay that, according to *Signé, Malraux* and *Chambre sourde*, are at work in Malraux. Beware of the pathos of horror—this was always Lyotard's reservation about Bataille. Naming what precedes all naming as "unnamable," or even *qualifying* it as unnamable, lets one off too lightly, with a supplement of virility from having been up to facing and thus mastering the horror, the horror. This is the danger that lies in wait for any proposal of the formless as a form adequate to the communication of *before*, as its representation in extremis. Beware pathos, when the pathos is determined or fixed: what Lyotard is looking for in Kant's Third *Critique* in the 1980s is an as yet indeterminable pathos, a pathos of *pathein* in general, before any determination, what he comes to call an "unconscious" affect at the time of his rereading of Freud at the end of the 1980s, unconscious affect linked to so-called originary repression, close to the sublime, which, he says, "cannot be located temporally" (*HLJ*, 61).

Could there be here the principle of an objection to be leveled at Lyotard's immense "early" work *Discours, figure*? In that book, the "deepest" level of the figure, after the *figure-image*, which occurs in the space of representation, after the *figure-forme*, which works at the level of that space itself, the constitution of that space, we get to the most inaccessible level (in fact radically inaccessible as such), the mysterious *figure-matrice*, which, while being "difference itself," is also apparently none other than the originary fantasy of a given subject: "The works of a man are only ever the offspring of this matrix; it can perhaps be glimpsed through their superimposition, in depth" (*DF*, 278–79). Swarming putrefaction would thus bring us close to Malraux's matrix-figure, and we could set off looking for such figures in others too, as for example in Lyotard's strange text in *Des dispositifs pulsionnels*, about Bachelard:

> One can assume that this form which organizes the problematic is the constant factor in the work: a sort of representational machine, an apparatus for producing fantasy, made from a soft medium with a hard surface, or a nocturnal element capped by an overexposed shot, or a diffuse warmth interrupted by a burning flash, or a flowing liquidity onto which is brandished the energy of a wave, or a region of immanence in contact with a region of transcendence, or. . . . And the whole question of Bachelard's desire bears on the *contact* between these two spaces. The recurrence of a doctrine of contact and the displacement of the partition [*la paroi*][20] of the contacts across his oeuvre attest to the fact that desire and interdiction are especially invested in the drama of sexual difference.[21]

What of Lyotard himself? Is not that what I am proposing here: a still ultimately—if not narratively—biographical hypothesis as to his originary fantasy and its avatars throughout his texts? On this hypothesis, will we say that Lyotard's matrix-figure, figured in his late texts by childhood, is not other that the matrix-figure *itself*, difference *itself*, on which *Discours, figure* dreams of "getting its hands" (*DF*, 328) pure *before*, the absent of all fantasy, childhood absent from all childhood, something absolutely early finally arrived at only late on? A fantasy of fantasy overcome by critical or philosophical work? Which would still really be in line with *Discours, figure* itself, and other texts of the same period, which are constantly extolling the *critical* function of the work, here its operation of *retournement* (turnaround, turning inside out, rather than simple reversal [*renversement*]) on what would otherwise be control by fantasy.[22] *Discours, figure* follows the birth of this critical function in the work of Klee, from a more or less direct expression of fantasy (a *clinical* rather than a *critical* matter, in a then common distinction), to a critical working through, which, as he will repeatedly say of the sublime or the postmodern later in his work, ends with "the invisible to be made visible, and no longer the fantasy to be recognized" (*DF*, 229)—this should obviously be placed alongside the "present that there is the unpresentable" of the texts on the postmodern: is it a coincidence that this process in Klee (as in Bachelard, as in Malraux) should pass through a mythology or a haunting of sexual difference that is maintained through the "critical" moment as its truth? And is the very term matrix-figure (*matrice* in French signaling more clearly than matrix in English to the womb, the maternal, *mater*)—is this term not already the discreet index of the existence of a similar mythology or haunting in Lyotard himself?

But if we should not rush toward the imaginary fulfillment of the fantasy of finding and exhibiting the matrix-figure or the primal fantasy of Lyotard himself—nor indeed of anyone else, on pain of falling ourselves into a banal fantasy *about* the primal fantasy, of getting into the clinical just when the point is to keep a watch that is critical—we will nonetheless not escape for all that the contingency of something like the singularity of the matrix-figure that will have marked Lyotard's texts with a singular seal, a proper name (the proper name was always for him the best mark of singularity),[23] or a signature. And just this is the sense of childhood *surviving*. My debt to childhood, which is irreducible, will always somewhere inscribe me, my life-as-survival, in my texts. So I am not trying to save Lyotard from himself, or from his fantasies, his signature, his oeuvre, by simply turning him into a transcendental philosopher after all, supposedly escaping from *his* matrix-figure by thinking *the* matrix-figure *in general*. And indeed another aspect of *Discours, figure* would *already* discourage us from so doing, in that it puts forward a concept of truth as aberrant with respect to philosophy[24] and exhibits a suspicion of the order of the concept that translates across Lyotard's work as a whole into the admiration he shows for all types of "artistic" practices. In Lyotard, critique does not give rise to doctrine, and this is why he very early turns against the critical motif—already in the preface to *Dérive à partir de Marx et Freud*,[25] before *Économie libidinale* and *Rudiments païens*[26]—and, despite appearances, does not really come back to it around the time of *Le différend*, where the "critical watchman" is no longer the agent of the transcendental. "The biographical" is thus ineluctably inscribed in the work that also tries to measure up to it, to liberate itself from it, or to *ruse* with it, as in the figure of the Greek *metis* that Lyotard likes to quote from Vernant and Vidal-Nacquet, which is an integral part of what he used to call "paganism" ("That's paganism. You do not know to whom you are speaking, you have to be very prudent, you need negotiation and ruse"),[27] and which dictates the work in the 1970s on rhetoric and its capacity to turn situations around, for example to make the weaker party into the stronger.[28] The work can be an event, and thereby a work, on condition of turning itself inside out like the fish-fox described in *Le mur du pacifique*,[29] or turning inside out its fantasy that is never for all that simply absent or simply sublated: *exposed*, rather, confessed. This exposure can be more or less direct and even confrontational, more or less discreet and secret, but even the transcendental philosopher will on this account make his work from desire, in a state or figure of desire which is not an absence of desire, but which is close to absolute or pure desire.[30]

Before, before the name, then, names nothing ("The thing is never in the name, under the name one gives it" [*SMX*, 337]). Saying *before* here, I am neither naming nor calling. I do not call *before*: it is *before* that calls me. From before, *before* calls me from its time before time. From the depths of time, as he sometimes writes, and even the depths of the depths of time, like Duras's *main négative* that cries out on the wall of the cave from the depths of time, *before* calls and calls me. This call or cry gives something to be read, even if as such it is unreadable. Which is why one reads texts rather than deciphering messages, why the philosophers of communication provoke his anger and consternation. And what infuses an element of "biography" into every piece of writing. So we must read to wonder why, at a given moment of his life, Lyotard launched himself, to my surprise and I imagine to everybody's surprise ("no one would have expected it" says a note on the book's cover) into the project of a biography of Malraux, finding in it the material for an intermittent but insistent reflection on the biographical in general. *Before* calls me, always ahead of me perhaps, but always behind me, more or less secretly, quietly, even shiftily, and the call that comes from behind me, back of me, pushes me forward, surprised.

Like in that example given in *Le Différand*, which is no doubt more than an example, because it is an example his readers quote to each other, recall like a watchword or a sign of recognition in humour: "The officer shouts *Charge!* [*Avanti!*] and jumps out of the trench; the soldiers, impressed, shout *Bravo!* without moving" (*LD*, 43). Memorable example perhaps because we would like to think of him as the brave one, he whose intellectual and political courage never failed, to whom perhaps too often we were tempted to say "Bravo!," to applaud instead of following, to watch instead of acting.

But of course it is not simply a matter of *following*. Lyotard managed fairly well to avoid all institutionalization of his name—unless I am mistaken, there will not really have been any "Lyotardians," except perhaps for those—especially in England, maybe—who thought they could use *Économie libidinale* as the gospel he thought he'd done everything to avoid writing, or perhaps the so-called postmoderns who read *The Post-*

modern Condition much too quickly and were then astonished by what came later (that is, according to that after, *before*). "But writing and reading are slow, advancing backward in the direction of the unknown thing 'inside'" (*LI*, 10–11). "One advances, but the past in words is waiting there ahead" (*LI*, 209).

Before thus lodges the (auto)biographical in writing. This can be more or less explicit, as in *Pérégrinations*, where Lyotard gives an example which is transparent to one with a modicum of knowledge of his life at that time: "To love a woman, for example, to want her to give you the child she wants to give you, to make a new life for yourself so that a life shared between her and the child is possible, is also a way of 'phrasing'" (19). But insofar as even this type of surface exposure of the biographical is in continuity with the more mysterious thematic of *before*, here via the figure of a childhood that survives, and whose true eventhood is in its survival or repetition beyond its time, in a time out of joint, then this very biographical element, which I am suggesting is irreducible, will also sooner or later upset any attempt to write a biography (which does not mean one should not even try: on the contrary). In *La confession d'Augustin*, which can always also be read (and which it is difficult not to read) as Lyotard's confession too, he explains that the event of the Other, the overturning brought about by the visit of what Augustine supposedly calls God only "because that's the custom" (56–57)—this raises a host of questions about how such a custom might have started, but also about the relationship of Lyotard's thought to monotheism on the one hand, and the polytheism vaunted (against Augustine, precisely) in, for example, *Économie libidinale*—he explains that such an event prevents any *dating* and even any *relation*:

> What could the soul placed outside itself in its own home, out of place and out of time, intrinsically—what could it localize, fix, have memorized of an avatar that abolishes the natural conditions of perception and cannot therefore be perceived as an event? How would the soul know whether the syncope takes place once or is repeated, given that the syncope deprives it of the power to gather the diversity of instances into one temporality [*durée*]? Where to situate an absolute visit, place it in relation, in a biography? Relate it? . . . The course of real life, biography, resists durably the improbable event of your coming. (*CdA*, 22, 31)

So that, *on the one hand*, the event cannot really be located, and certainly not in the present ("The assault of your eternity scarcely signs itself, with a syncope, nothing really, in the calendar of days. A tiny wing come from elsewhere brushes that calendar with your presence, and does not withdraw it from the preoccupations of its dead life. Your visitation is almost indiscernible from the slow routine of habit and the dissipations of desire" [*CdA*, 33–34]), and *on the other* it cannot but dissimulate itself (dissimilate itself, as he said in *Économie libidinale*), and so one therefore always runs the risk of being wrong about it: *before* is almost indiscernible—its event has a chance of being read only after the fact, before us, never established, at most, to use one of his favorite words, *alleged* in our readings still to come.

Let us beware, though, of slogans, and therefore stupidity. *Before* as childhood is perhaps always before us, still to come, an infinite task or unpayable debt. And it will of course call us to what he sometimes calls a working-through or a task of anamnesis which is neither forgetting nor forgetful memorializing.[31] But this schema evidently runs the risk of falling back into the old metaphysical assurances that *before* undoes. The point is that, even though it is before us, *before* is never properly and frankly in front of us, as an object over-against, nor even as the horizon of a continuous asymptotic approach.[32] It is the object neither of a concept nor of an Idea in the Kantian sense. Before does not mean in front, available to the subject I am supposed to be or to have become on leaving childhood. On the contrary, *before* befalls me like an event—but not, as might have been supposed, from on high, in the dimension of height, from the most high, but in much more dubious fashion, from behind. *Before* may well be before me, to come, but just as we were feeling brave and uplifted by that prospect, *before* turns out rather to mean behind. As we shall see, *before* comes at me from behind. Before is interminably before only by being always already behind. However quickly I turn round, before is never in front of me, never facing me, never face-on. The originary delay that means that we always run after *before* also means not only that we are always behind it, but that *before* is also behind us, the Other never presents itself face on, but will rather take us from behind.[33] And it is this more troubled dimension that complicates the figure of childhood with that of sexual difference, which always in Lyotard shows up as violence and extreme disorder. If we now look to the passage that comes just before, or just behind, the long derivation of childhood I took from the text on Hannah Arendt, then we find that the "event" I placed in suspense is "the event of sexed reproduction in the history of living beings. And in individual ontogenesis, the echo of sexual difference, which is the event whose savagery the entire life of the individual is taken up with 'sorting out' [*régler*]."[34] This event of sexual difference and its disorder generates a good deal of disorder in Lyotard's writing. For example, *La confession d'Augustin* speaks

> of what *jouissance* the rape perpetrated by the Other is the act. What is more, this ravishing is undergone by surprise, there's no need to stand up, to affront the Other face on—on the contrary—to experience the delicious torture.
>
> To the being in itself recumbent in its consuetude, nothing can happen except from behind. (*CdA*, 42–43)

Nothing can happen except from behind: for it is *also* from behind that come all the resistances to the event of the Other: vanity too, concupiscence murmur softly in one's ear, from behind one's back:

> Sly provocations *a dorso mussitantes*, whispered from behind. As though, he pretends to think, they wanted him to turn round toward them. Not so: they and he are used to being taken backward, to being oneself only by surprise, the dirty habit itself has no need of a contract, it is contracted *a tergo*. (*CdA*, 43)

How, then, are we to distinguish between the dirty habit and the true visitation of the Other? Love story or dirty story: *histoire d'amour* or *histoire de cul*?

It is a variation on the same figure that he finds in Malraux, in the depths of Malraux:

> The horror of remaining a girl among women and one day to have to be impregnated, by a man lost in advance, of a son lost in advance, and to have to weep for this son at the edge of a hole in the mud. "Men do not have children." An anguish clenched in the child without his realizing it, in these so-called women's phobias, about spiders and squid, insects, snakes, and rats. Everything that embraces you and penetrates you shadily from behind, figures of so sweet a rape. (*SMX*, 13)

To what extent is this figure of a penetration *a tergo* merely a fantasy of the subject Malraux? To the extent that it is, it would be one of the figures, alongside the disgusting, seething rot, of an individuality, a more or less secret key that it would be the biographer's task to pick up and bring out, what *Discours, figure* called the matrix-figure, and what the biography of Malraux calls, glossing Malraux himself, a "scarcely conscious matrix which obstinately moulds the impressions and expressions of a writer and which give his writing its secret singularity" (*SMX*, 241). The more so in that in Malraux's case the biographer has at his disposal the explicit narrative, in the novel *Les conquérants*, of a scene of anal rape, recounted by the "Malraux" character and linked to a juridical experience like Malraux's own in Indochina, and an admission of obsession on this subject ("This trial has got to him in his fantasy of a penetration *a tergo*" [*SMX*, 153–54]: if I am before the law, the law is right behind me). A fantasy of symbolic penetration (this time assented to) is also discreetly invoked around the relationship of Malraux and De Gaulle (*SMX*, 303). But, like any figure of *before*, this one must have a certain generalizing virtue, must escape from the purely idiomatic, if only in order to be recognized by the reader or biographer (and allow, for example, the massive and sustained use of free indirect discourse in *Signé, Malraux*, and more still in *La confession d'Augustin*, so that "signé Malraux" can be reapplied to the book that is also "signé Lyotard," and, as the French allows, *singé Malraux*—it's worth pointing out that the single explicit reflection on free indirect discourse in the book bears on the infiltration of a woman's voice into a man's voice)—so that we should not be surprised to find traces, and more than traces, of this elsewhere in Lyotard's work, in *Économie libidinale*, for example, and, as we have just seen, around Augustine. And this generalizability of the figure means that it tends to escape from its idiomatic localization, and so can figure in Lyotard something more general, for example what he calls "the sexual," or sexual difference, itself often assimilated to ontological difference,[35] from which point it can tend to dominate all other figures of *before*.

For if *before* had seemed, with its irreducible biographical moment, to find its privileged figure in childhood in the complex sense we have laid out, we must now find that privilege threatened with displacement by "the sexual," sexual difference, always in Lyotard referred to violence and savagery, to "the event of castration." *Signé, Malraux* refers (perhaps referring this view to Malraux, undecidably because of the free indirect discourse we have mentioned) to "the sexual differend, which is the ultimate driving force of every drama" (*SMX*, 227) and thereby, one might suspect, of every differend in general, the force that turns difference into differend, the force that remains nameless in *Le différend* itself.[36] Is this why, in *La confession d'Augustin*, Lyotard says so elliptically and mysteriously that time is bound up with "the sexual," and that Augustine, beneath the phenomenology of internal time consciousness, sketched out a "libidinal-ontological constitution of temporality" (38)? Now, what does "the sexual" do?

> The sexual continuously surprises, takes from behind, works behind one's back. It lets right resolutions, probity, and face-to-face promises have their say, they will pass. (*CdA*, 38)

To "take from behind" is, then, not simply a more or less idiomatic fantasy of Malraux or anyone else, but a figure of the sexual, and therefore of *before* in general: no surprise, then, to find in this motif the dominant figure of sexuality in Lyotard's work more generally, from at least *Économie libidinale* onward. We could follow this in *Économie libidinale* via the analysis of the Schreber case, of Schreber's "vertigo of anal eroticism," his "solar anus" or "mad anus" (76–77), through the section called " 'Use Me,' " in which we find, for example, "the erect member above the loins" (80), "buttocks, anus, passage offered by the woman bent double" (81). And further on, the anal ring is the dominant feature of the analysis of the Greek city (and by extension of politics more generally) in its homoerotic economy, its "annulatory perversion: annulling through movement on the ring [*l'anneau*] of the city. Circumversion" (194):[37] this is insistent to the point at which we might suspect that everything in *Économie libidinale* that comes down to the form of the circle—and even the dominant figure of the zero thus traced out—would be haunted by the ring of the anus. "The philosophy we're doing is one of sodomists [*enculés*: faggots] and women" (307), says the end of *Économie libidinale*, and it would be easy to show that the figure of *a tergo* penetration recurs every time the point is to affirm a certain anonymity of the sexual. The drama of sexual difference is played out from behind, and this dorsal perspective is what troubles any certain identification of the sexes involved.[38] *Before* gets me from behind, penetrates and unseats me from what *Économie libidinale* calls "the despotic fantasy of the master, of placing himself in the supposed place of the central zero and thus to identify himself with the matricial Nothing" (254). Despotic fantasy of seeing only a hole to fill,[39] anus-matrix, supposedly virile filiation, obviously doomed to fail, haunted by what is around it, in its borderlands, its *pagus*, placing the center in question:

The Voice at the Virile center . . . speaks only of these limits of the Empire (i.e., women) and we have ceaselessly to combat their exteriority. If this is the case, is it not because this object is unconsciously endowed with what we call activity? And does not the potential for ruse we allow it betray the secret overturning of our role by theirs? (Is there not a desire on the part of Western man to get himself sodomized by the woman?) Is not the outside of men's theater the most important, including for men? Is that not where he finds his "origin"? And is it not necessary that this origin be female? Is the mother not the originary woman? I.e., the way the external sex is represented in theory: ground, itself ungrounded, in which meaning is engendered? Meaningless Being?[40]

So what inscribes the biographical in the work, ineffaceably, is not *before* in an abstract sense, but *before* as an event of birth, as a childhood that resolves into the existence of a sexed body, marked by the event of castration, the fact that there are men and women, and not Man. This is duly what in part motivates "Her" objections to the idea that thought could go on without a body (see *LI*, 28–31): one *is* and therefore thinks on the basis of an existence that is aesthetic in the broadest sense, affective, in primary passivity, one is and so one has a body: and this body is constitutively marked by sexual difference.

Behind childhood, then (*before* is always behind), there is the sexual as the essential feature of bodily existence. "In love," as *Signé, Malraux* says again, "the enemy does not advance face forward. . . . The sexual is unnamable, the unnamable, perhaps" (245). The sexual arrives *essentially* from behind, as penetration *a tergo*. And this could be a reason for not completing a biography of a man already a biographer:

> What were these gentlemen writers asking for, the Drieus, Martin du Gards, Gides, Lawrences, Montherlants, in terms of [sexual difference]? An idea of femininity that would not upset the misogynous homosexuality, be it concealed or declared? Impossible biography no doubt, but a compromising one too: the indecent propensity hidden under the "virile fraternity" would have been too visible. (*SMX*, 279)

Before—childhood, unnamable, sexual, inscribes the biographical into the life that thereby becomes more or less legendary, through writing, a fantasy of virile filiation through the signature on a work—and thereby improper for the biography it also calls up because of that very gesture. Impossible biography from the moment *graphe* is the very gesture of defiance (hopeless defiance, at best in the "as if" attributed to childhood in the text on Hannah Arendt) against the murderous *bios* that condemns me to death and rotting. I write a biography to show that its possibility is none other than its impossibility, that the work I sign against my dead life, for the sake of my legend, is torn by the signature from the matrix of the female matrix. But I write a biography (and Lyotard, unlike Malraux, finished his), a compromising biography, at the price of the affirmation of an impossible, more or less shamefully or joyously perverse virility, dissimulated or dissimilated, perhaps homosexual, let's say more or less "gay." "It is possible," he says, "that from the moment you write, you are obliged to be a man. Writing is perhaps a thing of virility. Even if you write about femininity. Even if you write 'femininely.'" (*RP*, 213). But this "obligation," obligation itself, is endlessly ambiguous: can one be a man—and will one ever have finished confessing it, that is, exposing oneself to the surprise of what always might arrive from behind, from the other?

This is what means that a man is not man, and that man is not mankind, not the human. "Human sex is nonhuman," "inhuman," says *Discours, figure* already, commenting on Marx, against the Hegelian dialectic (138–41), already in infancy the entirety of what we have been trying to say?

> The question of this difference [i.e., sexual difference] is the question of castration, and every religion, as cultural fact, aimed at the absorption of castration in the advent of the condition of the son, i.e., the recuperation of meaning and violence into signification. So that by imagining real difference as the difference between human sex and nonhuman sex, Marx gets very close to what will be the object of Freud's research, since he refuses to scar over the difference of the sexes into a masculine/feminine opposition, since he imagines, if only for a moment, that there is, in the fact of human sex (masculine as well as feminine) an irremissible violence, a reference to an exteriority, nonhuman sex, which cannot find its place in the conscious order of what is legitimate, since, finally, he admits that the question of sex is not at all that of polarization between the sexes, but on the contrary that of their non-attraction and their non-thinkable separation.
>
> [Lyotard's note:] The Freudian theme of *Nachträglichkeit* must be attached to this concept of a difference outside the system. If the scene of seduction for example (to the extent that it exists) acts after the fact, this is not because we are always in the gap [*écart*], but because human sex is nonhuman. (*DF*, 140–41)

Bear witness to this, or confess it, in writing which condemns one to the obligation of being a man, of putting childish things behind one. Bear witness badly, naturally. Endlessly. I confess. Last sentence of *The Inhuman*: "The witness is a traitor."

Notes

NOTES TO "INTRODUCTION"

1. Jean-François Lyotard, *The Inhuman: Reflections on Time*, trans. Geoffrey Bennington and Rachel Bowlby (Stanford, CA: Stanford University Press, 1991), 204.

2. See Jean-François Lyotard, "The Survivor," trans. Robert Harvey and Mark S. Roberts, in Jean-François Lyotard, *Toward the Postmodern*, ed. Robert Harvey and Mark S. Roberts (Atlantic Highlands, NJ: Humanities Press, 1993), 144–63, at 146.

3. Jean-François Lyotard, *Postmodern Fables*, trans. Georges Van Den Abbeele (Minneapolis: University of Minnesota Press, 1997), 232; hereafter cited as *PF*.

4. See Jean-François Lyotard, *Misère de la philosophie* (Paris: Galilée, 2000), 115.

5. Jean-François Lyotard, "German Guilt," trans. Bill Readings and Kevin Paul Geiman, in *Political Writings*, trans. Bill Readings with Kevin Paul Geiman (Minneapolis: University of Minnesota Press, 1993), 127–34; hereafter cited as *PW*.

6. See Jean-François Lyotard, *The Differend: Phrases in Dispute*, trans. Georges Van Den Abbeele (Minneapolis: University of Minnesota Press, 1988); hereafter cited as *D*.

7. Jean-François Lyotard, *The Confession of Augustine*, trans. Richard Beardsworth (Stanford, CA: Stanford University Press, 2000); hereafter cited as *CA*.

8. See Jean-François Lyotard and Jacques Monory, *The Assassination of Experience by Painting: Monory* (London: Black Dog, 1998), 85–86.

9. Augustine, *Confessions*, 2 vols., trans. William Watts (Cambridge: Loeb Classical Library, 1989), 2: bk. X, vi, 87–89; translation modified.

10. Jean-François Lyotard, *The Postmodern Condition: A Report on Knowledge*, trans. Geoff Bennington and Brian Massumi (Minneapolis: University of Minnesota Press, 1984); hereafter cited as *PC*.

11. Immanuel Kant, *Critique of Judgment*, trans. Werner S. Pluhar (Indianapolis: Hackett, 1987); hereafter cited as *C3*. Unless otherwise stated, quotations are from Pluhar's translation. In all cases, subsequent reference is made to the *Akademie* pagination.

12. Here I refer to Meredith's translation of *Ak* 245. See Immanuel Kant, *The Critique of Judgement*, trans. James Creed Meredith (Oxford: Oxford University Press, 1952), 127.

13. See especially the chapter titled "The Sign of History," in *D*, 151–81.

14. Jean-François Lyotard, *Heidegger and "the jews,"* trans. Andreas Michel and Mark Roberts (Minneapolis: University of Minnesota Press, 1990), 26.

15. Jean-François Lyotard, *Signed, Malraux*, trans. Robert Harvey (Minneapolis: University of Minnesota Press, 1999); hereafter cited as *SM*.

16. Jean-François Lyotard, "Adrift," trans. Roger McKeon, in Jean-François Lyotard, *Driftworks*, ed. Roger McKeon (New York: Semiotext(e), 1984), 10.

17. In light of Lyotard's later discussions of this figure, one would have to add that the milieu is not merely to be found between the islands. In the form of rivers, it cuts through the surface of those islands; underground streams, long occluded from view, occasionally rise up; even in the apparently rarefied heights, clouds drift by, casting their shadows. The various islands, then, are bathed in the waters of the milieu. See *PF*, 5, 123–47; Jean-François Lyotard, *Peregrinations: Law, Form, Event* (New York: Columbia University Press, 1988), 1–15.

18. Quoted in *D*, 134; and Jean-François Lyotard, "Judiciousness in Dispute, or Kant after Marx," trans. Cecile Lindsay in *The Lyotard Reader*, ed. Andrew Benjamin (Cambridge: Blackwell, 1989), 324–59, at 329–31.

19. See Jean-François Lyotard, "A Svelte Appendix to the Postmodern Question," in *PW*, 25–29, at 28–29.

20. Jean-François Lyotard, *Que peindre? Adami, Arakawa, Buren* (Paris: Editions de la différence, 1987), 43; my translation. I wish to thank Dolorès Lyotard for having called my attention to these lines in the speech that she gave at the memorial service held at Emory University. See also Jean-François Lyotard, *Libidinal Economy*, trans. Iain Hamilton Grant (Bloomington: Indiana University Press, 1993); hereafter cited as *LE*. Speaking of his own writing in *LE*, Lyotard writes: "It would be like the bottle thrown in the sea, but . . . without its launch being a last attempt to signal and communicate a message entrusted to it. There would be no message in our bottle; only a few energies, whose transmission and transformation was [*sic*] left and was desired to be unpredictable" (255).

NOTES TO "LYOTARD AND *US*"

This title was chosen after the talk was first given; it was originally delivered without a title. The paper was first delivered at the Collège International de Philosophie in Paris in March 1999, and then again, after some minor modifications, in October 1999 at Emory University in Atlanta.

1. Jean-François Lyotard, *The Differend: Phrases in Dispute*, trans. Georges Van Den Abbeele (Minneapolis: University of Minnesota Press, 1988), 99; hereafter cited as *D*. [Georges Van Den Abbeele's translation of *The Differend* has, with just a couple of minor modifications, been used throughout here, and his

translation of most key Lyotardian terms retained. For example, the French *phrase* is translated throughout here as "phrase" rather than "sentence." See Van Den Abbeele's justification of this choice on 194.—*Trans.*]

2. I once heard my friend Serge Margel ask a similar question, but in the context of another space of thinking and set of references. See his essay "Les dénominations orphiques de la survivance: Derrida et la question du pire," in *L'animal autobiographique*, ed. Marie-Louise Mallet (Paris: Editions Galilée, 1999), 441–68.

3. Outline of the argument I was not able to spell out during the conference: death obligates; it would thus be the other original name of absolute obligation. Unconditional engagement binds only to the one who ("who" rather than "what"), from the place of death, becomes at once the absent origin and the destination of the absolute, unconditional, unnegotiable obligation, beyond any transaction. Absence without return would thus open onto the unconditional. Terrifying. Terror. This would be the meaning of "God is dead," the association of the name of God, as the place of the unconditional, with death. A desperate conclusion, perhaps: the unconditional (which I distinguish here from the sovereign, even if the distinction remains improbable) signifies the death of the dead, death without mourning: there shall be no mourning. One is under an unconditional obligation only toward the dead. One can always negotiate conditions with the living. Upon death, there is a rupture of symmetry: truth, the impossibility of pretending anymore. But does one ever really deal with the dead? Who could swear to it? The impossible death perhaps means that what is living conditions everything.

4. *Revue philosophique de la France et de l'étranger* 2 (April–June 1990), special issue "Derrida," ed. Catherine Malabou. Translations are modified from "Translator's Notes," trans. Roland-François Lack, in *Pli: The Warwick Journal of Philosophy* 6 (Summer 1997): 51–57; hereafter cited as *TN*.

5. [As in the Grimms' tale "Hansel and Gretel," *le Petit Poucet* drops pebbles to mark his path and so avoid becoming lost.—*Trans.*]

6. Jean-François Lyotard, *Signed, Malraux*, trans. Robert Harvey (Minneapolis: University of Minnesota Press, 1999), 286, 288.

NOTES TO "SAVING THE HONOR OF THINKING"

1. With respect to this last phase of Lyotard's writing, Gérald Sfez remarks: "One can almost speak of a second philosophy of the differend, whose role is not to resolve the contradictions, the aporias, and the already existing dissonant voices involved in the use of the term—it was never designed for this—but to encounter them again otherwise. One witnesses a shift in accent that neither resolves nor discredits the previous thought. The differend undergoes a change of aspect" (Gérald Sfez, "Writings of the Differend," p. 89, this volume).

2. *The Inhuman: Reflections on Time*, trans. Geoffrey Bennington and Rachel Bowlby (Stanford, CA: Stanford University Press, 1991), 128.

3. *The Differend: Phrases in Dispute*, trans. Georges Van Den Abbeele (Minneapolis: University of Minnesota Press, 1988), xiii; hereafter cited as *D*. For Lyotard's reservations regarding the linguistic discipline of pragmatics, and his attempt to distinguish his own phrastic approach from it, see "Discussions, or Phrasing 'After Auschwitz,'" in *The Lyotard Reader*, ed. Andrew Benjamin (Cambridge: Blackwell, 1989), 371–72.

4. For a discussion of Lyotard's shift from the use of the Wittgensteinian notion of "language games" in *The Postmodern Condition* to the notion of "phrase" in *The Differend*, see, e.g., Niels Brügger, "Où sont passés les jeux de langages?," in *Lyotard: Les déplacements philosophiques*, ed. Niels Brügger, Finn Frandsen, and Dominique Pirotte (Brussels: De Boeck-Wesmael, 1993), 33–53.

5. Lyotard discusses the distinction between articulated and nonarticulated phrases in "Examen Oral: Entretien avec Jean-François Lyotard," in *Lyotard: Les déplacements philosophiques*, 144–46.

6. *The Postmodern Condition: A Report on Knowledge*, trans. Geoff Bennington and Brian Massumi (Minneapolis: University of Minnesota Press, 1984), 23; hereafter cited as *PC*. For a description that betokens the essentially pragmatic nature of the instances of a phrase universe, see *PC*, 23–24, where Lyotard discusses a phrase whose regimen submits to the rules of scientific knowledge.

7. These are Lyotard's words (transcribed by himself) in the debate that followed the presentation of his "Discussions, or Phrasing 'After Auschwitz'" at Cerisy-la-Salle, on the occasion of a colloquium on the work of Jacques Derrida in 1980. See *Les fins de l'homme: A partir du travail de Jacques Derrida*, ed. Philippe Lacoue-Labarthe and Jean-Luc Nancy (Paris: Galilée, 1981), 314.

8. For a discussion of the resurgence of the norm of honor in contemporary social, cultural, and political life, see *Ehre: Archaische Momente in der Moderne*, ed. L. Vogt and A. Zingerle (Frankfurt/Main: Suhrkamp, 1994).

9. Jean-Jacques Rousseau, *Emile, or on Education*, trans. Allan Bloom (New York: Basic Books, 1979), 272.

10. *The Postmodern Explained: Correspondence, 1982–1985*, translation ed. Julian Prefanis and Morgan Thomas (Minneapolis: University of Minnesota Press, 1993), 72; hereafter cited as *PE*.

11. Kathleen Freeman, *Ancilla to the Pre-Socratic Philosophers* (Cambridge, MA: Harvard University Press, 1983), 19.

12. For an analysis of the shift from the code of honor to the concept of dignity in contemporary democratic societies, see Peter Berger, "On the Obsolescence of the Concept of Honour," in *Revisions: Changing Perspectives in Moral Philosophy*, ed. Stanley Hauerwas and Alasdair MacIntyre (Notre Dame, IN: University of Notre Dame Press, 1983), 172–81.

13. Aristotle, *The Complete Works*, ed. J. Barnes (Princeton, NJ: Princeton University Press, 1985), 2164 (1361a 25–30).

14. Aristotle, *The Complete Works*, 1731 (1095b 20–25), 1773 (1123b 20).

15. If honor is only the highest of all exterior goods, and not the highest in general (the highest good is truth, and is of the order of the *bios theoretikos*), it is because it is, after all, "superficial": "it is thought to depend on those who bestow honour rather than on him who receives it, but the good we divine to be something of one's own and not easily taken from one" (Aristotle, *The Complete Works*, 1731 [1095b 20–30]).

16. Jean-François Lyotard with Jean-Loup Thébaud, *Just Gaming*, trans. Wlad Godzich (Minneapolis: University of Minnesota Press, 1985), 54–55.

17. Theodor W. Adorno, *Negative Dialectics*, trans. E. B. Ashton (New York: Continuum, 1997), 381.

18. Theodor W. Adorno, *Metaphysik. Begriff und Probleme* (Frankfurt/Main: Suhrkamp, 1998), 61.

19. Adorno, *Negative Dialectics*, 391–95.

20. Adorno, *Metaphysik*, 196.

21. Ibid., 35.

22. Ibid., 42.

23. Ibid., 109.

24. Ibid., 34–35.

25. Ibid., 81; see also 140.

26. Adorno, *Negative Dialectics*, 391–92.

27. The restrictive locution "at least" (*du moins*) in "at least . . . to save the honor of thinking," suggests a defeat of all attempts (by thinking and other efforts) to give the differend its due. In this, the maxim "to save the honor of thinking" conforms to the current use in French of *sauver l'honneur*, which is used on the occasion of defeat (of a soccer team, for instance), and marks an effort not to lose face.

28. Jacob Rogozinski, "Lyotard: Differend, Presence," *L'esprit créateur* 31, no. 1 (Spring 1991): 107–21, at 110.

29. Ibid., 112–13.

30. For Geoffrey Bennington's and Jean-François Lyotard's responses to Rogozinski's paper at the Centre Sèvres, see *Témoigner du différend: Quand phraser ne se peut; Autour de Jean-François Lyotard*, ed. Pierre-Jean Labarrière (Paris: Editions Osiris, 1989), 85, 123, 126.

31. Geoffrey Bennington, *Lyotard: Writing the Event* (New York: Columbia University Press, 1988), 144–45, 153.

32. Jean-François Lyotard, *Questions au judaïsme: Entretiens avec Elizabeth Weber* (Paris: Desclée de Brouwer, 1996), 205–6.

33. This priority is explicable insofar as the cognitive discourse is the locus of truth. Tilman Borsche, in a superb essay, has shown that Lyotard's achievement in *The Differend* consists in having displaced the problematic of truth from its locus in the proposition or statement, a locus that it has enjoyed since Plato (who unseated the Pre-Socratics' assumption that the locus of truth is in the name), or

rather since Platonism until today. Lyotard situates its locus in actual discourse, that is, in the temporal interlinkage of phrases, by departing from the Platonist model of truth according to which truth is an invariable and is independent of the addressor and addressee of phrases. In thus focusing on the event of phrases, Borsche argues, Lyotard is much closer to Plato himself, that is, to the dialectic in the dramatic shape in which it can be found in Plato's dialogues. See Tilman Borsche, "Orte der Wahrheit, Orte des Widerstreits: Zur diskursiven Bestimmung von Bedeutung nach Lyotard," in *Fremde Vernunft. Zeichen und Interpretation*, vol. 4, ed. Josef Simon and Werner Stegmaier (Frankfurt/Main: Suhrkamp, 1998), 113–38.

34. Alain Badiou, "Custos, quid noctis?," *Critique* 450 (November 1984): 851–63, at 860. See also p. 854. Bennington makes a similar remark in *Lyotard: Writing the Event*. He writes: "In general, this insistence on the application of the rules of the cognitive genre to cases which might not come under its jurisdiction is the most common form of *différend* discussed by Lyotard (despite his insistence on their multiplicity)" (145).

35. When Lyotard remarks that to "distinguish between phrase regimens . . . comes down to limiting the competence of a given tribunal to a given kind of a phrase" (*D*, 5), it is clear that this distinction serves to keep illicit demands in check and to recall a tribunal (or a genre of discourse) to the area in which it can make reasonable demands. A main rationale for distinguishing between phrase regimens is to prevent unnecessary and irrational differends. Such fundamentally illicit differends arise from demands to account that are legitimate in certain discourses, to objects that, by contrast, and that for essential reasons, defy such demands. Thus there clearly are avoidable differends.

36. See also *PE*, 61–62.

37. If the cognitive phrase comes after a silence, it is (perhaps) because all phrases hold at bay the threat that nothingness could be a real possibility.

38. This is the moment where a brief reflection on the role of the Notices in *The Differend* may be appropriate. Under the entry "Reader," in the "Preface: Reading Dossier," Lyotard offers up *The Differend* to any philosophically interested reader, "philosophical" here involving only the minimal agreement of not seeking to be "done with 'language' and not to 'gain time.'" Yet, he adds, "for the Notices, a little more professional a reader" is required (*D*, xiv). The main body of the work, with its continual fragments of dialogue, in a style not unlike Wittgenstein's *Philosophical Investigations*, is addressed to the general public. The Notices, set in lowercase letters and addressed to the professional philosophers, would at first seem to concern only those who are at some remove from the public or the judge's eye, and who, rather like the intimate circle of the Platonic truth seekers, discuss and instigate the rules for public discourse. Yet, as we have seen from the three Notices discussed so far, they are the spaces in which Lyotard brings to light the hidden presuppositions of the *dialegesthai* and draws the reclusive institution of truth seeking into the open and agonistic space of the *agora*.

39. Adorno, *Negative Dialectics*, 402, 404.
40. Ibid., 364.
41. Ibid., 392 (translation modified).
42. Ibid., 362 (translation modified).
43. Adorno, *Metaphysik*, 180–81.
44. Adorno, *Negative Dialectics*, 365.
45. Ibid., 391–92.
46. Tilman Borsche concludes his essay on Lyotard by explaining: "The 'Problem' of thinking does thus no longer consist in discovering 'the' truth of 'the' things, because these are, in the same way, as truth, conditioned, that is, epiphenomena of different discourses. In contrast, what is at stake in the discourse that 'we' are, and through its suitable (conscientious, responsible) linkages, is 'to save the honor of thinking' " ("Orte der Wahrheit," 138).
47. This demarcation of Lyotard's reflections on thinking after Auschwitz from the similar concerns of Adorno imposes itself because Lyotard's reflections admittedly take off from Adorno's elaborations on this issue in *Negative Dialectics*. Nevertheless, an inquiry into what sets Lyotard's reflections apart from Heidegger's attempts to reconceive of the task of thinking may also be warranted, in spite of the disturbing absence of "Auschwitz" from Heidegger's meditations on why we are "not yet capable of thinking." Undoubtedly, the attempt to overcome metaphysical thinking by way of a meditation on the unthought of metaphysics, and the subsequent determination of the nature and task of thinking from the question of Being, has all the looks of a "merely" philosophical exercise, which would be oblivious to certain historical events and thus to their possible unsettling impact on the certitudes of thinking. However, Heidegger's discussion of the nature of metaphysical thought as representational thought in the first part of his 1951 and 1952 lectures on *What Is Called Thinking* (trans. J. G. Gray [New York: Harper & Row, 1968]) conjures up a state of affairs as regards the human being's relation to what is. Given the distress and the violence that characterize this state of affairs, it is not without resemblance to what both Adorno and Lyotard seek to address, and that seems to confer an urgency that is not simply "theoretical" upon the effort to go beyond metaphysical thinking. In the context of a debate with Nietzsche, from whom he takes his major clues concerning the reasons why we still do not think, Heidegger determines the kind of relation of the human being that has come to dominate modernity (and, hence, the metaphysics of the subject) as representational relating. Such relating not only passes over the human being, but causes thinking to face what it sets in front of itself as something to be resisted and opposed. Having suggested "that such representing [*Vorstellen*] at bottom sets upon everything it sets before itself, in order to depose and decompose it [*herabzusetzen und zu zersetzen*] [. . . and that] it sets all things up in such a way that fundamentally it pursues and sets upon them [*nachstellt*]," he asks: "What is the spirit of this manner of representation? What type of thinking is it that in thought pursues everything in this manner? Of what

kind is the pursuit of thought by man so far?" (84, translation modified). To this question concerning the spirit of the kind of thinking whose aim it is to hunt down whatever it sets before itself, Heidegger answers with Nietzsche that it is "'*the spirit of revenge* [des Geist der Rache].'" He writes: "The pursuit of thought, re-presentation, by the human being so far is determined by revenge, the onset, the attack" (85, translation modified). Heidegger wonders toward the end of these lectures whether Nietzsche has truly achieved the deliverance he sought from the spirit of revenge—a revenge which is neither psychological nor moralistic, but, as Heidegger explains, metaphysical—with his doctrine of the superman and the eternal recurrence of the same. It is thus safe to say that the Heideggerian attempt to reconfigure the task of thinking in the second part of the lectures must be understood against the background of the Nietzschean determination of the vengeful nature of all thinking up to the present. The notion of thinking that emerges from the last part—a thinking that answers the call of Being—is a thinking that has twisted itself free from the spirit of revenge that has dominated representational thinking. For Heidegger, the representational turn of thinking, which climaxes in the world picture of technology, is not a regrettable accident; in a manner similar to Adorno and Lyotard's perception of the effects of thinking, he sees it as intimately tied to the very nature of Western thinking. However, the effort to reach back to a more fundamental conception of thinking leads neither to an all-out discrediting of metaphysics and a subsequent saving of thinking as micrological thinking, nor to seeking the salvation of the honor of thinking by giving the differends caused by thinking their due.

48. Lyotard, *Témoigner du différend*, 119.

NOTES TO "LENDING AN EAR TO THE SILENCE PHRASE"

Note on Ficowski, "Seven Words," in *A Reading of Ashes*, trans. Keith Bosley and Krystyna Wandycz (London: Menard, 1981). According to the author, the poem was inspired by the testimony of a survivor who overheard the seven words of a child being pushed into the gas chamber in Bergen-Belsen: "Mamusiu! Ja przecież byl¯em grzeczny! Ciemno, ciemno!" (Mommy! But I was good! It's dark, dark in here!).

1. Jean-François Lyotard, "Discussions, or Phrasing after Auschwitz," in *The Lyotard Reader*, ed. Andrew Benjamin (Cambridge: Blackwell, 1989), 360–92; hereafter cited as *LR*.

2. Binjamin Wilkomirski, *Fragments: Memories of a Wartime Childhood*, trans. Carol Brown Janeway (New York: Schocken, 1995). In the wake of revelations that Wilkomirski's book is not based on personal experience, *Fragments* was downgraded from Holocaust memoirs to "fake," and the ensuing controversy prompted the publishers, first in Germany and then in the United States, to withdraw it from print. For a balanced account of the controversy, see Stephen Maechler's "definitive report" based on his investigation into Wilkomirski's life, *The Wilkomirski Affair: A Study in Biographical Truth* (New York: Schocken, 2001).

3. Norman Finkelstein, *Holocaust Industry: Reflections on the Exploitation of Jewish Suffering* (New York: Verso, 2000).

4. Allen Dunn, "A Tyranny of Justice: The Ethics of Lyotard's Differend," *boundary 2* 20, no. 1 (1993): 193–220.

5. Lyotard explains the provenance of the term "pagan" from *pagus*, "a border zone where genres of discourse enter into a conflict over the modes of linking. It' s in the *pagus* that the *pax* and the pact are made and unmade. The *vicus*, the *home*, the *Heim*, is a zone in which the differend between the genres of discourse is suspended"; Jean-François Lyotard, *The Differend: Phrases in Dispute*, trans. Georges Van Den Abbeele (Minneapolis: University of Minnesota Press, 1988), 63; hereafter cited as *D*.

6. Jean-François Lyotard, *Lessons on the Analytic of the Sublime*, trans. Elizabeth Rottenberg (Stanford, CA: Stanford University Press, 1994).

7. Immanuel Kant, *Critique of Judgment*, trans. J. H. Bernard (New York: Hafner, 1951), 82.

8. Jean-François Lyotard, *Heidegger and "the jews,"* trans. Andreas Michel and Mark Roberts (Minneapolis: University of Minnesota Press, 1990), 32; hereafter cited as *HJ*.

9. Jean-François Lyotard, "L'inarticulé ou le différend même," in *Figures et conflits rhétoriques*, ed. Michel Meyer and Alain Lempereur (Bruxelles: Université de Bruxelles, 1990), 201–7.

10. David Carroll, "Foreword: The Memory of Devastation and the Responsibilities of Thought," in *HJ*, vii–xxix, at x.

11. Elie Wiesel, *Night* (New York: Bantam Books, 1982), 32.

12. Avital Ronell cites Lanzmann's *Shoah* as an example of a cinematic work that creates conditions for such meetings to occur. The feeling released in between the frames of the film is what allows the Nazi phrase and the Jewish phrase to cohabit in the viewer, that is, to remember. "The Differends of Man," *Diacritics* 19, no. 3–4 (1989): 65–75.

13. Under the impact of burgeoning trauma theory in recent years, historical studies of the Holocaust have now emerged that have challenged the sole mastery of the cognitive genre, most notably the works of Dominick LaCapra. See LaCapra, *Representing the Holocaust: History, Theory, Trauma* (Ithaca, NY: Cornell University Press, 1994), and *Writing History, Writing Trauma* (Baltimore, MD: Johns Hopkins University Press, 2001).

14. Ida Fink, "The Table," in *A Scrap of Time*, trans. Madeline Levine and Francine Prose (Evanston, IL: Northwestern University Press), 141, 149, 156.

15. Krystyna Żywulska, *Przeżyłam Oświęcim* (Oświęcim: Muzeum Narodowe w Oświęcimiu, 1998).

16. Moshe Weiss, *From Oświęcim to Auschwitz* (Oakville, Ontario: Mosaic Press, 1994).

17. Based on my own and my students' experiences of reading *Fragments*, I would counter the assertions of readers such as Philip Gourevitch and Stephen

Maechler that once exposed as a "fake," Wilkomirski's book deteriorates into kitsch.

18. Isabella Leitner, *Fragments of Isabella: A Memoir of Auschwitz* (New York: Dell, 1978).

19. Jean-François Lyotard, *Just Gaming*, trans. Wlad Godzich (Minneapolis: University of Minnesota Press, 1989), 17.

20. Jean-François Lyotard, "The Survivor," in Lyotard, *Toward the Postmodern*, ed. Robert Harvey and Mark S. Roberts (Atlantic Highlands, NJ: Humanities Press, 1993), 144–63; hereafter cited as *TP*.

21. In Lyotard's obituary, Matthew Pateman describes the philosopher's own project in similar terms: "Never so stuck to an idea that he could not unchain himself, Lyotard was a philosopher always on trial"; *Parallax* 5, no. 1 (1999): 130.

22. David Carroll, "Memorial for the *Différend*: In Memory of Jean-François Lyotard," *Parallax* 6, no. 4 (2000): 10.

23. Dunn, "Tyranny of Justice," 220.

24. Lyotard is advocating here nonrepresentational modes of speaking about the unspeakable, and he cites Lanzmann's *Shoah* as an example of perhaps the only work that heeds this imperative. This generous assessment, albeit well deserved, is also rather uncritical of the film's shortcomings and unfair to other nonrepresentational works inspired by the Shoah, such as, for example, Mindy Weisel's abstract paintings or Samuel Bak's Holocaust surrealism.

25. In *The Gates of the Forest*, Wiesel tells a story of a rabbi who intercedes with God to save his people, although he has forgotten the words of the prayer: "Then it fell to Rabbi Israel of Rizhyn to overcome misfortune. Sitting in his armchair, his head in his hands, he spoke to God: 'I am unable to light the fire and I do not know the prayer; I cannot even find the place in the forest. All I can do is to tell the story, and this must be sufficient.' And it was sufficient." Elie Wiesel, *The Gates of the Forest*, trans. Francis Frenaye (New York: Holt, Rinehart and Winston, 1966), epigraph.

26. Lyotard speaks of the aftermath of the disaster experienced by the survivors by using an analogy with an earthquake in which all instruments for the measurement of the cataclysm have been destroyed and therefore it cannot be ascertained scientifically (*D*, 56). It reminds me of an anecdote in Julian Stryjkowski's novel *Wielki strach* [Great Fear] (Warsaw: Czytelnik, 1990), in which the elder of a Jewish community pleads for assistance after the village has been razed to the ground in a fire. When asked for a report on the fire, he answers that the report has burnt with the village; the conflagration is absolute, while skepticism remains.

27. Jean-François Lyotard and Eberhard Gruber, *The Hyphen: Between Judaism and Christianity*, trans. Pascale-Anne Brault and Michael Naas (Amherst, NY: Humanity Books, 1999); hereafter cited as *H*.

28. Art Spiegelman, *Maus: A Survivor's Tale*, vol. 2, *And Here My Troubles Began* (New York: Pantheon Books, 1991), 45.

NOTES TO "TOWARD A FEMINIST ETHICS OF DISSENSUS"

For the longer version of this essay, see Ewa Płonowska Ziarek, *An Ethics of Dissensus: Postmodernity, Feminism, and the Politics of Radical Democracy* (Stanford, CA: Stanford University Press, 2001), 83–116.

1. Seyla Benhabib, *Situating the Self: Gender, Community and Postmodernism in Contemporary Ethics* (New York: Routledge, 1992), 204.

2. Ibid., 213.

3. Ibid., 229.

4. Seyla Benhabib, "Democracy and Difference: Reflections on the Metapolitics of Lyotard and Derrida," *Journal of Political Philosophy* 2 (1994): 1–23, at 23.

5. Nancy Fraser and Linda J. Nicholson, "Social Criticism without Philosophy: An Encounter between Feminism and Postmodernism," in *Feminism/Postmodernism*, ed. Linda J. Nicholson (New York: Routledge, 1990), 24.

6. bell hooks, *Yearning: Race, Gender, and Cultural Politics* (Boston: South End Press, 1990), 21.

7. Fraser and Nicholson, "Social Criticism," 34–35.

8. This comment was made in Tina Chanter's response, entitled "The Politics of Thinking through New Imaginary Communities," at a session titled "Thinking Ethics and Politics: A Close Encounter with Ewa Ziarek," 2004 meeting of the International Association for Philosophy and Literature, Syracuse. I am grateful for this important intervention into the limitations of the feminist politics of difference.

9. hooks, *Yearning*, 55.

10. Jean-François Lyotard, *The Postmodern Condition: A Report on Knowledge*, trans. Geoff Bennington and Brian Massumi (Minneapolis: University of Minnesota Press, 1984), 40; hereafter cited as *PC*.

11. Ernesto Laclau and Chantal Mouffe, *Hegemony and Socialist Strategy: Towards a Radical Democratic Politics* (London: Verso, 1994).

12. Jean-François Lyotard, *The Differend: Phrases in Dispute*, trans. Georges Van Den Abbeele (Minneapolis: University of Minnesota Press, 1988), 140; hereafter cited as *D*.

13. Ernesto Laclau, *New Reflections on the Revolution of Our Time* (London: Verso, 1990), 17.

14. We can explain this double function of antagonism—the rupture of the event and the partial constitution of historical objectivity—in terms of Laclau's distinction between the dislocation of social relations and their contingent historical sedimentation, achieved through the naturalization of hegemonic power structures. See Laclau, *New Reflections*, 34–51.

15. As Lyotard writes in *The Postmodern Condition*, one can find a Nietzschean problematic already in Kant if one rereads antinomies of Kant's acknowledgment of the irreducible conflict of Reason with itself.

16. Emmanuel Levinas, *Totality and Infinity: An Essay on Exteriority*, trans. Alphonso Lingis (Pittsburgh, PA: Duquesne University Press, 1969), 23.

17. For a discussion of the limits of historical knowledge brought by Lyotard's revision of the sign of history, see David Carroll, "Rephrasing the Political with Kant and Lyotard: From Aesthetic to Political Judgments," *Diacritics* 14:4 (1984): 74–88, 78.

18. Immanuel Kant, "An Old Question Raised Again: Is the Human Race Constantly Progressing?," in *On History*, ed. Lewis White Beck (New York: Bobbs-Merrill, 1963), 143.

19. Jean-François Lyotard, "The Sign of History," trans. Geoffrey Bennington, in *Post-Structuralism and the Question of History*, ed. Derek Attridge, Geoffrey Bennington, and Robert Young (London: Cambridge University Press, 1987), 165; hereafter cited as *SH*.

20. To mark the inappropriateness of the term enthusiasm for "our history," Lyotard exposes the limits of the very concept of the sign and necessitates its revision as the differend. "Other names are now part of our history . . . the preliminary question would be: are 'we' today still able to give credence to the concept of the sign of history?" In response to this question that occurs in the last chapter of *The Differend*, Lyotard claims that "[the differend] is not a sign. But it is to be judged, all the way through to its incomparability" (*D*, 181).

21. As Bill Readings aptly puts it, the prescription to be just is "incommensurable with the description of the true" (Readings, *Introducing Lyotard: Art and Politics* [New York: Routledge, 1991], 108). Furthermore, "the confusion of prescriptive justice" with "descriptive *justification*" leads to injustice (112).

22. Jean-François Lyotard, "Levinas' Logic," trans. Ian McLeod, in *The Lyotard Reader*, ed. Andrew Benjamin (Oxford: Blackwell, 1989), 308.

23. Jacques Derrida, "Force of Law: The 'Mystical Foundations of Authority'," in *Deconstruction and the Possibility of Justice*, ed. Drucilla Cornell, Michel Rosenfeld, and David Gray Carlson (New York: Routledge, 1992): 3–68.

24. *Peregrinations: Law, Form, Event* (New York: Columbia University Press, 1988), 15.

25. For an excellent discussion of the shift in Lyotard's thought from the libidinal economy to the question of justice, see Stephen Watson, "The Adventures of the Narrative," in *Philosophy and Non-Philosophy since Merleau-Ponty*, ed. Hugh Silverman (London: Routledge, 1988), 174–89. Although I agree with Watson's argument, I think we need to take into account the opposite movement in Lyotard's work, characteristic of the essays in *The Inhuman*, which seeks the analogon for the complexity of justice in the sexed body.

26. Jean-François Lyotard, "Can Thought Go On without a Body?," in *The Inhuman: Reflections on Time*, trans. Geoffrey Bennington and Rachel Bowlby (Stanford, CA: Stanford University Press, 1991), 12–13; hereafter cited as *CTGWB*.

27. Jean-François Lyotard, "One of the Things at Stake in Women's Struggles," trans. Deborah Clarke, in *The Lyotard Reader*, ed. Andrew Benjamin (Oxford: Blackwell, 1989), 112; hereafter cited as *TSWS*.

28. Jacques Lacan, *Encore: On Feminine Sexuality; The Limits of Love and Knowledge*, trans. Bruce Fink (New York: Norton, 1998).

29. Emmanuel Levinas, *Outside the Subject*, trans. Michel B. Smith (Stanford: Stanford University Press, 1994), 97. For my analysis of incarnation in Levinas's thought, see Ziarek, *Ethics of Dissensus*, 48–62.

30. For Lyotard, this concept of the body changes the relation between transcendence and immanence. What opens the possibility to transcend the given is no longer the fiction of metalanguage abstracted from the body and limited only by the needs of survival but the possibility of desire.

31. For a fuller articulation of such an ethics, see Ziarek, *Ethics of Dissensus*.

NOTES TO "THE WRITINGS OF THE DIFFEREND"

1. [The French term *l'essai*, like the English term "essay," need not refer solely to a type of interpretive literary composition but might also be translated as "experiment" or "trial." These various meanings will be operative throughout this essay.—*Trans.*]

2. *Témoigner du différend: Quand phraser ne se peut; Autour de Jean-François Lyotard*, ed. Pierre-Jean Labarrière (Paris: Editions Osiris, 1989), 118.

3. [In Latin, *vocatur* means "to be called." It is a reference to a passage in *Que peindre?*, where Lyotard, speaking of Adami, writes "He is called, *vocatur*." See *Que peindre? Adami, Arakawa, Buren* (Paris: Éditions de la différence, 1987), 37; hereafter cited as *QP*.—*Trans.*]

4. Jean-François Lyotard, *Le différend* (Paris: Minuit, 1983), 9; hereafter cited as *LD*. Published in English as *The Differend: Phrases in Dispute*, trans. Georges Van Den Abbeele (Minneapolis: University of Minnesota Press, 1988), xi; hereafter cited as *D*.

5. See Gérald Sfez, *Jean-François Lyotard: La faculté d'une phrase* (Paris: Galilée, 2000).

6. Jean-François Lyotard, *L'inhumain: Causeries sur le temps* (Paris: Galilée, 1988), 15. Published in English as *The Inhuman: Reflections on Time*, trans. Geoffrey Bennington and Rachel Bowlby (Stanford, CA: Stanford University Press, 1991), 7.

7. Jean-François Lyotard, "Devant la loi, après la loi," in *Questions au judaïsme: Entretiens avec Elisabeth Weber*, ed. E. Weber (Paris: Desclée de Brouwer, 1996), 209–10.

8. Jean-François Lyotard, *Moralités postmodernes* (Paris: Galilée, 1993), 171; hereafter cited as *MP*. *Postmodern Fables*, trans. Georges Van Den Abbeele (Minneapolis: University of Minnesota Press, 1997), 199; hereafter cited as *PF*.

9. [The French expression *faisait signe* is here translated as "make a sign." Both the French and the English translation convey a number of meanings, such as "to signify," "to signal," or even "to make a gesture." Yet, in this context, it is important to remember that, in Lyotard's work, the term *signe* is often used in

the Kantian sense of "a sign of history." See Jean-François Lyotard, "The Sign of History," in *The Lyotard Reader*, ed. Andrew Benjamin (Cambridge: Blackwell, 1989, 393–411.—*Trans.*]

10. [The French expression *faire geste* is here translated as "make a gesture." It too carries the sense of "to signal" or "to make a sign." It need not be taken merely as the physical act of gesturing; rather, it can also carry the sense of making a gesture which is just a sign of what cannot (or will not) be realized.—*Trans.*]

11. [A crucial theme in the late work of Lyotard, the French term *pâtir* comes from the Greek *pattein*. In Lyotard's work, it is synonymous with "affect," which is how it is translated in this text. It can also be taken, as indicated by the singular verb, as synonymous with "the passibility to the event."—*Trans.*]

12. Jean-François Lyotard, "L'extrême réel: Entretien avec Gérald Sfez," *Rue Descartes*, special issue, "Passions et politique," ed. Gérald Sfez and Marcel Hénaff, 12–13 (May 1995): 200–204; hereafter cited as *ER*.

13. Blaise Pascal, *Pensées*, ed. Louis Lafuma (Paris: Seuil, l'Intégrale), 82–299.

14. [Merleau-Ponty cites this quote from Cézanne; see Maurice Merleau-Ponty, "Eye and Mind," in *The Merleau-Ponty Aesthetics Reader: Philosophy and Painting*, ed. Michael B. Smith, trans. Galen A. Johnson (Evanston, IL: Northwestern University Press, 1993), 139.—*Trans.*]

15. [Merleau-Ponty cites this quote from Michaux; see "Eye and Mind," in *The Merleau-Ponty Aesthetics Reader*, 143.—*Trans.*]

16. [This is another quote attributed to Cézanne by Merleau-Ponty; see Merleau-Ponty, "Cézanne's Doubt," in *The Merleau-Ponty Aesthetics Reader*, 67. It is also quoted by Jean-François Lyotard, "Formule charnelle," *Revue des sciences humaines* 243 (July 1996): 173–80, at 178.—*Trans.*]

17. Maurice Merleau-Ponty, *Phénoménologie de la perception* (Paris: Gallimard, 1945), 248. Published in English as *Phenomenology of Perception*, trans. Colin Smith (London: Routledge, 1989) 214; translation modified.

18. Jean-François Lyotard, *Flora Danica: La sécession du geste dans la peinture de Stig Brøgger* (Paris: Galilée, 1997), 10; hereafter cited as *FD*.

19. [The term *virtù* comes from Machiavelli, for whom it means simultaneously efficiency and courage or fortitude.—*Trans.*]

20. [The phrase "trait of the soul" (*trait d'âme*) is a neologism. It plays on the French expression *trait d'esprit*, which translated literally would mean "trait of mind," but which commonly means "a witticism." In coining this term, Sfez plays with Lyotard's understanding of the distinction between mind (*esprit*) and soul (*âme*): if a witticism is a trait of mind insofar as it is a sign of intelligence or wit, the feeling of presence would likewise be a trait of soul insofar as it is a sign of a passibility to affect.—*Trans.*]

21. Jean-François Lyotard, "Le visuel touché," *Rue Descartes*, special issue, "Passions et politique," ed. Gérald Sfez and Marcel Hénaff, 12–13 (May 1995): 219–35; hereafter cited as *VT*.

22. *QP*, 51. English translation by David Macey, *The Lyotard Reader*, 224.

23. [In English in the original.—*Trans.*]

24. [See Jean-François Lyotard, *Lectures d'enfance* (Paris: Galilée, 1991), 109–26. Published in English as "On What Is 'Art,'" trans. Robert Harvey, in *Toward the Postmodern*, ed. Robert Harvey and Mark S. Roberts (Atlantic Highlands, NJ: Humanities Press, 1993), 164–75.—*Trans.*]

25. [Leonardo da Vinci distinguished painting from sculpture by opposing two methods: the method *via di porre* (to add) and the method *via di levare* (to subtract). It is an opposition that Freud will later transpose into the domain of psychoanalysis: hypnosis, which adds; analysis, which subtracts and which is preferable for this reason.—*Trans.*]

26. James Joyce, *Giacomo Joyce*, trans. André du Bouchet (Paris: Gallimard, 1973), 2.

27. [In French, *soûl*, which is being used as a noun in the phrase *le soûl de l'âme*, is an adjective, which could also be translated as "satiation."—*Trans.*]

NOTES TO "THE INARTICULATE AFFECT"

1. See Lyotard's comments on the back cover of *Le différend* (Paris: Minuit, 1983), and the early editions of its English translation, *The Differend: Phrases in Dispute*, trans. Georges Van Den Abbeele (Minneapolis: University of Minnesota Press, 1988).

2. Jean-François Lyotard, "Emma: Between Philosophy and Psychoanalysis," trans. Michael Sanders et al., in *Lyotard: Philosophy, Politics and the Sublime*, ed. Hugh J. Silverman (New York: Routledge, 2002), 23–45; hereafter cited as *E*. "Emma" was first published in *La nouvelle revue de psychanalyse* 39 (1989) and later included in Jean-François Lyotard, *Misère de la philosophie* (Paris: Galilée, 2000), 55–95; hereafter cited as *MPH*. All translations from the essays from *MPH* are my own.

3. See Sigmund Freud, "Project for a Scientific Psychology" (1895), in *The Standard Edition of the Complete Psychological Works of Sigmund Freud*, trans. and ed. James Strachey et al., 24 vols. (London: Hogarth, 1966) 1:283–397.

4. Ron Katwan, "The Affect in the Work of Jean-François Lyotard," *Surfaces* 3, no. 13 (1993): 1–22, at 4.

5. Jean-François Lyotard, "La phrase-affect (D'un supplément au *Différend*)," in *MPH*, 43–54.

6. Jean-François Lyotard, "La peinture, anamnèse du visible," in *MPH*, 97–115.

7. Geoffrey Bennington, "The Same, Even, Itself . . . ," *Parallax* 17 (2000): 88–98, at 91–92.

8. Jean-François Lyotard, *Lectures d'enfance* (Paris: Galilée, 1991), 134; hereafter cited as *LdE*. All translations from *LdE* are my own.

9. See Jean-François Lyotard, *Moralités postmodernes* (Paris: Galilée, 1993), 191. See also *MPH*, 51.

10. See *LdE*, 109–26.

11. André Green, *The Fabric of Affect in the Psychoanalytic Discourse* (London and New York: Routledge, 1999), 3.

12. For more on this "debt of affect," see *LdE*, 146; *MPH*, 103. See also Plínio Walder Prado Jr., "La dette d'affect," in *Jean-François Lyotard: L'exercice du différend*, ed. Dolorès Lyotard, Jean-Claude Milner, and Gérald Sfez (Paris: Presses Universitaires de France, 2001), 57–75.

13. See Jean-François Lyotard, *Heidegger and "the jews,"* trans. Andreas Michel and Mark Roberts (Minneapolis: University of Minnesota Press, 1990), 65; *MPH*, 103.

14. Cited in *LdE*, 145.

15. Cited in ibid., 146.

16. Jean-François Lyotard, "Gesture and Commentary," trans. Stephen Adam Schwartz, in *Between Ethics and Aesthetics: Crossing the Boundaries*, ed. Dorota Glowacka and Stephen Boos (Buffalo: State University of New York Press, 2002), 73–82, at 80.

17. Sigmund Freud, "On the Psychical Mechanism of Hysterical Phenomena: Preliminary Communication," in *The Standard Edition*, 2:17.

NOTES TO "JEAN-FRANÇOIS'S INFANCY"

1. See Walter Benjamin, "Berliner Kindheit um Neunzehnhundert," in *Gesammelte Schriften*, vol. 4, 1, ed. Tillman Rexroth (Frankfurt-am-Main: Suhrkamp Verlag, 1972), 235–304.

2. Jean-François Lyotard, "Prescription," in *Lectures d'enfance* (Paris: Galilée, 1991), 35–56; hereafter cited as *LdE*. "Prescription" is collected in *Toward the Postmodern*, ed. Robert Harvey and Mark S. Roberts (Atlantic Highlands, NJ: Humanities Press, 1993), 176–92; hereafter cited as *TP*.

3. I refer to my *Infant Figures* (Stanford, CA: Stanford University Press, 2000).

4. Let me add that this belated recognition of the lesson was probably also enabled by that fact that I had received one like it many years before from Kenneth Burke. Burke suggested to me in my very first semester of graduate study that if I wanted to discover my intellectual vocation, my particular path in literature and philosophy, I should translate. I began to learn the truth of that striking suggestion by translating Blanchot (while reading Hölderlin on translation)—the lesson being that one finds one's language through encounter with the language of the other. Jean-François prompted me, I believe, to a comparable experience, though I think that the added dimension of the forcefulness of his pedagogical intervention is best understood from the notion of usage Heidegger develops when he speaks of a freeing relation to another being. The reference to Heidegger, in any case, helps underscore that the experience—the encounter and

the discovery—involves a form of *poiesis* or *praxis* (Heidegger's notion of usage is a recasting of these latter terms).

5. This practical dimension of the complex "lesson" to which I have referred is developed perhaps nowhere more powerfully than in the essay by Emmanuel Levinas, "The Temptation of Temptation," in *Nine Talmudic Readings*, trans. Annette Aronowicz (Bloomington: Indiana University Press, 1990), 30–51.

6. Jean-François Lyotard, *Le postmoderne expliqué aux enfants* (Paris: Galilée, 1986). Translated as *The Postmodern Explained: Correspondence, 1982–1985*, translation eds. Julian Pefanis and Morgan Thomas. (Minneapolis: University of Minnesota Press, 1993); hereafter cited as *PE*. The English translation omits the crucial reference to children in the title.

7. See Jean-François Lyotard, *The Inhuman: Reflections on Time*, trans. Geoffrey Bennington and Rachel Bowlby (Stanford, CA: Stanford University Press, 1991), 184; hereafter cited as *I*.

8. Jean-François Lyotard, "Voix," in *LdE*, 129–53.

9. The question of the relation between sexual difference and ontological difference proved to be one of the nodal points of concern at the conference at Emory University at which the paper was delivered on which this essay is based. It would be impossible to address this issue satisfactorily here, but let me suggest that I understand Jean-François's argument to be comparable to that of Luce Irigaray as it is articulated in *Speculum of the Other Woman*, trans. Gillian G. Gill (Ithaca, NY: Cornell University Press, 1985). Neither author reduces the one difference to the other; rather, they think the "experience" of sexual difference as something like the bodily threshold (a threshold that is never fully crossed) for the relation to ontological difference. I attempt to articulate Irigaray's understanding of this relation in *Language and Relation: . . . That There Is Language* (Stanford, CA: Stanford University Press, 1996).

10. One could perfectly well invert this question and note that something like "thought"—defined as entailing an openness to alterity—would not itself be thinkable without something like infancy, and that thought always knows this insufficiency. A logic that says that only the adult can know childhood (proleptically) will proceed from the logic of thought's necessary debt (by reason of its finitude, it must have an infancy, etc.). But Jean-François starts from the exigency of infancy, from its bodily "fact." Hence the order of questioning that I obey here.

11. Jean-François Lyotard, *Discours, figure* (Paris: Editions Klincksieck, 1974), 328–54.

12. I have translated Jean-François's *comme si* with "as though" because I understand it in relation to the notion of supposition to which I have referred. I will have to develop on another occasion his appropriation of the Kantian *als ob*, whose standard translation is "as if."

13. Maurice Blanchot, *The Writing of the Disaster*, trans. Ann Smock (Lincoln: University of Nebraska Press, 1986), 116.

14. "Saying yes to the gift of the undecipherable message, to the election that the request is, the (impossible) alliance with the other who is nothing, signifies the assumption of the I's fracture . . . 'the assumption [of passivity] nowhere exceeds passivity'" (Jean-François Lyotard, *The Differand: Phrases in Dispute*, trans. Georges Van Den Abbeele [Minneapolis: University of Minnesota Press, 1988], 112–13; hereafter cited as *D*).

15. Blanchot, *Writing of the Disaster*, 72.

16. "The diaspora, persecution, the Shoah, all these accelerated modes of dispatching into nothingness, leave the soul without the support of a tradition; they leave to its desolation only the responsibility of saying yes or no to abjection, only the infancy of the mind, the capacity of judging, which is true filiation" (*LdE*, 154; translation modified).

NOTES TO "ON THE UNRELENTING CREEPINESS OF CHILDHOOD"

1. I discuss the relation of idiocy and its correlates to philosophy more fully in *Stupidity* (Champaign: University of Illinois Press, 2001).

2. Jean-François Lyotard, *The Inhuman: Reflections on Time*, trans. Geoffrey Bennington and Rachel Bowlby (Stanford, CA: Stanford University Press, 1991), 4; hereafter cited as *I*.

3. Jean-François Lyotard, "Mainmise," in Jean-François Lyotard and Eberhard Gruber, *The Hyphen: Between Judaism and Christianity*, trans. Pascale-Anne Brault and Michael Naas (Amherst, NY: Humanity Books, 1999); hereafter cited as *H*. It may be useful to consider the translator's note: "*Mainmise*—from the French *main* and *mettre*: 1. A term from feudal jurisprudence referring to the action of taking hold of or seizing someone because of infidelity or lack of devotion to the feudal lord. 2. The action of laying a hand upon or striking someone. 3. The freeing of slaves by their lords (Emile Littré, *Dictionnaire de la langue française*, edited by Encyclopaedia Britannica, Chicago: 1978). The *Pluridictionnaire de Larousse* adds that *mainmise* can also refer to the action of laying a hand on and having an exclusive influence over something or someone—as in a state's *mainmise* over certain businesses (Paris: Librairie Larousse, 1975)" (quoted in *H*, 12).

4. In this regard a careful reading of Jean-Luc Nancy, *L'expérience de la liberté* (Paris: Galilée, 1988), would complicate the trajectories we are pursuing. Freedom is linked to the singular experience of existence, an experience that does not obey the logic of *fact* that would be opposable to the law.

5. This becomes one of the fixed points of the ethics of psychoanalysis. See Jacques Lacan, *Le séminaire*: *L'éthique de la psychanalyse, livre VII* (Paris: Editions du Seuil, 1986). Published in English as *The Seminar of Jacques Lacan,* book 7, *The Ethics of Psychoanalysis, 1959–1960*, trans., Dennis Porter (New York: Norton, 1992).

6. For more on addiction, see Avital Ronell, *Crack Wars: Literature, Addiction, Mania* (Lincoln: University of Nebraska Press, 1992).

7. Martin Heidegger, *Sein und Zeit* (Tübingen: Max Niemeyer, 1979). See also Christopher Fynsk, *Heidegger: Thought and Historicity* (Ithaca, NY: Cornell University Press, 1986).

8. Jean-François Lyotard, *Peregrinations: Law, Form, Event* (New York: Columbia University Press, 1988), 9; hereafter cited as *P.*

9. My last conversation with Lyotard concerned depletion, his and mine, that is, my chronic fatigue and the preparations he was making to teach a course at Emory University the following semester on fatigue.

10. One of the chapters in *Peregrinations* bears the title "Clouds." Lyotard links cloud formations to thought.

11. There is a sense in which freedom wins out: "But modern emancipation did at least open up an horizon. An horizon, let's say, of freedom. Of a freeing of freedom. Yet as this freedom 'wins out' over itself, as it extends its *mancipium*, its grip, as we approach what I tried to designate, and very poorly, by the name postmodernity, this horizon (historicity) in turn disappears. And it is as if a paganism without any Olympus or Pantheon, without *prudentia*, fear, grace or debt, a *desperate* paganism, were being reconstituted in the name of something that is in no way testamentary, that is neither a law nor a faith but a fortuitous cosmological rule: development" (*H*, 9).

12. George Steiner, *Comment taire?* (Geneva: Éditions Cavaliers Seuls, 1986). The title homonymically combines "How to Keep Silent" with "Commentary."

13. Franz Kafka, "Abraham," trans. Clement Greenberg, in *Parables in German and English* (New York: Schocken, 1946), 36–41; hereafter cited as *A*.

14. Jacques Derrida, *The Gift of Death*, trans. David Wills (Chicago: University of Chicago Press, 1995), 58.

15. Søren Kierkegaard, *"Fear and Trembling" and "The Sickness unto Death,"* trans. Walter Lowrie (Princeton, NJ: Princeton University Press, 1981), 35.

16. Although the Bible does not make Abraham clean his room before he can go out, it turns out that Kierkegaard does. "It was early in the morning, and everything in Abraham's house was ready for the journey." Søren Kierkegaard, "Exordium," in *Fear and Trembling/Repetition*, ed. and trans. Howard V. Hong and Edna H. Hong (Princeton, NJ: Princeton University Press, 1983), 14.

17. For Freud and his analysis of the *Geschenk*, see his *Jokes and Their Relation to the Unconscious*, in *The Standard Edition of the Complete Psychological Works of Sigmund Freud*, ed. James Strachey and Anna Freud, 26 vols. (London: Hogarth, 1964), 8:166. On the connectedness of the gift and laughter, see Jean-Luc Nancy, "Laughter, Presence," in *Birth to Presence*, trans. Brian Holmes et al. (Stanford, CA: Stanford University Press, 1993): "Laughter is thus neither a presence nor an absence. It is the offering of a presence in its own disappearance. It is not given but offered" (383).

18. See also Kafka's parable "Die Prüfung (The Test)" in *Parables and Paradoxes* (New York: Schocken, 1958), 80: "'Bleib,' sagte er, 'das war ja nur eine Prüfung. Wer die Fragen nicht beantwortet, hat die Prüfung bestanden'" ["Hold

on," he said; "That was just a test. Anyone who didn't answer the question passed it"].

19. In *The Last Trial: On the Legends and Lore of the Command to Abraham to Offer Isaac as a Sacrifice: The Akedah*, trans. Judah Goldin (Woodstock, VT: Jewish Lights, 1993), Shalom Spiegel describes the way in which the rabbinic tradition has engaged the puzzle of Abraham descending—to all intents and purposes *alone*—from Mount Moriah. ("So Abraham returned to the young men" [Genesis 22:19]). Spiegel shows how significant was the interpretation that considered Isaac to have been wounded or indeed killed by Abraham, an interpretation that began to emerge in early rabbinic commentaries. By the twelfth century, Abraham Ibn Ezra saw a need to defend the verse against this interpretation: "'And Abraham returned'—And Isaac is not mentioned. . . . But he who asserts that Abraham slew Isaac and abandoned him, and that afterwards Isaac came to life again, is speaking contrary to writ" (quoted in Spiegel, *The Last Trial*, 8).

20. Take still another Abraham, one who stages a collusion between the imaginary and real fathers—the depriving and castrating ones, the father, according to Lacan, elevated to the rank of Great Fucker. ("If we are sufficiently cruel to ourselves to incorporate the father, it is perhaps because we have a lot to reproach this father with. . . . It is this imaginary father [the one associated with the experience of privation] and not the real one which is the basis of the providential image of God. And the function of the superego in the end, from its final point of view, is hatred for God, the reproach that God has handled things so badly"). Finally: "What is in question is the moment when the subject quite simply perceives that his father is an idiot or a thief, as the case may be, or quite simply a weakling or, routinely, an old fogey, as in Freud's case." Or Abraham's. Lacan, *The Ethics of Psychoanalysis, 1959–1960*, 307–8.

NOTES TO "PASSAGES OF THE MAYA"

1. André Malraux, *Antimémoires* (Paris: Gallimard [NRF "Blanche"], 1967), 114. [All translations in this essay are my own.—*Trans.*]

2. André Malraux, *Les voix du silence* (Paris: Gallimard, 1951), 418.

3. Ibid., 416.

4. André Malraux, *Le démon de l'absolu*, in *Oeuvres complètes*, vol. 2 (Paris: Gallimard [Pléiade], 1996), 2, 1293.

5. Jean-François Lyotard, *Signé, Malraux* (Paris: Grasset et Fasquelle, 1996), 9; hereafter cited as *SMX*. Published in English as *Signed, Malraux*, trans. Robert Harvey (Minneapolis: University of Minnesota Press, 1999).

6. Louis-Ferdinand Céline, *Entretiens avec le Professeur Y* (Paris: Gallimard [NRF], 1955), 101.

7. Louis-Ferdinand Céline, *Les beaux draps* (Paris: Nouvelles éditions françaises, 1941), 148.

8. André Malraux, *Fragments d'une réflexion sur les "Antimémoires,"* in *Oeuvres complètes*, vol. 3 (Paris: Gallimard [Pléiade], 1996), 897.

9. Blaise Cendrars, *Trop c'est trop*, in *Oeuvres complètes* (Paris: Le Club Français du Livre, 1969), 15, 152.

10. Céline, *Entretiens*, 67.

11. On the occasion of the reissue of this title in the paperback "Folio" collection, in 1972, and at the same moment that Malraux reinterprets his works in terms of Buddhism.

12. André Malraux, *Les chênes que l'on abat* (Paris: Gallimard [Soleil], 1971), 61.

13. "My gratitude to those who, in one way or another, helped me to write this 'hypobiography'" (*SMX*, 355).

14. In an interview given in August 1996 to *Magazine littéraire* ("Malraux et sa légende"), no. 347: "a hypobiography is a hypothetical biography" (27).

15. Malraux, *Les chênes que l'on abat*, 96.

16. Ibid., 95.

17. Malraux, *Antimémoires*, 193.

18. André Malraux, *Le miroir des limbes* (Paris: Gallimard [Pléiade], 1976), 361.

19. André Malraux, *Les noyers de l'Altenburg*, in *Oeuvres complètes*, vol. 2 (Paris: Gallimard [Pléiade], 1996), 764.

20. Malraux, *Le miroir des limbes*, 727.

21. Malraux, *Les voix du silence*, 452.

22. Malraux, *Le miroir des limbes*, 707.

23. Jean-François Lyotard, "Nécessité de Lazare," in *Albert Ayme: Les nuicts* (Paris: Traversières, 1995), 63.

NOTES TO "LYOTARD ARCHIPELAGO"

This essay was first presented at a memorial session for Jean-François Lyotard at the Society for Phenomenology and Existential Philosophy, Eugene, Oregon, October 7, 1999.

1. See Jean-François Lyotard, *La confession d'Augustin* (Paris: Galilée, 1998).

2. I have cited here only figures or proper names that are treated in some depth in Lyotard's work and have left aside all those thousands of figures in margins, notes, or parentheses, or referred to in passing or summed up in an ellipsis, often with an astonishing lucidity and power of synthesis.

3. See Jean-François Lyotard, "A Bizarre Partner," in *Postmodern Fables*, trans. Georges Van Den Abbeele (Minneapolis: University of Minnesota Press, 1997), 146–47.

4. Lyotard's unfinished text on Augustine's *Confessions* bears witness to this in a striking way.

5. Jean-François Lyotard, *Signed, Malraux*, trans. Robert Harvey (Minneapolis: University of Minnesota Press, 1999); hereafter cited as *SM*.

6. Jean-François Lyotard, *Chambre sourde: L'antiesthétique de Malraux* (Paris: Galilée, 1998); hereafter cited as *CS*. All translations from this text are my own.

Published in English as *Soundproof Room: Malraux's Anti-Aesthetics*, trans. Robert Harvey (Stanford, CA: Stanford University Press, 2001).

7. André Malraux, *Lazarus*, trans. Terence Kilmartin (New York: Holt, Rinehart and Winston, 1977), 79; hereafter cited as *L*.

8. Jean-François Lyotard, "Several Silences," trans. Joseph Maier, in *Driftworks*, ed. Roger McKeon (New York: Semiotext(e), 1984), 90–110, esp. 99–101.

9. Jean-François Lyotard, *Political Writings*, trans. Bill Readings with Kevin Paul Geiman (Minneapolis: University of Minnesota Press, 1993), 5; hereafter cited as *PW*. Lyotard in the essay "Born in 1925" calls Malraux and Breton "prophets," "foretelling the future and calling forth being through their speech. . . . Speaking often takes on this power at the dawn and twilight of civilizations" (*PW*, 87).

10. Note that Malraux speaks more than once of Augustine's *Confessions* in this work—yet another point of intersection in the trajectories of these two thinkers.

11. See Malraux's references to autobiography in *L*, 67.

12. André Malraux, *Man's Fate*, trans. Haakon M. Chevalier (New York: Random House, 1961), 54; hereafter cited as *MF*.

13. This scene is treated again at some length in *SM*. See, e.g., 135, 204, 210–12.

14. The foot sticking out from the netting "lived like a sleeping animal" (*MF*, 4). Ch'en mistakes a drop of blood running down his arm for an "insect running over his skin" (*MF*, 5). After the attack, something "prevented him from returning to the world of men" (*MF*, 7; see also 11). Shanghai is later described as "a silence full of lives at once remote and very near, like that of a forest saturated with insects" (*MF*, 90).

15. Interestingly, Kyo already, albeit obscurely, holds the key to this exteriorization and alienation of the voice. He "knows" that it's a question of the throat: "that record, *his* voice which he had not recognized a while ago. . . . He thought of it with the same complex uneasiness that he had felt when, as a child, he was shown his tonsils which the surgeon had just removed" (*MF*, 26).

16. Jean-François Lyotard, *L'inhumain: Causeries sur le temps* (Paris: Galilée, 1988), 10. (my translation). Published in English as *The Inhuman: Reflections on Time,* trans. Geoffrey Bennington and Rachel Bowlby (Stanford, CA: Stanford University Press, 1991).

17. In his *Note on Malraux,* Blanchot argues that Malraux is perhaps always looking only for himself in his novels, though he finds himself in the history and events of his time. See Maurice Blanchot, *La part du feu* (Paris: Gallimard, 1984), 204–7.

18. See Malraux's description of anxiety, which is not unlike that of Heidegger in *Being and Time*: "And yet the feeling, the awareness of death exists: a feeling without an object, like anxiety, one that invents its object" (*L*, 106).

19. This metonymy of death is evoked by such things as the striped hospital clothing, which reminds Malraux of the shadows found in the concentration camps in 1945 (*L*, 70).

20. Lyotard refers explicitly to Roland Barthes' *La chambre claire* and his use of the notion of the *punctum*; it thus seems as if Lyotard's title, which substitutes the ear for the eye, were an attempt to reinscribe the *punctum*, the I-without-me that breaks all codes and narratives (*CS*, 110).

21. Lyotard writes at the end of *Des dispositifs pulsionnels* (Paris: Christian Bourgois, 1980), 304, in the context of an essay on Nietzsche: "The *voyage* is a passage without trace, a forgetting, snapshots that are multiple only for discourse, not for themselves. That is why there is no *representation* for this voyage, for this nomadism of intensities."

NOTES TO "CHILDISH THINGS"

1. Jean-François Lyotard, "La mainmise," in *Lyotard: Les déplacements philosophiques*, ed. Niels Brügger, Finn Frandsen, and Dominique Pirotte (Brussels: De Boeck, 1993), 125–36, at 131; translated in Jean-François Lyotard and Eberhard Gruber, *The Hyphen: Between Judaism and Christianity*, trans. Pascal-Anne Brault and Michael Naas (Amherst, NY: Humanity Books, 1999), 7; hereafter cited as *H*.

2. Jean-François Lyotard, *Signé, Malraux* (Paris: Grasset et Fasquelle, 1996), 25; hereafter cited as *SMX*. All translations from this text are my own. Published in English as *Signed, Malraux*, trans. Robert Harvey (Minneapolis: University of Minnesota Press, 1999).

3. Jean-François Lyotard, "Retour," in *Lectures d'enfance* (Paris: Galilée, 1991), 11–33; hereafter cited as *LdE*: "filiation obeys the general principle that it is reversible. The father is thus his son's son, as the son is his father's father. They engender each other. One might say that they are the same engendering itself" (23; my translation). Cf. too "On a Hyphen," in *H*, on St. Paul: "Paul's suffering, his own passion, consists in having to kill the father of his own tradition, or at least in having to pronounce him dead. And to engender the true father revealed by Jesus. This is the suffering of a son who must become the father of his father" (16), and "La mainmise" (132ff [*H* 7ff]).

4. Jean-François Lyotard, foreword to Andrew Benjamin, *The Lyotard Reader* (Oxford: Blackwell, 1989), xiii; here retranslated from the French version, "Directions to Servants," in *Moralités postmodernes* (Paris: Galilée, 1988), 131–41, at 140. See also "*Domus* et la mégapole," in *L'inhumain: Causeries sur le temps* (Paris: Galilée, 1988), 203–15; hereafter cited as *LI*: "Thought wakes up in the middle, the *milieu*, of words that are very old, laden with a thousand domesticities. . . . Thinking, which is writing, means awakening in them a childhood that these oldies have not yet had. . . . One advances, but the past in words is waiting there ahead" (209). All translations from this text are my own. Published in English as *the Inhuman: Reflections on Time*, trans. Geoffrey Bennington and Rachel Bowlby (Stanford, CA: Stanford University Press, 1991).

5. Jean-François Lyotard, *La confession d'Augustin* (Paris: Galilée, 1998), 63; hereafter cited as *CdA*. All translations from this text are my own. Published in

English as *The Confession of Augustine*, trans. Richard Beardsworth (Stanford, CA: Stanford University Press, 2000).

6. Lyotard, *SMX*, 42, 335, 340, 341.

7. Jacques Derrida, "Préjugés: Devant la loi," in Jacques Derrida, Vincent Descombes, Garbis Kortian, Philippe Lacoue-Labarthe, and Jean-Luc Nancy, *La faculté de juger* (Paris: Minuit, 1985).

8. Cf. too "La mainmise," which links childhood more obviously to the question of "the jews," an issue I am sidestepping here (but see my "Lyotard and 'the Jews,'" in *Modernity, Culture and "the Jew,"* ed. Brian Cheyette and Laura Marcus [Cambridge: Polity Press, 1998], 188–96): "By childhood, I understand not only, like the rationalists, an age deprived of reason. I understand that condition of being *affected* when we do not have the means—language and representation—to name, identify, reproduce and recognise what affects us. I understand by childhood that we are born before being born to ourselves. And therefore born of others, but also born to others, given over defencelessly to others" (127; my translation [*H*, 2]).

9. *SMX*, 38; Jean-François Lyotard, *Chambre sourde: L'antiesthétique de Malraux* (Paris: Galilée, 1998), 30; hereafter cited as *CS*. All translations from this text are my own. Published in English as *Soundproof Room: Malraux's Anti-Aesthetics*, trans. Robert Harvey (Stanford, CA: Stanford University Press, 2001).

10. Jean-François Lyotard, *Heidegger et "les juifs"* (Paris: Galilée, 1988), 68; hereafter cited as *HLJ*.

11. "La mainmise," 127; (*H*, 2–3).

12. But compare an early remark from the opening of Jean-François Lyotard, *Discours, figure* (Paris: Klincksieck, 1971), hereafter cited as *DF*: "In its radicality, this return to scripture understood as allocution of the Other and as promise, in which Jewish thought and demythologized Christian thought come together, even gives up on the eye listening. Master of illusion, slave of illustrations, always the 'evil eye.' First and last philosophy is, as E. Levinas says, morality, the face-to-face of the face because the face is presence of the absolutely Other, the only Gegenstand worthy of the name. . . . This book is a defense of the eye . . . there is no absolutely Other" (10–11).

13. This was the burden of Elisabeth de Fontenay's assessment in her paper at the Jean-François Lyotard conference in Paris on March 23–25, 1999.

14. Especially in English, perhaps, given its late translation date (1991).

15. Jean-François Lyotard, *La phénoménologie* (Paris: Presses Universitaires de France, 1954), 43 (my translation).

16. For an interesting translator's reflection on the problems of this motif of *la redite*, see Robert Harvey, "Lyotard in Passing," *October* 86 (Fall 1998): 19–23, at 21.

17. Geoffrey Bennington, *Lyotard: Writing the Event* (Manchester: Manchester University Press, 1988); see Lyotard's comments in *Lyotard: Les déplacements philosophiques*, 138. See also the interview with Richard Beardsworth, "Nietzsche

and the Inhuman: An Interview with Jean-François Lyotard," in *Journal of Nietzsche Studies* 7 (1994): 67–130, at 89.

18. Cf. Jean-François Lyotard, *La condition postmoderne* (Paris: Minuit, 1979), 8, 99, 106; Jean-François Lyotard, *Le différend* (Paris: Minuit, 1983), Notice Kant 3; hereafter cited as *LD*. All translations from this text are my own. Published in English as *The Differend: Phrases in Dispute*, trans. Georges Van Den Abbeele (Minneapolis: University of Minnesota Press, 1988).

19. Lyotard, *La phénoménologie*, 43 (my translation).

20. Any attempted symptomatic reading of Lyotard himself would have to pursue this motif of the *paroi*, which in the plural gives a subtitle to a section of the book on Duchamp, *Les transformateurs Duchamp* (Paris: Galilée, 1977), 43–58, where sexual difference is again the issue. See also Jean-François Lyotard, *L'assassinat de l'expérience par la peinture, Monory* (Paris: Le Castor Astral, 1984), 12ff.

21. Jean-François Lyotard, "'L'eau prend le ciel': Proposition de collage pour figurer le désir bachelardien," in *Des dispositifs pulsionnels* (Paris: Christian Bourgois, 1980), 149–69, at 156; hereafter cited as *DP*.

22. The symptomatic reading would have to follow too this motif of *retournement*, and no doubt link it to the almost equally persistent motif of a rotation through 90 degrees. See, e.g., *DF*, 23, 70, 94, 100, 117–18; Jean-François Lyotard, *Dérive à partir de Marx et Freud* (Paris: Union Générale d'Edition, 1973), 83, 91, 109, 113, 128–29, 156, 307; Jean-François Lyotard and Jacques Monory, *Récits tremblants* (Paris: Galilée, 1977), 59. This motif is partially thematized in "La place de l'aliénation dans le retournement marxiste," in *Dérive*, 78–166, at 84–85; 97–98; 105–7; 109–10, and explicitly linked to the 90-degree or right-angle motif, but the symptomatic reading would have to follow it further, up to and including the "cul de charogne retourné" in *CdA*, 45.

23. Cf. the remark made at the 1972 Cerisy-la-Salle conference, published in *Nietzsche aujourd'hui? 1. Intensités* (Paris: Union Générale d'Editions, 1973): "Les noms propres, c'est le vrai pluriel: le singulier indéclinable" (177).

24. "Truth shows up as an aberration measured by the standards of meaning and knowledge. It clashes . . . if truth does not appear where it is expected, and if no discourse can exhibit it as a rounded meaning because it does not belong to its field, then this book is not true, insofar as this book obviously tries to produce articulate meanings. . . . A good book, in order to let truth be in its aberration, would be a book in which linguistic time . . . would itself be deconstructed. . . . This book is not that good book, it still stands in meaning, it is not an artist's book, deconstruction doesn't operate in it directly, it is *signified*. It is still a book of philosophy, by that fact" (*DF*, 18).

25. Lyotard, *Dérive*, 14ff.

26. Cf. Jean-François Lyotard, *Économie libidinale* (Paris: Minuit, 1974), 165, hereafter cited as *EL*. All translations from this text are my own. Published in English as Libidinal Economy, trans. Iain Hamilton Grant (Bloomington: In-

diana University Press, 1993); Jean-François Lyotard, *Rudiments païens* (Paris: Union générale d'édition, 1977), 29, 77, 103, 115, 234; hereafter cited as *RP*.

27. Jean-François Lyotard and Jean-Loup Thébaud, *Au juste* (Paris: Christian Bourgois, 1979), 83.

28. See especially Jean-François Lyotard, "Expédient dans la décadence," in *RP*, 115–56, and Jean-François Lyotard, "Sur la force des faibles," *L'Arc* 64 (1976): 4–12.

29. "The Greeks and their doxographers recount the ruse of the fox-fish: 'It unfolds its internal organs, turns them out, taking off its body like a shirt.' . . . The labyrinth is not a complicated building in which one gets lost, but a power of the body to undo its apparent voluminosity and evaginate itself: what exactly occupies the place of the fox-fish's heart when it has accomplished its ruse and all its entrails are outside?" Jean-François Lyotard, *Le mur du pacifique* (Paris: Galilée, 1979), 45–46 (my translation). This should evidently be compared to the memorable opening of *EL*.

30. This absolute or pure desire is perhaps best described in terms of the 'apathy' that Lyotard discusses often, in *EL* and *RP*, and that *Pérégrinations* reveals to have been, in the form of the theme of *indifference*, the subject of his master's thesis (cf. Jean-François Lyotard, *Pérégrinations: Loi, forme, événement* [Paris: Galilée, 1990], 27, where the link between this thematic and the later question of melancholia is also raised; hereafter cited as *PLFE*. All translations from this text are my own. Published in English as Preregrinations: Law, Form, Event (New York: Columbia University Press, 1988).

31. Cf. *LI*, 64–67; *HLJ*, passim.

32. "It is tempting to imagine an event as a face-to-face with nothingness. A sort of presence to death. But things are not so simple. Many events happen without one's being able to look the in the face [*dévisager*]. . . . They come to us hidden in the externals of the everyday" (*PLFE*, 41).

33. Already the preface to *DF* casts doubt on Levinas's thematic of the Other presenting itself in the face-to-face: the claim there that "il n'y a pas d'absolument Autre," which is hardly worked out with respect to Levinas, is still at work in the more recent writing we are examining. See too in *PLFE*: "the great forgetting that Hölderlin detected: God and man divided in their conjunction, each cut from the other and turning his back on him . . . there is no monk who does not wonder if God is turning to him, to us, his front or his behind" (18).

34. *LdE*, 64. See also the derivation in "La mainmise," 131–32 [*H*, 7–8], which moves directly from childhood to the theme of infantile seduction.

35. See especially *LdE*, 30–31.

36. See "Examen oral," in *Lyotard: Les déplacements philosophiques*, 137–53, and its discussion of the expression "le différend même" (140ff). Is it a coincidence that this is called up by reference to a paper by Jacob Rogozinski, first husband of Lyotard's second wife?

37. Cf. also *RP*, 219, 228; *DP*, 256–57, etc.

38. See for example *EL*, 173–74, and Lyotard, *Récits tremblants*, 54, 97–98, 103.

39. See too the reference to the "horrors" contained in Malraux's Lawrence biography: "assassinations, scalpings, Lawrence's murder of the Arab, the blocked asshole of the Sassanian kings" (*SMX*, 273).

40. Jean-François Lyotard, "'Féminité' dans la métalangue," in *RP*, 213–32, at 220–21.

GEOFFREY BENNINGTON is Asa G. Candler Professor of Modern French Thought at Emory University. He is the author of half a dozen books, among them *Lyotard: Writing the Event* (Manchester University Press, 1988), *Legislations: The Politics of Deconstruction* (Verso Books, 1994), and *Interrupting Derrida* (Routledge, 2000). He has also translated Jean-François Lyotard's *The Postmodern Condition* (University of Minnesota Press, 1984, with Brian Massumi) and *The Inhuman: Reflections on Time* (Stanford University Press, 1991, with Rachel Bowlby), along with several books by Jacques Derrida (*The Truth in Painting, Of Spirit: Heidegger and the Question*, and *Jacques Derrida*, all published by the University of Chicago Press).

PHILIPPE BONNEFIS is Asa G. Candler Professor of French at Emory University. His most recent books are *Pascal Quignard: Son nom seul* (Galilée, 2001), *Métro Flaubert* (Galilée, 2002), *Le cabinet du docteur Michaux* (Galilée, 2003), and *Cinq portraits "perfectionnés" de Guy de Maupassant* (Galilée, 2004).

JACQUES DERRIDA was director of studies at the École des Hautes Études en Sciences Sociales, Paris, and professor of humanities at the University of California, Irvine. Some of his most recent books include *Veils* (written with Hélène Cixous), *Of Hospitality* (written with Anne Dufourmantelle), and *Negotiations: Interventions and Interviews, 1971–1998* (edited by Elizabeth Rottenberg), all published by Stanford University Press.

CHRISTOPHER FYNSK is professor of comparative literature and modern thought and director of the Center for Modern Thought at the University of Aberdeen. He is the author of *Heidegger: Thought and Historicity* (Cornell University Press, 1986; 2nd ed., 1993), *Language and Relation: . . . That There Is Language* (Stanford University Press, 1996), and *Infant Figures* (Stanford University Press, 2000). He has also co-edited, with Philippe Lacoue-Labarthe, *Typography: Mimesis, Philosophy, Politics* (Harvard University Press, 1989; paperback ed., Stanford University Press, 1997). His most recent book is *The Claim of Language: A Case for the Humanities* (University of Minnesota Press, 2004).

RODOLPHE GASCHÉ is Eugenio Donato Professor of Comparative Literature at the State University of New York at Buffalo. His recently published books include *Of Minimal Things: Studies on the Notion of Relation* (Stanford University Press, 1999) and *The Idea of Form: Rethinking Kant's Aesthetics* (Stanford University Press, 2003). He has just completed another book entitled *The Honor of Thinking* and is currently working on a book-length study on the philosophical concept of Europe.

DOROTA GLOWACKA is associate professor in the Contemporary Studies Programme at the University of King's College in Halifax (Canada). She has published many articles on Holocaust literature in the context of continental theory. She is a co-editor of *Between Ethics and Aesthetic: Crossing the Boundaries* (SUNY Press, 2002).

MICHAEL NAAS is professor of philosophy at DePaul University in Chicago. He is the author of *Turning: From Persuasion to Philosophy* (Humanities Press, 1998) and *Taking on the Tradition: Jacques Derrida and the Legacies of Deconstruction* (Stanford University Press, 2002). He is also the co-translator of several works by Jacques Derrida (including *Rogues* [Stanford University Press, 2005]) and of Jean-François Lyotard and Eberhard Gruber's *The Hyphen: Between Judaism and Christianity* (Humanity Books, 1999).

CLAIRE NOUVET is associate professor in the Department of French and Italian at Emory University, where she is a Fellow in the Psychoanalytic Institute. She is the editor of *Literature and the Ethical Question* (*Yale French Studies* 79, 1991) and the author of articles on topics ranging from medieval French literature to contemporary thinkers such as Jean-François Lyotard and Gayatri Chakravorty Spivak.

AVITAL RONELL is professor of German, English, and comparative literature at New York University, where she taught an annual course with Jacques Derrida. Chair of the German department, she is a regular contributor to *ArtForum, MLN*, and several other leading journals and has published *The Telephone Book: Technology—Schizophrenia—Electric Speech* (University of Nebraska Press, 1989), *Crack Wars: Literature, Addiction, Mania* (University of Nebraska Press, 1992), *Stupidity* (University of Illinois Press, 2002), and *The Test Drive* (University of Illinois Press, 2005). She works on video and film in New York City and is professor of philosophy and media at the European Graduate School in Saas Fee, Switzerland.

GÉRALD SFEZ teaches at the Institute of Political Studies in Paris. He is the author of *Machiavel: Le prince sans qualités* (Kimé, 1997), *Machiavel: La politique du moindre mal* (Presses Universitaires de France, 1999), and most recently of *Léo Strauss: Lecteur de Machiavel, la modernité du mal* (Ellipses, 2003). One of his recent books is *Jean-François Lyotard: La faculté d'une phrase* (Galilée, 2000). He is also a co-editor, with Dolorès Lyotard and Jean-Claude Milner, of *Jean-François Lyotard: L'exercice du différend* (Presses Universitaires de France, 2000).

KENT STILL is a doctoral candidate in philosophy at Emory University and co-editor of *Addressing Levinas* (Northwestern University Press, 2005).

ZRINKA STAHULJAK is assistant professor of French at the University of California, Los Angeles. She is the author of *Bloodless Genealogies of the French Middle Ages:* Translatio, *Kinship, and Metaphor* (University Press of Florida, 2005).

EWA PŁONOWSKA ZIAREK is Julian Park Professor of Comparative Literature and director of Humanities Institute at the State University of New York at Buffalo. She is the author of *The Rhetoric of Failure: Deconstruction of Skepticism, Reinvention of Modernism* (SUNY Press, 1995) and *An Ethics of Dissensus: Feminism, Postmodernity, and the Politics of Radical Democracy* (Stanford University Press, 2001); an editor of *Gombrowicz's Grimaces: Modernism, Gender, Nationality* (SUNY Press, 1998); and a co-editor of *Revolt, Affect, Collectivity: The Unstable Boundaries of Kristeva's Polis* (SUNY Press, 2005). She has published numerous articles on Kristeva, Irigaray, Derrida, Foucault, Levinas, and Fanon, and, more generally, on the relation of feminism, ethics, and deconstruction. Currently she is working on a book devoted to feminist aesthetics.